THE **STRUCTURAL FOUNDATIONS** OF **MONETARY POLICY**

The Hoover Institution gratefully acknowledges the following individuals and foundations for their significant support of the **Working Group on Economic Policy** *and this publication:*

Lynde and Harry Bradley Foundation

Preston and Carolyn Butcher

John A. Gunn and Cynthia Fry Gunn

Stephen and Sarah Page Herrick

Michael and Rosalind Keiser

Koret Foundation

William E. Simon Foundation

THE STRUCTURAL FOUNDATIONS OF MONETARY POLICY

EDITED BY

MICHAEL D. BORDO
JOHN H. COCHRANE
AMIT SERU

CONTRIBUTING AUTHORS

Michael D. Bordo
James Bullard
Martin Eichenbaum
Jesús Fernández-Villaverde
Laurie Simon Hodrick
Andrew T. Levin
Charles I. Plosser
Daniel Sanches
Kevin Warsh

Markus Brunnermeier
John H. Cochrane
Charles L. Evans
Stanley Fischer
Arvind Krishnamurthy
Lee E. Ohanian
Eric Rosengren
John B. Taylor
Volker Wieland

WITH ADDITIONAL DISCUSSANTS

HOOVER INSTITUTION PRESS
STANFORD UNIVERSITY   STANFORD, CALIFORNIA

www.hoover.org

Hoover Institution Press Publication No. 687
Hoover Institution at Leland Stanford Junior University,
Stanford, California 94305-6003

First printing 2017
26 25 24 23 22 21 20 19   10 9 8 7 6 5 4 3 2

Manufactured in the United States of America

Library of Congress Cataloging-in-Publication Data

Names: Bordo, Michael D., editor, author. Cochrane, John H. (John Howland), 1957– editor. Seru, Amit, editor.
Title: The structural foundations of monetary policy.
Description: Hoover Institution Press casebound edition. | Stanford, Calif. : Hoover Institution Press, 2018.
Identifiers: LCCN 2018285761 | ISBN 9780817921347 (cloth : alk. paper) | ISBN 9780817921361 (epub) | ISBN 9780817921378 (mobi) | ISBN 9780817921385 (PDF)
Subjects: LCSH Monetary policy.
LC record available at https://lccn.loc.gov/2018285761

♾ This paper meets the requirements of ANSI/NISO Z39.48—1992 (Permanence of Paper).

Contents

Preface

Michael D. Bordo, John H. Cochrane, and Amit Seru

Each spring, the Hoover Institution hosts a monetary policy conference. The conference is an annual series started in 2014 by John Taylor, Michael Bordo, and Lee Ohanian.

This year's conference, titled "The Structural Foundations of Monetary Policy," examined the long-run monetary issues facing the world economy. The presentations and discussion were wide ranging, focusing on nearly everything *but* short-term issues, such as whether the Federal Reserve will or should raise interest rates another twenty-five basis points at the next meeting. Instead, participants focused on deep, unresolved structural questions. Their presentations and the discussions that followed are reproduced in this volume.

Chapter 1 addresses the Federal Reserve balance sheet. Should Fed officials keep lots of interest-paying reserves outstanding? Should they shrink the balance sheet, and if so, how fast? Should the Fed return to procedures with very small reserves and not pay interest? What kind of assets should the Fed buy or keep? Should it buy lots of assets and expand the balance sheet again in the next recession? Should the Fed periodically swap risky assets back to the Treasury?

Chapter 2 examines long-run interest rates. We seem to be facing globally lower long-run real interest rates. How should monetary policy adapt? Should we aim now for a 3 percent long-run nominal interest rate rather than 4 percent? Or should we keep "headroom" over the zero bound and raise the inflation target so interest rates can still head toward 4 percent? Or perhaps further lower the inflation target?

Chapter 3 studies the puzzle of the last eight years in the United States and the last twenty in Japan: the long, quiet zero bound, the fact that the Fed's forecasts have been wrong year after year, and what that means for monetary policy.

Chapter 4 explores the payment system. How will monetary policy adapt to blockchain and other innovations in payment systems? Will fintech take over from banks in providing transaction services? Will that eliminate or exacerbate worries about demand deposits? Should the Federal Reserve Wire Network clear transfers using blockchain, or should the Fed offer blockchain-cleared transactions directly? How will instant settlement of financial assets affect the monetary system? Should the Fed create its own digital currency?

In chapter 5, John Taylor explains how to make monetary policy decisions when there are wildly different views and models. The military will tell you it's a bad idea to take one forecast and then count on it being true. Fog of war wisdom is probably appropriate in central banking.

Other chapters give Fed policy makers a chance to weigh in. Chapter 6 features Stanley Fischer, vice chair of the Federal Reserve System. Commenting on the central question of rules versus discretion, he comes out largely in favor of the latter.

In chapter 7, Markus Brunnermeier focuses on structural issues in the euro. He contrasts the economic policies of France and Germany to illustrate the power of ideology in driving states with congruent economic interests toward fundamentally different policies. In chapter 8, Kevin Warsh warns Federal Reserve decision makers that being prepared for future economic crises means avoiding a complacent climate of opinion.

Chapter 9 begins with a panel discussion moderated by John Cochrane with Federal Reserve Bank presidents James Bullard (St. Louis), Charles Evans (Chicago), and Eric Rosengren (Boston). The chapter engages a wide spectrum of big-picture questions, including monetary policy rules—a subject no Hoover monetary conference could ignore. What should rules look like? When should the Fed deviate from them? Panelists also address proposed structural reforms, such as the 2017 Financial CHOICE Act, and add a practical perspective to many of the academic questions raised in other sessions.

For inspiring the conference and this volume, we thank John Taylor. We also thank the *real* organizers of the conference, Marie-Christine Slakey, Denise Elson, and Eryn Witcher Tillman; Kristen Weiss for transcribing each session; Kyle Palermo for making a complete book manuscript out of a series of transcriptions; our summer intern Will Nagle for his excellent assistance; and Hoover's director, Tom Gilligan. We also extend special thanks to Hoover's donors for picking up the check—without them, we would not be here.

CHAPTER ONE

THE BALANCE SHEET

· ·

SECTION ONE

The Risks of a Fed Balance Sheet Unconstrained by Monetary Policy

Charles I. Plosser

Last fall I was invited to give a talk at the Swiss National Bank in honor of Karl Brunner on the occasion of the hundredth anniversary of his birth. Karl, of course, was a famous Swiss economist, often associated with coining the term "monetarism." I first met Karl at the Hoover Institution, where he and Robert Barro were visiting in 1978. They recruited me to the University of Rochester. Between 1978 and his death in 1989, I was fortunate to be a colleague of Karl's at Rochester and learned a great deal from him over those years—not only about economics but many other things, including his views of the professional responsibilities associated with being a journal editor. Having founded the *Journal of Money, Credit, and Banking* and the *Journal of Monetary Economics*, he felt strongly about the important role played by high-quality refereed academic journals. Karl's interests also spanned political science, sociology, and the philosophy of science. He was truly a committed scholar and had an amazing intellect.

You might ask what all this has to do with the Fed's balance sheet. Karl had a deep interest in policy, and he tried to encourage academics to take an interest in policy-related research. He founded the Carnegie-Rochester Conference Series on Public Policy with Allan Meltzer, his student and longtime collaborator. The two of them also created the Shadow Open Market Committee in 1971 to bring policy insights out of the academic environment and make them accessible to the press and broader public. One theme Karl stressed in his discussions of policy was that institutions matter. He thought it important to recognize that policy makers are not the romantic "Ramsey planners" that we economists often assume in our models but actors responding to incentives and subject to institutional constraints, both of which shape policy choices and outcomes. Karl felt we needed to understand that environment to provide useful policy advice. Little did I know during those years at Rochester that I would end up in a policy-making role at the Fed during one of the most challenging times for our central bank.

This preface is relevant because I found Karl's message, which I heard so many years ago, to be more germane than I imagined. And consequently, it has helped shape my thinking about policy and the current debates over monetary reform, including alternative operating regimes for implementing monetary policy.

I have often spoken about important institutional aspects of our central bank.[1] In particular, I have stressed the importance of Fed independence and how institutional arrangements influence it. I have stressed that in a democracy, independence must come with limitations on the breadth and use of authorities. These constraints must be chosen carefully to preserve independence and the ability to achieve objectives while limiting actions that go beyond accept-

---

1. See, for example, Charles Plosser, "A Limited Central Bank," delivered at the Cato Institute's 31st Annual Monetary Conference, November 14, 2013; and Charles Plosser, "Balancing Central Bank Independence and Accountability," in *Central Bank Governance and Oversight Reform*, ed. John H. Cochrane and John B. Taylor (Stanford, CA: Hoover Institution Press, 2016).

able boundaries. For example, I have suggested limiting the Fed's mandate to price stability and restricting the composition of the asset side of its balance sheet to Treasuries. Such limitations would constrain discretion and largely prevent the Fed from engaging in credit allocation policies that, in a democracy, should be in the hands of the marketplace or elected officials.

My focus today is on the Fed's balance sheet and how institutions, and the incentives they create, matter for how it is managed. Since 2006, the balance sheet of our central bank has grown about fivefold, primarily because of the Fed's unconventional policies during the financial crisis and subsequent recession. Once the Fed had reduced the targeted fed funds rate to near zero in December 2008, it embarked on a program of large-scale asset purchases. Initially, those purchases were motivated by a desire to provide liquidity and maintain financial market stability. Those goals were largely achieved by mid-2009, yet quantitative easing (QE) continued and expanded. It was justified not on the grounds of financial market dysfunction but as a means to provide more monetary accommodation to speed up the recovery.

STRUCTURE OF THE FED'S BALANCE SHEET

Currently, the Fed's balance sheet is roughly $4.5 trillion, compared to about $850 billion prior to the financial crisis. The composition of the balance sheet is also quite different today than it was prior to the crisis. In 2006, the asset side of the balance sheet was predominately US Treasury securities. Today, approximately 40 percent of the balance sheet is composed of mortgage-backed securities (MBS), while Treasuries account for most of the rest. In addition, at various points during the crisis the Fed held hundreds of billions of dollars of other private-sector securities or loans, although most of these private-sector securities have rolled off the balance sheet, leaving primarily Treasuries and MBS.

The liability side of the balance sheet also reflects the impact of QE. In 2006, currency accounted for more than 90 percent, or $785 billion, of the $850 billion, and bank reserves just about 2 percent, or $18 billion, almost all of which were required reserves. Today, currency represents about $1.5 trillion, or just 33 percent of the balance sheet, while reserves have risen to about $2.6 trillion, or about 60 percent of the balance sheet, of which only $180 billion are required.[2] So there is about $2.4 trillion in excess reserves today compared to zero in 2006.

Thus, currency has doubled (growing about 6 percent a year) over the last ten years, yet reserves have grown by a factor of about ten (growing about 26 percent per year).

As for the Fed's assets, holding predominately Treasuries was historically viewed as neutral in the sense that no sector of the economy was favored over another, and the maturity structure was chosen so that the yield curve was not affected.[3] The purchase of MBS during QE, however, was a deliberate effort to improve the housing sector, while acquiring other private-sector securities as part of the rescues of Bear Stearns and AIG was intended to aid the creditors of those institutions. In the rescues, the Fed sold off Treasuries to purchase private-sector securities and make loans. These were highly unusual actions in support of specific parties even though the broader goal was to stabilize the financial system. Regardless of the rationale, the actions amounted to debt-financed fiscal policy and a form of credit allocation. Thus, such changes in the mix of assets held by the Fed are frequently referred to as credit policy.

---

2. I have counted outstanding reverse repurchase agreements as part of total reserves as they are simply a mechanism for temporarily reducing excess reserves.

3. That is, the Fed's holding of Treasuries mostly reflected the same mix of bonds and bills as issued by the Treasury.

OPERATING REGIMES AND THE
ROLE OF THE BALANCE SHEET

How big should the Fed's balance sheet be? In part, this depends on the Fed's goals and objectives and on the operating regime for monetary policy. Prior to the crisis, the Fed operated with a relatively small balance sheet. Its size was determined by the demand for currency and the demand for required reserves. The Fed supplied currency elastically and supplied reserves in a way that achieved the target for the fed funds rate (the interbank lending rate). That is, it expanded or shrank reserves in the banking system to achieve its funds rate target. This operating procedure required the Fed to increase or decrease its balance sheet accordingly. The size of the balance sheet was integral to setting the instrument of monetary policy—the fed funds rate.

The Fed has not provided much in the way of guidance regarding the role it sees for the balance sheet going forward. In its exit principles, the Fed has stated that "the size of the securities portfolio and the associated quantity of bank reserves are expected to be reduced to the smallest levels that would be consistent with the efficient implementation of monetary policy."[4] This is not helpful without knowing how the Federal Open Market Committee (FOMC) will ultimately choose to implement monetary policy. Will it return to the prior framework of targeting the fed funds rate or will it adopt some other target or instrument? What will determine the size of the balance sheet? Different approaches will have different implications for the balance sheet.

As to the preferred instrument of monetary policy going forward, the FOMC seems to have suggested that it would like to

---

4. Federal Open Market Committee, "Policy Normalization Principles and Plans," September 2014, https://www.federalreserve.gov/monetarypolicy/files/FOMC_Policy Normalization.pdf.

restore the federal funds as its primary instrument but has not committed to this strategy. How will the FOMC then achieve its target? With the current large balance sheet flooding the market with reserves, trading in the fed funds market is quite thin compared to the precrisis period.

Several economists (including former Fed chair Ben Bernanke, now at the Brookings Institution, and John Cochrane at the Hoover Institution) have argued that since the Fed now has the ability to pay interest on bank reserves, it is possible, desirable, and perhaps more efficient to maintain a large balance sheet and use the interest rate paid on reserves (IOR) as the instrument of monetary policy rather than the fed funds rate. The basic idea is that by setting the interest rate it pays on bank reserves, the Fed establishes a floor for short-term risk-free rates. In such a regime, as long as the balance sheet is of sufficient size to satiate the demand for reserves, it can be arbitrarily large (that is, operate with significant amounts of excess reserves) without affecting the conduct of monetary policy. This operating regime is often referred to as a "floor system." Under this type of system, the fed funds market as we know it would likely disappear. Indeed, as I noted, due to QE and the current large balance sheet, the funds market is mostly moribund today.

The precrisis system of targeting a fed funds rate could also be implemented in a world where interest is paid on reserves. In such a regime, the fed funds target could be set slightly above the interest rate paid on reserves (say twenty-five to fifty basis points). However, to achieve a funds rate higher than the floor, or IOR, the balance sheet (more precisely, reserves) would have to shrink. This method of setting the interest rate target is often referred to as a "corridor" or "channel system." This is because the instrument (the fed funds rate) is in a corridor above the IOR but less than the discount or primary credit rate, which is the rate at which the Fed is willing to lend reserves to depository institutions.

How big might the balance sheet be today under such a corridor system? As a reference point, one can think of a balance sheet today composed of currency plus required reserves as about $1.7 trillion. Adding $100 billion or so for the Treasury's general account suggests that we might expect a Fed balance sheet of $1.8–$1.9 trillion as the size necessary to return to the precrisis operating regime. The arguments for a large balance sheet, composed of significant quantities of excess reserves, untethered to monetary policy, generally focus on financial stability factors. One argument is that large amounts of riskless reserves ensure ample safe assets in the system, which presumably provides liquidity and reduces systemic risk (whatever that may mean). It is argued that a scarcity of safe assets contributed to financial fragility in the crisis.[5] Moreover, paying interest on reserves mitigates the distortionary effects of the tax on deposits caused by reserve requirements.

RISKS OF A LARGE BALANCE SHEET

The theoretical arguments for a floor system and a large balance sheet are straightforward, and while I disagree with some elements of the economic arguments, my major concerns arise from the institutional arrangements and incentives engendered by such a system at the Fed and in other parts of the government. Who will determine the amount of excess reserves created and how will they do it, since the monetary policy instrument will be the IOR? Unfortunately, there is little discussion or analysis of how to determine the appropriate amount of excess reserves that should be created. Is it $10 billion, $100 billion, or $1,000 billion?

---

5. This argument is not compelling to me. Buying up short-term Treasuries in exchange for bank reserves would seem to simply swap one safe asset for another and thus lead to no net increase in safe assets. Only if the Fed was purchasing "risky assets"—for example, long-term Treasuries, corporate debt, or equities—does this argument seem to apply. Even so, such actions just shift risk to the taxpayer.

Making the Fed's balance sheet unrelated to monetary policy opens the door for the Fed to use its balance sheet for other purposes. For example, the Fed would be free to engage in credit policy through the management of its assets while not impinging on monetary policy. Indeed, the Fed's balance sheet could serve as a huge intermediary and supplier of taxpayer subsidies to selected parties through credit allocation. It also opens the door for Congress (or the Fed) to use the balance sheet for its own purposes. Let me elaborate by articulating several concerns raised by pursuing an operating regime that tolerates a large and unconstrained balance sheet. Some of these concerns could be mitigated through legislation, while others are not so easily addressed.

First and foremost, an operating regime where the Fed's balance sheet is unconstrained as to its size or holdings is ripe for misuse, if not abuse. A Fed balance sheet unconstrained by monetary policy becomes a new policy tool, a free parameter if you will. Congress would be free to lobby the Fed through political pressure or legislation to manage the portfolio for political ends. Imagine Congress proposing a new infrastructure bill where the Fed was expected, or even required, to buy designated development bonds to support and fund the initiative so taxes could be deferred. This would be very tempting for Congress. Indeed, in testimony before Congress I was asked why the Fed shouldn't contribute "its fair share" to an infrastructure initiative. Image the lobbying for the Fed to purchase "build America bonds" issued by the Treasury to fund infrastructure initiatives.

More generally, the temptation would be to turn the Fed's balance sheet into a huge hedge fund, investing in projects demanded by Congress and funded by forcing banks to hold vast quantities of excess reserves on which the central bank pays the risk-free rate. Of course, this just represents off-budget fiscal policy.

Consider the European Central Bank's holdings of sovereign debt. This policy seems to have been designed to prop up the financial positions of countries in fiscal distress. Imagine if Illinois or California were on the verge of default. Would Congress decide that Fed purchases of state and local bonds constituted an acceptable tactic to delay and defer undesirable turmoil? Imagine the moral hazard and perverse incentives such a policy might induce.

Another recent example of these pressures can be found in Switzerland. The Swiss National Bank (SNB) has grown its balance sheet, which is composed mostly of foreign exchange reserves. Political pressure is being applied to "use" the reserves to invest in various initiatives, such as Swiss companies or other politically attractive activities. The arguments are often couched in the language of "risk management" or "appropriate diversification" of the SNB's balance sheet.

Congress will undoubtedly find many "appropriate" uses for the Fed's balance sheet and could do so and claim it doesn't interfere with the independence of monetary policy. Recall that in 2015 Congress raided the Fed's balance sheet to help fund a transportation bill. In 2010, the resources for the Consumer Financial Protection Bureau were found in Fed revenues. These were all efforts to exploit the central bank for fiscal policy purposes.

Imagine the political debates over appointments to the Board of Governors. Hearings might focus on the nominees' views on the investment policy for the balance sheet rather than monetary policy. Political pressure to purchase various forms of securities to support favored projects or initiatives could be enormous and fraught with controversy. Fed independence is fragile and is gradually being eroded further. Offering the fiscal authorities a balance sheet to conduct fiscal policy or credit allocation off budget is akin to opening Pandora's box.

With a big balance sheet, the Fed would also be paying banks large amounts of interest that would otherwise flow to the Treasury. For example, an increase of one percentage point in IOR with $2.4 trillion in excess reserves would increase payments to the banking system by $24 billion that "otherwise" would have gone to the US Treasury. Congress might complain that they want access to those revenues rather than "subsidizing" the banking system for holding excess reserves. The fact that a large portion of excess reserves is held by foreign banks will not help matters. Of course, appropriate economic analysis tells us this is a fallacious argument from the standpoint of the government's consolidated balance sheet. That is because if the Fed didn't hold the Treasuries, the public would; thus, the interest payments going to the Fed and then to the banks would be going to the public (maybe not the banks), and the Treasury is no better or worse off. In any event, that outcome is unlikely to stop Congress. Again, remember the case of the Consumer Financial Protection Bureau, which was funded from Fed income to avoid the appropriation process. Worse, imagine if Congress decided to cap or eliminate the authority to pay interest on reserves.

One way to mitigate some of these concerns is to require the Fed to maintain an all-Treasuries portfolio. Such a restriction would give the Fed some protection and grounds for saying no to proposals that would require the Fed to either acquire private-sector securities or engage in some types of credit allocation. But it may not prevent Congress from requiring the Fed to purchase Treasuries to support specific fiscal initiatives, such as "build America bonds." After all, Congress could argue that requiring such purchases didn't matter for monetary policy, and hence independence is not compromised.

These risks are what some would call political economy issues, but that does not mean we should ignore them. The risks posed for our institutions are serious and could adversely affect economic outcomes.

IMPLEMENTING MONETARY POLICY
WITH A BIG BALANCE SHEET

I have other concerns surrounding the implementation of monetary policy under a big-balance-sheet regime. The evidence accrued to date suggests that the IOR does not provide a firm floor for the funds rate or other short-term rates. Several reasons have been offered for this outcome. Some of them are regulatory related. For example, depository institutions are required to pay a tax to the FDIC based on total assets. This means that these firms have less incentive to hold reserves compared to those firms that are not depository institutions. This seems to be one reason nondepository foreign banks are holding a large fraction of the excess reserves. Capital requirements have also influenced market equilibrium in other ways. When some banks are required to hold capital against total assets, including reserves, flooding the banking system with excess reserves increases the capital these banks must hold.

One way the Fed has sought to address these problems is by increasing its interventions into the short-term money markets and creating the opportunity to, in effect, pay interest on reserves to a broader range of short-term market participants. The idea is that this broadens participation and improves the arbitrage. This program is the reverse repo program, or RRP. This program allows non-depository institutions to borrow Treasury securities from the Fed overnight (which soaks up reserves) with an agreement that the Fed will repurchase the securities the next day. The Fed pays an interest rate on the transaction. The consequence is a reduction in reserves overnight or for the duration of longer-term repos. This program effectively gives many financial institutions the ability to earn interest on reserves even though they are not depository institutions. It also means that many more market participants are interacting and trading with the Fed.

Thus, we have some evidence that the floor system currently in place does not provide a firm floor and must be supported by the RRP program, which effectively drains reserves from the banking system on an ongoing basis. Will the necessity of the RRP decline as the balance sheet shrinks? If it does, will the Fed continue to use it? And if so, to what purpose?

The Fed has become a larger and more deeply embedded participant in the short-term financial markets than ever before. Some say that is a good thing because it gives the Fed more insight and the ability to intervene when and where it feels appropriate. Some also argue that such dominance allows the Fed to influence more rates more quickly, making the monetary transmission mechanism more effective. Others say this is a worrisome development, as RRPs give large financial firms a safe and reliable place to flee in times of volatility—and making it easy to do so may increase systemic risk rather than reduce it. It also places the Fed in a powerful position, so that markets may focus more on the Fed and less on fundamentals. Put slightly differently, such dominance reduces market influences and feedback while broadening the role of price setting by the Fed.

These are legitimate concerns that deserve broader consideration than they have been given to date. They are important because they go to the fundamental question of how short-term institutional arrangements are likely to evolve under the floor system, perhaps accompanied by a large ongoing RRP program. In particular, what should the role of the Fed be? What should be the limits to its discretionary authority? Or more simply, how big does the Fed's footprint in the markets need to be? The unintended consequences may prove larger and more worrisome than we think.

The floor system also poses some governance issues that are as yet unresolved. The instrument of monetary policy in a floor system is the interest paid on reserves. Unlike the funds rate, the IOR is an administered rate rather than a market rate. Under current law, the IOR is set by the Board of Governors, not the FOMC. In other words, it is the Board of Governors rather than the FOMC that technically determines monetary policy. Under a pure floor system, the FOMC would become irrelevant.

Both Bernanke and Janet Yellen have understood this but have acted to preserve the role of the FOMC in practice by tying the IOR decision to a funds rate decision of the FOMC. This has been healthy for governance but is not required going forward. The structure of the FOMC, which includes the presidents of the Federal Reserve Banks, is an important characteristic that sustains monetary policy independence. Gutting the FOMC's role in monetary policy would undermine independence and result in monetary policy becoming far more political. Obviously, legislation can fix this, and some reform bills have included provisions that require FOMC approval for IOR decisions. My view is that it would be a huge mistake to adopt a floor system without addressing this governance issue in legislation.

The FOMC is currently operating a floor system out of necessity. QE flooded the banking system with reserves. The argument for doing so was that at the zero lower bound it was the way the FOMC sought to provide additional accommodation. The zero lower bound is no longer a binding constraint, and the Fed is seeking to raise rates. Yet the FOMC continues to stress that the large balance sheet makes the stance of policy more accommodative. How does this accommodation come about? One mechanism stressed by the Fed is that the cumulative purchases of longer-term assets (Treasuries and MBS) lowered long rates more broadly through some sort of portfolio balance mechanism. Michael Woodford and others have argued that QE is theoretically of dubious value at best.

Those who support a large balance sheet argue that using interest on reserves as the policy instrument allows monetary policy to be conducted independent of the size of the balance sheet. Yet if, as the Fed has argued, the large balance sheet is providing accommodation, that has implications for how the Fed sets the IOR. It would suggest that the policy instrument, IOR, might have to be higher than it would be with a small balance sheet—fewer excess reserves—to achieve any specified degree of accommodation. If that is the case, then how should IOR be set as a function of the size of the balance sheet? Why does it make sense to substitute increases in short-term rates to avoid reducing the balance sheet if you think it is providing accommodation through its pressure on long rates? The Fed has not offered any clues as to how it would calibrate IOR policy depending on the balance sheet.

One possibility is that the effectiveness of QE and thus the balance sheet's impact on monetary policy depend on the composition of the balance sheet. For example, the Fed purchased mostly longer-duration assets in an effort to directly influence long rates or the term premium and purchased MBS to target the housing sector. It might be the case, for example, that as the duration of the Fed's holdings declines with time, the degree of monetary accommodation from the portfolio balance effect diminishes.[6]

CONCLUSIONS

The large effect of unconventional monetary policy on the Fed's balance sheet and on short-term money markets has raised many questions about the future of monetary policy. These are healthy discussions and have opened the door to reconsidering important features of the way the Fed implements policy.

A particularly important and pressing question revolves around the future size and composition of the balance sheet. Some have argued that using interest on reserves as the instrument of monetary policy allows the Fed to maintain a large balance sheet

---

6. If this is the view of the FOMC, then it should explain it and consider eliminating the reference to the balance sheet in its post-meeting statement.

unconstrained by monetary policy. They argue that this offers an opportunity to improve financial stability and efficiency. But what constraints should be in place on the size and composition of the balance sheet? Advocates of a floor system have yet to offer an answer. As I noted at the beginning, freedom or independence of the central bank must be accompanied by constraints on discretionary authorities. It is best to make those constraints clear at the outset rather than wait for a disaster.

On the other hand, the Fed has argued through the crisis and recession that the large balance sheet is providing accommodation and thus is important for the conduct of monetary policy. In that view, how does one conduct monetary policy with two instruments working through perhaps different channels? With such a complicated framework, it would be important to understand and to communicate to the public and markets how policy would be implemented before adopting such a regime for the longer term.

I have tried to highlight some concerns regarding the Fed's approach to its balance sheet and its choice of operating regimes. Many of these concerns stem from the nature of our institutions and the incentives of political actors and policy makers who must operate within them. A large Fed balance sheet that is untethered to the conduct of monetary policy creates the opportunity and incentive for political actors to exploit the Fed and use its balance sheet to conduct off-budget fiscal policy and credit allocation. Such actions would undermine Fed independence and politicize the Fed to a far greater degree than it currently is. Without changes in the Federal Reserve Act, it would shift the conduct of monetary policy to a more politicized Board of Governors and away from the FOMC. Finally, it seems to require that the Fed play a much larger, directive role in the functioning of short-term money markets, potentially reducing the traditional role of market forces. For these reasons, I think the economy would be better served if the Fed returned to an operating regime based on a smaller footprint, where the balance sheet is more directly linked to the conduct of monetary policy.

Political independence is an essential element of sound monetary policy decision making. But with that independence must come constraints on broad discretionary authorities that could be subject to political abuse and interference. For example, the Fed should not be allowed to engage in fiscal policy actions that rightly belong to the fiscal authorities. Without carefully established constraints on the size and composition of the Fed's balance sheet, credit allocation and off-budget fiscal policy represent discretionary opportunities ripe for abuses that would undermine the case for political independence. Such authorities are likely to prove detrimental to our institutions and the economy.

· ·

SECTION TWO

Alternatives for Reserve Balances and the Fed's Balance Sheet in the Future

John B. Taylor

Since this is a chapter on the Fed's balance sheet, I begin by looking at the Fed's balance sheet today and reviewing how it has changed in the years since the global financial crisis. I then discuss alternative balance sheet sizes and configurations for reserve balances in the future, and consider alternative ways to get there. I explain why a balance sheet size and configuration for reserve balances in which the short-term interest rate is determined by market forces should be considered for the future as an alternative to one in which the short-term interest rate is administered through the interest payments on excess reserves.

THE BALANCE SHEET TODAY
AND HOW WE GOT HERE

The upper panel in Table 1.2.1 shows the balance sheet of the Fed today. The lower panel shows the balance sheet as it was on a date before the financial crisis in May 2006—eleven years ago. The numbers are exactly those reported for these dates in the Fed's Consolidated Statement of All Federal Reserve Banks, but I have aggregated the assets and liabilities into key categories to focus on the central developments.

The "size" of the balance sheet usually refers to total assets, and you can see in the left column that the size of the balance sheet has exploded from $842 billion to $4,470 billion in these eleven years. The reason for that explosion is that the Fed engaged in large-scale asset purchases, sometimes called quantitative easing, in an attempt to drive down long-term interest rates. These purchases are shown

TABLE 1.2.1. Fed's balance sheet (billions of dollars)

Fed's Balance Sheet (Billions of Dollars)

April 26, 2017

Assets		Liabilities	
Securities Held Outright	4,246	Federal Reserve Notes	1,496
Other	224	Reserve Balances	2,201
		Other	733
Total Assets	4,470	Total Liabilities	4,430

May 10, 2006

Assets		Liabilities	
Securities Held Outright	760	Federal Reserve Notes	758
Other	82	Reserve Balances	14
		Other	41
Total Assets	842	Total Liabilities	813

Source: Consolidated Statement of All Federal Reserve Banks, Federal Reserve Statistical Release H.4.1, Table 5, April 26, 2017; Table 2, May 11, 2006, Selected Items

as "Securities Held Outright." The holdings grew from $760 billion to $4,246 billion over the same span of time as the Fed bought both mortgage-backed securities and Treasury securities.

To finance these purchases, the Fed borrowed from banks in the form of reserve balances, or bank deposits at the Fed on which the Fed pays interest. You can see these reserve balances in the right-hand "Liabilities" column. Before quantitative easing began, reserve balances were $14 billion, an amazingly small number for the balance sheet these days. They're now equal to $2,201 billion. This explosion of reserve balances has important implications for monetary policy, as I explain below.

Also shown on the balance sheet are Federal Reserve notes (currency). These have increased from $758 billion to $1,496 billion, which is about a 6 percent average annual growth over this period of time. That rate of growth is not that unusual. The demand for currency grows steadily as the economy grows, and the Fed supplies currency to meet this demand. What is unusual is the explosion of reserve balances to finance the purchases of securities.

Figure 1.2.1 is a plot of these reserve balances from 2000 to the present. The graph shows a small jump at the time of the 9/11 attacks and the resulting damage on Wall Street (it was considered a big $60 billion jump at the time). It shows a bigger jump during the panic in the fall of 2008 as lender of last resort loans were made domestically and internationally by the Fed. The part of the graph labeled "with liquidity support only" is what I estimate would have happened had this liquidity support been the only intervention, as it was at the time of 9/11. The liquidity facilities automatically phased away when the need for them disappeared.

But then quantitative easing (QE) began in earnest in 2009. You can see the impact of the three big bouts of QE1, QE2, and QE3 on reserve balances as these were used to finance the asset purchases. As each QE ended, the jump in reserve balances also ended, and then reserve balances gradually declined over time as currency

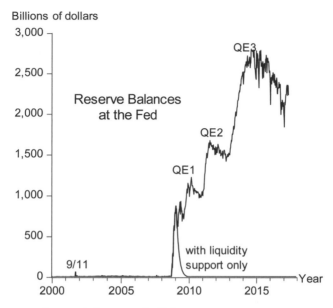

FIGURE 1.2.1. Reserve balances at the Fed

increased and the need for reserve balances to finance the stock of securities thereby diminished.

Some of the volatility in reserve balances during these downward trajectories is due to changes in Treasury balances at the Fed or to the use of overnight reserve repurchase (ON RRP) agreements. When the Fed conducts an ON RRP, it sells a security to a counterparty and simultaneously agrees to buy the security back the next day. As explained in "Overnight Reverse Repurchase Agreement Facility" on the Fed's website, "There is a reduction in reserve balances on the liability side of the Federal Reserve's balance sheet and a corresponding increase in reverse repo obligations while the trade is outstanding." When the trade is over, reserve balances return to where they were. This decline and the reversal are quite noticeable on the right-hand side of the chart after QE3, when ON RRPs were used frequently. There is no functional difference between reserve balances and ON RRP as a means of financing securities held or purchased. The Fed used ON RRP because they can be sold to government-sponsored enterprises and mutual funds. Some argue that this gives the Fed a wider reach into the financial markets for better interest rate control. Others argue that this expansion is not appropriate for the Fed and has been used sparingly.

To be sure, the recent short-run ups and downs in reserve balances from month to month are not a reflection of the stance of monetary policy. The fact that the supply of reserves is so much greater than demand is what is important. And that will continue for at least a while. Demand is now probably a bit greater than the amount of reserve balances supplied before the explosion, but nowhere near the more than $2 trillion now supplied. Without changes in the amount of securities held, reserve balances will decline very slowly as currency demand increases, as illustrated by the downward trend since the end of QE3. If the size of the securities held declines, reserve balances will decline more quickly.

But as long as reserve balances are this high, there is no choice other than to use interest on excess reserves (IOER) to move the short-term interest rate up or down. Without IOER, the federal funds rate would drop to zero. One can understand this by looking at what happened in 2008, when the supply of reserves started growing rapidly. Figure 1.2.2 (from Taylor 2009a) shows how the federal funds rate moved in the last part of 2008 as the supply of reserve balances exploded well above the demand.

SHRINKING THE BALANCE SHEET IN PREDICTABLE AND STRATEGIC WAYS

Getting back to a balance sheet with reserves close to the normal level observed before the financial crisis will require that the Fed substantially reduce its securities holdings. If it waits the long period required for currency growth to create the normalization, the transition period will be so long that a high level of reserves

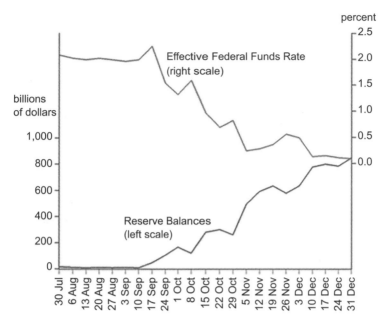

FIGURE 1.2.2. Reserve balances and the federal funds rate in 2008. Source: Taylor 2009a.

will seem permanent. It is therefore essential that the Fed reduce its holding of securities, and as argued in Taylor (2009b), this reduction should be conducted in a predictable and strategic way so as not to cause market turbulence. It should not be sudden or surprising. That was the lesson learned from the "taper tantrum" in 2013, when Ben Bernanke indicated it might be in "the next few meetings" that the size of the purchases of securities would diminish, and the markets went all over the place. As soon as the tapering became more strategic and the amount of tapering was more predictable, the markets digested it easily.

The Fed's statement in its September 2014 "Policy Normalization Principles and Plans," which said that the FOMC "intends to reduce the Federal Reserve's securities holdings in a gradual and predictable manner," was consistent with this approach and provided an improvement over vaguer statements, such as that the

Fed will keep "the size of the Federal Reserve's balance sheet at a high level for some time," as stated in the FOMC Minutes from the meeting of January 27–28, 2009.

The "Addendum to the Policy Normalization Principles and Plans," issued on June 14, 2017, provided useful details. The FOMC said it intends to gradually reduce the Fed's securities holdings by decreasing its reinvestment of principal payments to the extent that they exceed gradually rising caps:

> For payments of principal that the Federal Reserve receives from maturing Treasury securities, the Committee anticipates that the cap will be $6 billion per month initially and will increase in steps of $6 billion at three-month intervals over 12 months until it reaches $30 billion per month. For payments of principal that the Federal Reserve receives from its holdings of agency debt and mortgage-backed securities, the Committee anticipates that the cap will be $4 billion per month initially and will increase in steps of $4 billion at three-month intervals over 12 months until it reaches $20 billion per month. The Committee also anticipates that the caps will remain in place once they reach their respective maximums so that the Federal Reserve's securities holdings will continue to decline in a gradual and predictable manner until the Committee judges that the Federal Reserve is holding no more securities than necessary to implement monetary policy efficiently and effectively. Gradually reducing the Federal Reserve's securities holdings will result in a declining supply of reserve balances.

A BALANCE SHEET FOR THE FUTURE

While a statement that the supply of reserve balances will decline by set amounts reduces uncertainty and lowers the chances of market disruption, there is still a great deal of uncertainty about what kind of balance sheet the Fed is aiming for. As stated in the Addendum, the "Committee currently anticipates reducing the quantity of reserve balances, over time, to a level appreciably below that seen in recent years but larger than before the financial crisis; the level will reflect the banking system's demand for reserve balances and the Committee's decisions about how to implement monetary policy most efficiently and effectively in the future. The Committee expects to learn more about the underlying demand for reserves during the process of balance sheet normalization."

The Fed could be more specific about the eventual size and configuration of the balance sheet, as the range of uncertainty is still very large. There are different views about this, as explained by Powell (2017). One approach is for the Fed to say it is aiming for an eventual balance sheet and level of reserve balances in which the interest rate is determined by the demand and supply of reserves—in other words, by market forces—rather than by an administered rate under IOER. Conceptually this means the Fed would be operating under a framework with a balance sheet, as it did in the years before the crisis—for example, around 2006 and in the decades before. Most likely the level of reserve balances will be greater than the $14 billion observed in 2006 and will depend on liquidity regulations, but the defining concept of a market-determined interest rate is what is important.

I think the case can be made for such a framework. Peter Fisher ran the trading desk at the New York Fed for many years and knows well how these markets work. His assessment, as stated in the "General Discussion" below, is that such a framework would work: "We could go back and manage it with quantities; it's not impossible. We could just reengineer the system and go back to the way we were." I spent time in the markets for federal funds, watching how they operated in those days, and I wrote up an institutional description of how good, experienced people traded in these markets and developed a model showing how the market worked (Taylor 2001).

If we went back to that framework, there would not be any need for interest on excess reserves. If the Fed wanted to change the short-term interest rate, it would just adjust the supply of reserves. The amount of reserves would be set so that the supply and demand for reserves determine the interest rate.

The Fed could also provide liquidity support if it needed to do so in that framework. One way to see how this would work is to consider the example of 9/11. That little blip, which you can hardly see now in Figure 1.2.1, was viewed as gigantic back in 2001. It was so huge that Don Kohn came over from the Fed to the Treasury, where I was working, to tell me about it. So you can have that kind of liquidity support if you wanted to in such a regime.

In contrast, under a system where the supply of reserves remains above the demand, the interest rate must be administered through interest on excess reserves. It's not market determined. The method is sometimes called a "floor," as recently discussed by Powell (2017). But the federal funds rate is always below the floor, so it is not really a floor. In my view, we would be better off with a corridor or band with a lower interest rate on deposits at the bottom of the band, a higher interest rate on borrowing from the Fed at the top of the band, and most important, a market-determined interest rate above the floor and below the ceiling. Unlike current Fed policy, there would be a real floor because the actual rate would be market determined. If there was a corridor, the rate would be inside it. The interest rate at the top of the corridor would be the discount rate. See Kahn (2010) for a comparison of floor and corridor systems.

We want to create a connect, not a disconnect, between the interest rate that the Fed sets and the amount of reserves or the amount of money that's in the system. Because the Fed is responsible for the reserves and money, that connection is important. Without that connection, you raise the chances of the Fed being a multipurpose institution. In chapter 1, Plosser gives some scary examples of what that means. The Fed has already been involved in credit allocation with respect to mortgage-backed securities purchases in QE1, and it could do more than that. Hence that disconnect is problematic.

I think it does raise questions, at least for some people, about the Fed's independence. Why do you need an independent agency to do all these things? Independent agencies should have limited purposes. And indeed, it may be more appropriate for the Treasury, if we want such interventions, with Congress also approving in some cases.

There are other views, and the Fed needs to figure out what to do. Some analysts, for example Keister (2016), argue that we need a level of reserves greater than the amount needed to determine the interest rate for liquidity purposes. They say the payment system doesn't function right with a small amount of reserves. In the past, there were large daylight overdrafts, but with the right reforms, one could limit the size of the overdrafts, perhaps as a percentage of collateral. There also may be some regulatory changes that would reduce the mandated demand for liquidity.

Another view is that with a large balance sheet the Fed could provide depository services to regular people, just like it provides depository services to banks. But the Treasury could just as easily do that without interfering in the Fed's operations (see Cochrane 2014). And perhaps there is another way the service could be provided that prevents the disconnect between the interest rate and reserves.

Yet another view is that a permanently large balance sheet with a large amount of reserves would allow quantitative easing to be used regularly. I don't think quantitative easing has been that effective, and because there is uncertainty about its impact, it is hard to conduct a rules-based monetary policy with such interventions. Moreover, the way quantitative easing has spread to other central banks adds turbulence to exchange rates and the international financial system.

CONCLUSION

For all the reasons stated here, I think this proposal for the eventual size of reserve balances and the balance sheet makes sense. The key concept is that economic forces in the market for reserves, and for money more broadly, would determine the interest rate. We should not only be thinking about how to reduce the size of the balance sheet in a predictable, strategic way; we should be thinking about where we're going with reserve balances and the balance sheet. I would say that after this normalization period, after this transition is finished, interest rates should again be determined by market forces.

References

Board of Governors of the Federal Reserve System. 2014. "Policy Normalization Principles and Plans." September 16, https://www.federalreserve.gov /monetarypolicy/files/FOMC_PolicyNormalization.pdf.

Board of Governors of the Federal Reserve System. 2017a. "Overnight Reverse Repurchase Agreement Facility." February 21, https://www.federalreserve.gov /monetarypolicy/overnight-reverse-repurchase-agreements.htm.

Board of Governors of the Federal Reserve System. 2017b. "Addendum to the Policy Normalization Principles and Plans," press release, June 14, https://www .federalreserve.gov/newsevents/pressreleases/monetary20170614c.htm.

Cochrane, John. 2014. "Monetary Policy with Interest on Reserves." *Journal of Economic Dynamics and Control* 49 (December): 74–108.

Kahn, George. 2010. "Monetary Policy under a Corridor Operating Framework." *Economic Review* 95 (4).

Keister, Todd. 2016. "Interest on Reserves." Testimony before the Subcommittee on Monetary Policy and Trade, Committee on Financial Services, US House of Representatives, May 17.

Powell, Jerome H. 2017. "Thoughts on the Normalization of Monetary Policy." Paper presented at the Economic Club of New York, New York, June 1.

Taylor, John B. 2001. "Expectations, Open Market Operations, and Changes in the Federal Funds Rate." *Federal Reserve Bank of St. Louis Review* 83 (4): 33–47.

Taylor, John B. 2009a. "The Need to Return to a Monetary Framework." *Business Economics* 44 (2): 63–72.

Taylor, John B. 2009b. "The Need for a Clear and Credible Exit Strategy." In *The Road Ahead for the Fed*, edited by John Ciorciari and John Taylor, 85–100. Stanford, CA: Hoover Institution Press.

Taylor, John B. 2016a. "Unconventional Monetary Policy, Normalization, and Reform." Testimony before the Subcommittee on Monetary Policy and Trade Committee on Financial Services, US House of Representatives, December 7.

Taylor, John B. 2016b. "Interest on Reserves and the Fed's Balance Sheet." *Cato Journal* 36 (3): 711–20. Adapted from testimony with the same title before the Subcommittee on Monetary Policy and Trade, Committee on Financial Services, US House of Representatives, May 17.

· ·

SECTION THREE

The Size of the Fed's Balance Sheet

Arvind Krishnamurthy

My comments are focused on the size of the Fed's balance sheet. For this discussion, I assume that the Fed holds only Treasuries. I will argue in favor of a large balance sheet. There is a related but separate discussion about the composition of the balance sheet. In the interest of time, I do not discuss composition, although it is obviously also an important issue.

The question is, How large should a Treasuries-only balance sheet be?

I will make the case for a large balance sheet, around $2.5 trillion. I offer two sets of arguments, the first related to monetary policy pass-through and the second to financial stability.

Before the crisis, the Fed held reserve balances in the neighborhood of $50 billion and steered money market rates by altering the scarcity of reserves. Since the crisis, banks have had large excess reserves. Reserve balances are currently in excess of $2 trillion, and the Fed has steered money market rates by altering the interest it pays on reserve balances as well as the interest it pays in the reverse repo program (RRP).

We know in theory that to set a given fed funds rate on average, the Fed could set the quantity of reserves or the interest it pays on excess reserves. But the quantity approach will lead to much more volatility. Before the crisis, banks traded a small amount of reserves to settle an often large quantity of payments. This led to an elaborate game of musical chairs that often produced considerable volatility in interbank interest rates.

There is ample evidence that the excess reserve regime has reduced this volatility. There are fewer delays in settling interbank payments. There is less use of intraday credit from the Fed. All in all, settlement occurs with less friction and less musical chairs.

With currency of around $1.5 trillion in circulation and reserve requirements of around $100 billion, this calls for a balance sheet of at least $1.6 trillion, or somewhat larger to limit the money market volatility.

I think the balance sheet should be even larger. This is because of the RRP.

Traditionally, the Fed has focused on steering the federal funds rate and thereby steering other money market rates. In a theoretically frictionless benchmark, arbitrage should ensure that all money market rates, adjusted for economic risks such as credit risk, are the same.

In practice, the world is not at the frictionless benchmark. The connection between federal funds and other money market rates involves slippage. This is apparently empirical. There is dispersion in money market rates, caused by real-world frictions: imperfect competition, segmentation, institutional constraints, and regulatory frictions.

Darrell Duffie and I wrote a paper for last summer's Jackson Hole conference documenting dispersion and identifying some of the factors that drive dispersion. Figure 1.3.1 (Duffie and Krishnamurthy 2016) tracks a number of important money market

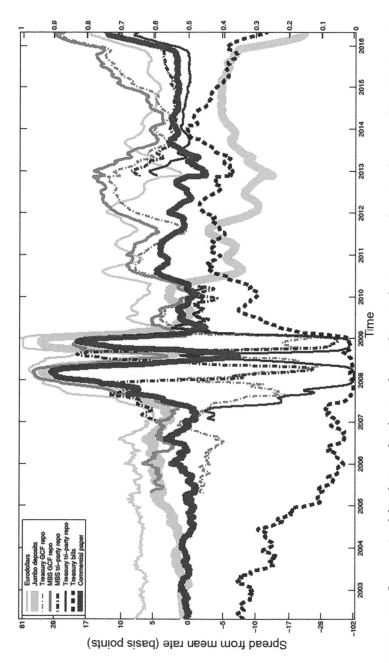

FIGURE 1.3.1. Cross-sectional distribution of a selection of overnight-equivalent money market rates, shown as rolling 120-day lagging averages. Source: Duffie and Krishnamurthy 2016.

rates, plotted as a spread from the mean rate at any given time, over a period from 2003 to 2016. These rates have been adjusted for credit and maturity differences. In theory, the spreads should all be zero, but they are not.

To give one example, we observe in the data that when the Fed increases its target for fed funds, short-term T-bill rates move up only slowly. This can be seen at the end of the sample. We ascribe this slow movement of T-bill rates to the fact that deposit rates move slowly because of imperfect competition across banks on the deposit side. Further, since T-bills and deposits are liquidity substitutes in investor portfolios, T-bill rates track the slow movements of deposit rates. This type of dispersion is the slippage in the monetary transmission mechanism.

Darrell and I show that the RRP can reduce dispersion. One can readily see why. The RRP effectively allows the nonbank public to deposit with the Fed, bypassing banks and leading to stickiness in deposit rates. RRP is a substitute for T-bills, so T-bill rates move more in line with the Fed's target rate.

In my paper with Darrell, we argue that some of the changes in the world over the last few years, including money market reform and the general rise in demand for safe assets, increase dispersion. The RRP is all the more valuable in today's world.

Let me link this back to balance sheet size. To offer an RRP, the Fed needs a large cushion of bank reserves in excess of reserve requirements. If the cushion is too small, sudden shifts in the demand for the RRP will drain reserves from the banking system, creating a liquidity squeeze. Thus, the framework needs sufficient excess reserves. How large? I am not sure, but for the sake of argument, let us say $1 trillion, which gives a balance sheet of about $2.5 trillion. That's large, but the current balance sheet is about twice that size.

These latter two arguments in favor of a large Treasuries-only balance sheet are arguments that IOER plus RRP aid in the efficacy of the monetary transmission mechanism.

I turn next to financial stability considerations. A growing literature in finance shows that investors have a special demand for safe short-term securities, such as bank debt, repo, and Treasury bills. In the finance term-structure literature, it is well understood that term structure models to fit the Treasury yield curve fail to price the shortest-term Treasury bills. To give an example, Greenwood, Hanson, and Stein (2015) document that investors accept low yields for holding one-week Treasury bills compared to alternatives such as six-month Treasury bills. My work with Annette Vissing-Jorgensen shows that this demand is satisfied by both government securities and private securities.

Figure 1.3.2 (Krishnamurthy and Vissing-Jorgensen 2015) plots the supply of government assets against the financial sector's short-term debt (net short-term debt), annually from 1875 to 2014. Both series are normalized by GDP and de-trended. The figure shows

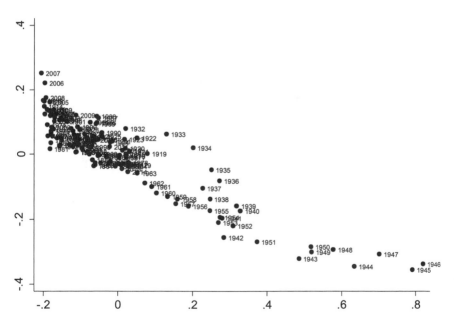

FIGURE 1.3.2. Government supply/GDP, de-trended. Source: Krishnamurthy and Vissing-Jorgensen 2015.

the strong substitution pattern between government securities and private securities. If the demand for safe assets is not satisfied by government securities, it will be satisfied by private securities. Annette and I show that shifts in safe asset demand are a significant factor driving the leverage of the banking system, and hence its fragility.

But private short-term financially engineered securities are a source of systemic risk, as we learned in the crisis. A financial system that has more equity and long-term debt, and less short-term runnable debt, is a safer system.

From this standpoint, operating a large Fed balance sheet, especially via the RRP, can satisfy investors' demand for safe assets and crowd out private financially engineered debt.

I do not have a target for balance sheet size but have suggested $2.5 trillion as a possibility. I think this should be on the agenda for the Fed to research. For example, the Fed could monitor safe asset premiums as a way to understand the private sector's incentives for financial engineering and size the balance sheet to counteract such premiums.

I have provided an argument grounded in monetary economics in favor of a large balance sheet. John Taylor acknowledges these points but views them as unimportant relative to the institutional design and mandate issues of the Fed. Charles Plosser is similarly concerned that opening the door to the types of concerns I have raised untethers the Fed's balance sheet.

These concerns can be addressed. Take the safe asset stability concern I mentioned. One way to tether the size of the balance sheet is to link the balance sheet to the size of safe asset premiums. That is, as noted, the Fed could systematically monitor safe asset premiums and link balance sheet size to these premiums, in the spirit of the Taylor rule. When safe asset premiums are high, the Fed would expand its balance sheet size to counteract the private sector's incentives for expansion, and the reverse. Right now, these premiums are relatively small, which indicates that currently we should have a relatively small balance sheet. As I have noted, something like $2.5 trillion may be appropriate. But in the period prior to the 2007–9 crisis, when safe asset premiums were high, my approach would have indicated that the Fed should have a much larger balance sheet to counteract the private sector's debt buildup.

Similarly, consider the mandate question: Should the provision of safe assets fall under the mandate of the Fed or the Treasury? I would argue that it should fall to the Fed. Why? Because such policy is fundamentally about financial stability, which is within the mandate of the Fed. It is about monitoring things like liquidity premiums and safe asset premiums, which is squarely within the Fed's expertise.

Thus, I conclude that the Fed operating a large balance sheet can deliver improvements in monetary policy pass-through and enhance financial stability. This can be done in a manner that tethers the Fed's balance sheet, allaying some of the concerns raised by John and Charlie.

References

Duffie, D., and A. Krishnamurthy. 2016. "Pass-through Efficiency in the Fed's New Monetary Policy Setting in Designing Resilient Monetary Policy Frameworks for the Future." Presented at the Federal Reserve Bank of Kansas City, Jackson Hole Symposium, August 25.

Greenwood, R., S. G. Hanson, and J. C. Stein. 2015. "A Comparative-Advantage Approach to Government Debt Maturity." *Journal of Finance* 70 (4): 1683–1722.

Krishnamurthy, Arvind, and Annette Vissing-Jorgensen. 2015. "The Impact of Treasury Supply on Financial Sector Lending and Stability." *Journal of Financial Economics* 118 (3): 571.

GENERAL DISCUSSION

JOHN COCHRANE: Thank you so much, Arvind. Now let's turn to questions. I particularly welcome questions on what I think are the two most central issues the panel raised. First, should the Fed go back to the system of controlling interest rates by rationing something like $14 billion of reserves and then letting that interest rate percolate out to the rest of the economy, as John said? Or should the Fed keep a large balance sheet so there's abundant liquidity and instead just set the interest rate on reserves as its operating mechanism for changing interest rates?

The second big question: Let's say we get a recession. Interest rates will be zero within about five minutes. Should the Fed embark on buying more assets? If it does, what should it buy? If the Fed wants 3 percent Treasury interest rates, maybe it should just open up the balance sheet. Bring us your Treasuries, in any quantity. We'll give you 3 percent reserves in return. That will nail the interest rate at 3 percent. Or should the balance sheet size be an independent tool and quantity?

Those seem to me to be the central questions.

DARRELL DUFFIE: First of all, kudos to the entire panel. I want to go to an interaction effect between the liquidity benefits you all spoke about and the monetary policy transmission issues that Arvind focused on. Arvind has a recent paper with Jennie Bai and Charles-Henri Weymuller that has data on the daily or weekly liquidity requirements of banks under the so-called liquidity coverage ratio rule.[7] This is a new regulation that is now interacting with everything the panel has talked about, because banks on a daily average basis are going to need to meet a very large liquidity requirement. And looking at those data, it looks like the daily volatility of that quantity is on the order of magnitude

---

7. Arvind Krishnamurthy, Jennie Bai, and Charles-Henri Weymuller, "Measuring Liquidity Mismatch in the Banking Sector." NBER Working Paper no. 22729, October 2016.

of the entire pre-2007 reserves. So if you went back to a small balance sheet and you steered interest rates using a very small rate of reserves, every day there would be a lot of bumping up and down from meeting these liquidity coverage ratio requirements, with banks lurching into and out of the reserves market to quickly meet their liquidity coverage ratio needs. This would make it very difficult for the Fed to steer rates merely by adding or subtracting reserves on a daily balance. They couldn't predict how much reserves they would need to have one day ahead. Arvind and I were recently discussing the implications of this for what would happen if we went back to a small balance sheet. And we ruminated that this would be a difficult issue for the Fed when steering rates.

JOHN TAYLOR: In answer to Darrell, yes, the ups and downs of my chart in Figure 1.2.1 are much larger in the more recent period. Some of the volatility in reserve balances during this period is due to the use of overnight reserve repurchase (ON RRP) agreements, which result in a reduction in reserve balances while the agreements are outstanding. There is a question as to whether that would make it harder for the Fed to influence the Feds rate, but if you add ON RRP to the chart I think it would indicate that the volatility is lower. Also, the liquidity coverage ratio itself is not nailed in stone.

JOHN COCHRANE: Darrell does have a good point. The old reserve requirement is not the binding constraint—banks have far more reserves than regulations require for their deposits. But now other constraints, such as liquidity and capital, may bind and force banks to hold reserves.

CHARLES PLOSSER: I guess I would just note that we're creating this problem, in part, for ourselves through our regulatory framework. In addition to liquidity ratio requirements, we have an FDIC tax on total assets that drives a wedge between depositary and non-depository institutions and thus is inhibiting the ability of interest on reserves to act as an effective floor for the funds rate and thus other short-term rates. And so, how necessary is that? Are we trying to change institutional and market arrangements to offset the unintended consequences of regulatory constraints imposed to accomplish unrelated objectives? Should the design of monetary policy be the handmaiden of the whims of regulations intended to address other issues? I think we should proceed with caution.

The other comment I'd like to make is about the RRP program. Clearly at some level, the more interest rates and short-term markets the Fed can intervene in to set a price and the interest rate, the more efficient or effective, in one sense I guess, monetary policy might be. But do we really want to move away from a world where markets are setting interest rates to one in which the Fed is playing an ever-bigger role? It seems to me, if you take this idea about improving the efficiency of monetary policy to its extreme, then why shouldn't the Fed intervene in all sorts of asset markets and security markets in order to get the prices where they think they ought to be? Wouldn't that really improve the "effectiveness" of monetary policy? But is controlling every interest rate really the goal? Why would you want to reduce market feedback and information? I'm not so sure that's a road we want to go down. The RRP is just a program to avoid congressional rules that say we can't pay interest on reserves to non-depository institutions. I just think we have to be very careful in wishing for a regime where we're inviting more and more intervention on the part of the Fed or even Congress and regulators, in setting all these prices. So I worry that these arguments are sort of a slippery slope where no limits are defined and institutional discretion could be vastly expanded.

MICHAEL DOTSEY: I have a comment that I'd like Arvind to respond to and then a question for him. In lots of our macro models, it's a quarterly interest rate that the Fed is operating on. And this sort of intraday volatility is not that important. Given that perspective, where do you think this intraday volatility is important?

And my question concerns excess reserves supplying safe assets. If we put out excess reserves and take these ten-day Treasury bills, that's not going to do much. So there's got to be some kind of maturity mismatch in order to supply safe assets with reserves. So what's the relationship between the right amount of maturity mismatch and the right amount of operations we should do?

ARVIND KRISHNAMURTHY: On the first question, the financial world has a bunch of activity that happens at a high frequency and ends up affecting security prices. The repo market is the perfect example of this. I would say that is a flaw of the macro model. It is missing important prices and quantity relations that are present in the world. And once you consider these, you start thinking about the issues I have pointed to as potentially important.

On the second question, I think you are asking, How much maturity mismatch should the Fed have? That's a fair question. I don't have an answer for that. One thing I can say is an important input would be to measure something like a safe asset premium. And there is a cost to be factored in, which relates to the points that Charlie and John brought up—that is, how much risk the central bank can take on its balance sheet. A cost-benefit trade-off would tell you how much maturity mismatch the central bank should take on.

PETER FISHER: Let me just make a few points, all intended to be provocative. I share John's perspective that we could go back and manage it with quantities; it's not impossible. We could just reengineer the system and go back to the way we were. I think we're arguing about whether it's desirable. I'll share two perspectives.

One, to Charlie's angst, a sort of good news and bad news. The good news is, once upon a time we had a Congress that cared about whether the Fed was going to do credit policy. It limited the instruments the Fed could use in open market operations to US Treasuries and agency mortgage-backed securities, because they cared about that. They didn't want the Fed doing that. We should all look carefully across the Atlantic to Europe, which made the terrible mistake when setting up the monetary union of treating each and every sovereign borrower as presenting equally good credit, and you got the same number of euros representing par on German government debt as on Spanish and Portuguese. And the mechanics of the crisis accelerated when they had to reverse that. So you can really mess things up by not understanding market prices and by what you do with your balance sheet.

To Arvind, I want to offer one thought. When I ran the open market desk, I was proud of the insight that I should care about intraday volatility and zero was the wrong number. And in retrospect, I suspect I repressed volatility too much, even though I was aware that the market was only going to work when I allowed it to have a certain amount. And so I'm deeply skeptical of the view that volatility is bad and the Fed can find the optimal level of volatility in the money markets by pressing it as low as possible.

So the Fed is running a large maturity mismatch across its balance sheet, by issuing short-dated liabilities and holding long-dated assets. You seem to think that, somehow, the Fed doing so will reduce the extent to which private financial intermediaries run maturity mismatches (engage in maturity transformation) across their own balance sheets. At best, this seems to me to be a very inefficient way of controlling private maturity transformation, and more likely, it is simply irrelevant: won't private intermediaries simply adjust the rest of their balance sheets to achieve their desired maturity mismatch?

ARVIND KRISHNAMURTHY: On the first comment about zero volatility, I would rephrase that as a footprint issue. How much of a footprint should the Fed have? If the Fed has too large a footprint, it is decreasing incentives for the private sector to do price discovery. So I share your view. Zero is probably not the right answer. Somewhere in the middle should be the right answer, as always. It strikes me that $14 billion in reserves was too far on the other side. Something healthy in the middle sounds like the right answer.

On the second point, the proposal of using the Fed's balance sheet to counteract the financial sector's maturity mismatch, which is what I was laying out, is a tool. It exists and can be used by the Fed. I think what you're suggesting is, maybe capital requirements, rather than the Fed's balance sheet, should be the tool used for financial stability. I understand that perspective, but we also know that capital requirements are an imperfect tool. For example, they only hit the regulated banking sector. Whereas something like using the Fed's balance sheet alters a market price, which is the price signal that drives maturity mismatch and would counteract any sector's maturity mismatches.

GEORGE SHULTZ: Governor Plosser indicated in his remarks that this large sum could be something that could finance, say, infrastructure or some other thing that comes along. In other words, the Fed has a honeypot to finance things. I think that's a very bad idea. Once used, there would be a great demand for the Fed to create another honeypot. It's a handy way of getting things you couldn't otherwise get. That, for me, is an argument for getting rid of it and learning to operate in the old-fashioned way.

CHARLES PLOSSER: I agree with you a hundred percent. The design of institutions is important. You want designs that enable and incentivize good outcomes, but you also should have constraints that reduce the likelihood of huge mistakes. Allowing a central bank's balance sheet to be unrelated to monetary policy invites abuses by the fiscal authorities (such as credit allocation or off-budget financing) or by the monetary authorities (credit allocation or discretionary interventions). You must understand the incentives at work and have well-defined constraints that act to limit potential abuses. That's the slippery slope. The incentives of different parties, when I was talking about how institutions matter—the incentives created here can be dangerous, and we need to be careful about them.

JOHN COCHRANE: I might add that the question is not just the quantities; it's the prices. The Bank of Japan is now buying stocks. And there's a lot of worry among the regulatory people that someone might sell stocks and the stock prices would go down. There would also be incentives for the Fed to buy in order to prop up stock prices.

JOHN TAYLOR: That was the reason for the MBS.

JOHN COCHRANE: Yes. And if that expands to stock and real estate and who knows what, that's even more dangerous.

WILLIAM NELSON: I also think the FOMC should go back to operating policy the way it used to. I'll add another perspective on one of the reasons.

I'm sensitive to the political risk of having a lot of reserves and paying a lot of interest. Another point I'd make is sort of the "if it ain't broke, why fix it" argument. Precrisis, the Fed operated in a small market. It conducted small reverse repos with broker-dealers. Those transactions were not that important to the broker-dealers. They weren't an important way they funded their balance sheet. Those transactions were transmitted to the interbank market for reserves, a whole different set of institutions, so that the market would clear. That was a small market. The banks did not see themselves in any sense as getting those reserves from the Fed, and the federal funds rate was transmitted beautifully to the other money market instruments in the rest of the economy. And there were lots of studies on whether the intraday volatility mattered, and of course we know as financial economists that it doesn't matter because it averages out almost immediately.

The alternative, as I see it, is the Fed being on either side of transactions throughout the economy. Instead of being a small, unimportant player, imagine that it is on both sides of a giant repo market, of LIBOR. It is engaged in all kinds of transactions that will leave a much larger footprint in the economy. I think the political risk they will be exposed to by being seen to be out there is also much higher. I see a risk to independence. I'm curious about perspectives on that issue.

I'm also sympathetic to the financial stability argument, and to the fact that the liquidity coverage ratio will increase the demand for the high-quality liquid assets (HQLA). But treasuries are also HQLA, so as the Fed sells Treasuries and reduces the quantity of reserves—it's kind of an open question what exactly will happen. And what I see as an important question the Fed faces now, as it pivots to reducing the size of its balance sheet toward the end of the year, is looking to see when market rates begin to open up and assessing the gap between that and interest on excess reserves (IOER). Maybe banks are going to want to hold a large quantity of reserves, because reserves are a convenient way to hold HQLA. Nonbanks, of course, can't hold reserves, but they can come to the RRP. But at the same time, I'm confident that if IOER was a hundred basis points below the fed funds rate, as was sort of a normal precrisis level, banks would find ways to economize on their reserves and meet their HQLA needs by other means or term out their borrowing beyond thirty days.

I agree that there's going to be a trade-off coming. I don't think the Fed can have a sort of smallish balance sheet floor system, which is one of the options people used to think they could have, and it's a good active debate, I think, to have as to how small it should be.

STEVE LIESMAN: I wonder if the panelists might address the size of the balance sheet relative to the current macro evidence. You've got a $4.4 trillion balance sheet, 2 percent inflation, an unemployment rate that's right around what's thought to be the potential 4.5 percent, and an economy growing right around potential 2 percent. What's wrong with that?

JOHN TAYLOR: I like those numbers.

But first, we're talking about other things that can be caused by the policy. Charlie and I gave a long list. And whether you could design the system so you don't get into that situation.

Second, it's not so much the size of the balance sheet; it's the large amount of excess reserves. It's the reserve balances that I showed you in Figure 1.2.1. The balance sheet could be large because of lots of currency being used. So reserve balances are the number to focus on. And I think all of the proposals we're working on here, including how you would have to operate this to have the connect between interest rate and reserves, are designed to prevent problems. Also I argue that the QE we had was not that helpful. Maybe it was counterproductive. Maybe it still is counterproductive. Lots of work is being done along those lines.

STEVE LIESMAN: Is the current economic performance telling you something about the necessary size of the balance sheet?

JOHN TAYLOR: The current size of the balance sheet is not informed by a particular unemployment number or a particular inflation number. It's informed by a desire to have monetary policy that is not limited in its purpose. It's a very expansive purpose, and many dangers could come from that—loss of independence, damage to other parts of the economy. So it's a question of wouldn't it be better—and I think it would—if we ran monetary policy like we did in the past? Obviously, the world is somewhat different. But Peter Fisher agrees we could do that, and I haven't heard reasons why we can't. There are issues around interest rate pass-through, but you don't want the pass-through to be exact. There's all sorts of things that happen from one market to another. There are many reasons for volatility. I think the question that Darrell raises about the volatility now is, to some extent, due to the different system for determining the interest rate. If you had to guide the supply of reserves so the interest rate was being determined by supply and demand, most likely you'd be offsetting a lot of those movements, and they would be smaller.

JOHN COCHRANE: I'd like to add that we have learned that huge amounts of reserves paying interest don't cause inflation. That was a worry we had going into this that turned out not to be true.

CHAPTER TWO
THE NATURAL RATE

. . . .

SECTION ONE

R-Star: The Natural Rate and Its Role in Monetary Policy

Volker Wieland

WHAT IS R-STAR AND WHY DOES IT MATTER?

The natural or equilibrium real interest rate has taken center stage in the policy debate on the appropriate stance for monetary policy in the United States and elsewhere. In Taylor-style rules for monetary policy, this rate is often denoted by r-star. This discussion draws on results from three recent research papers. The titles of these contributions speak directly to the available empirical evidence and the problems encountered in modeling and estimating r-star: "Finding the Equilibrium Real Interest Rate in a Fog of Policy Deviations" (Taylor and Wieland 2016), "Instability, Imprecision and Inconsistent Use of Equilibrium Real Interest Rate Estimates" (Beyer and Wieland 2017), and "Little Decline in Model-Based Estimates of the Long-Run Equilibrium Interest Rate" (Wieland and Wolters 2017).

The equilibrium real interest rate can be defined by using a simple aggregate demand relationship, as shown in Figure 2.1.1.

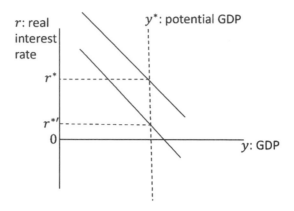

FIGURE 2.1.1. Aggregate demand, potential GDP, and r-star

The solid lines in Figure 2.1.1 display the aggregate demand curve in real interest rate and GDP space. The equilibrium rate r^* corresponds to the realization of aggregate demand—that is, the equilibrium of investment demand and aggregate savings—when GDP corresponds to the level of equilibrium output (potential GDP). Mathematically, this relationship can be expressed as follows:

$$y = y^* - \beta(r - r^*) + \alpha x \qquad (1)$$

The parameter β determines the sensitivity of aggregate demand to the real interest rate. The parameter α reflects the influence of other factors, which are denoted by x. This expression is easily rearranged to determine the level of the real interest rate r as a function of r^* and the other variables and parameters, as in Figure 2.1.1.

$$r = r^* - \beta^{-1}(y - y^*) + \alpha\beta^{-1}x \qquad (2)$$

If the aggregate-demand curve or savings-investment relationship shifts downward, the equilibrium rate r^* also declines. Of course, this downward shift of the aggregate demand curve could be temporary—for example, due to some economic shock. In this case, it would return fairly soon to the original level, and along with it the equilibrium rate. Or the shift could persist for a longer period, maybe due to fiscal policy or other persistent factors. Finally, it could be due to an essentially permanent change in the structure of the economy. Whether and how monetary policy would need to be adjusted depends on the nature of this shift and the degree of persistence.

Three different concepts of the equilibrium real interest rate that have received substantial attention in the literature are associated with different time horizons.

The first equilibrium rate concept is a purely short-run equilibrium. It is often referred to as the natural rate and is well formulated in New Keynesian dynamic stochastic general equilibrium (DSGE) models, where it corresponds to the value of the real interest rate that would be realized if prices are flexible (Neiss and Nelson 2003; Woodford 2003). This short-run equilibrium is influenced by temporary shocks other than monetary policy shocks. Estimates of this natural rate often exhibit greater variability than actual real interest rates, which are influenced by the presence of price rigidities. Some recent contributions have recommended that the central bank set policy rates in a way that drives the actual real interest rate to the value of this short-run natural rate (Barsky, Justiniano, and Melosi 2014; Curdia et al. 2015). Clearly, such a policy is highly model and shock dependent. It is not robust to model uncertainty but rather sensitive to the respective model specification.

Laubach and Williams (2003) introduced another equilibrium rate concept that has received much attention. This concept is of a medium-run nature. Its derivation is based on a mixture of atheoretical time-series methods and a simple Keynesian-style model consisting of an aggregate demand relationship and a Phillips curve relationship. The equilibrium rate is modeled as the function of potential growth and some preference parameters, similar to a fully specified general equilibrium model without imposing the cross-equation restrictions of such models. Equilibrium rate, potential GDP growth, and preference parameters are unobserved variables. How much they move depends on technical parameters of the unobserved components time-series specification. More recently, Laubach and Williams (2016) and Holston, Laubach, and Williams (2017) have provided updated estimates indicating a sharp decline toward values around 0 percent for the United States and lower values in the euro area. These estimates have had a substantial impact on policy making. Yet they are characterized by a large degree of imprecision, instability, and potential estimation bias (GCEE 2015; Taylor and Wieland 2016; Beyer and Wieland 2017).

A third concept is the long-run equilibrium rate or steady-state interest rate. The New Keynesian DSGE models that can be used to derive a short-run natural rate also include a long-run equilibrium rate or steady-state rate to which the short-run rate converges over time. This long-run equilibrium rate is a function of steady-state growth (per capita) and household rates of time preference and elasticity of substitution. Since the effects of price rigidities are temporary, the long-run equilibrium rate in New Keynesian DSGE models is equivalent to the equilibrium rate in a model of real economic growth (see, for example, Christiano, Eichenbaum, and Evans 2005; Smets and Wouters 2007).

This chapter focuses on estimates for medium-run and long-run equilibrium real rates that are often used as an element of monetary policy rules in order to prescribe a particular policy stance.

R-STAR, THE TAYLOR RULE, AND THE POLICY IMPACT OF THE LAUBACH-WILLIAMS ESTIMATES

Estimates of the medium-run equilibrium rate concept by Laubach and Williams (2003) have had an important influence on recent policy practice. The article originally referred to the Taylor (1993) rule for monetary policy to emphasize the role of the natural or equilibrium rate in measuring the policy stance "with policy expansionary (contractionary) if the short-term real interest rate lies below (above) the natural rate." The Taylor rule prescribes an expansionary (contractionary) stance for the federal funds rate (f) when inflation is below (above) a target rate (p^*) of 2 percent or output is below (above) its natural or equilibrium level (y^*). The response coefficients are 1.5 and 0.5, respectively.

$$f = r^* + p^* + 1.5(p - p^*) + 0.5(y - y^*)$$

$$= 2 + p + 0.5(p - 2) + 0.5(y - y^*) \qquad (3)$$

Taylor set the equilibrium rate r^* equal to 2 percent, which was "close to the assumed steady growth rate of 2.2 percent." He estimated this GDP trend growth rate over 1984:1 to 1992:3. The average real rate was also close to 2 percent over the 1984 to 1992 period. Interestingly, the average real federal funds rate from 1966:1 to 2016:4 stands at 1.91 percent. Thus, 2 percent is a candidate estimate for long-run equilibrium.

By contrast, Laubach and Williams (2003) have provided estimates that exhibit substantial time variation. As shown in Figure 2.1.2, values of the one-sided r-star estimate of their baseline model moved from a peak of 5 percent in the late 1960s to a bit below 2 percent by the late 1970s. After reaching another interim high of about 3 percent around 1990, the one-sided estimate dropped to values near 1 percent by 1995. Subsequently, it recovered to close to 3 percent by the year 2000. In terms of methodological contribution, Laubach and Williams emphasized that they estimated the natural rate of interest jointly with the natural level of output and natural rate of output growth. To a significant extent, changes in the r-star estimate were associated with changes in trend output growth. With regard to policy implications, they concluded

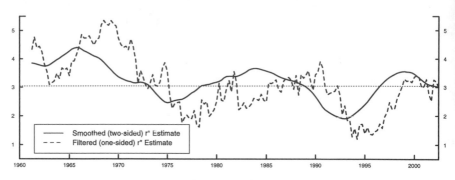

FIGURE 2.1.2. R-star estimates of Laubach and Williams 2003

that "estimates of a time-varying natural rate of interest . . . are very imprecise and are subject to considerable real-time mismeasurement. These results suggest that this source of uncertainty needs to be taken account of in analyzing monetary policies that feature responses to the natural rate of interest."

Estimates of a medium-run r-star using the Laubach-Williams methodology started to receive more attention after the Fed had kept the federal funds rate near zero for a few years following the global financial crisis. For example, referring to updated estimates available from the website of the Federal Reserve Board of San Francisco, Summers (2014) wrote that "their methodology demonstrates a very substantial and continuing decline in the [equilibrium] real rate of interest."

As shown in Figure 2.1.3, the one-sided estimate dropped from about 2 percent to 0 percent in 2009 and stayed there till 2014. Also, the estimates for the 1980s and 1990s had changed relative to the findings presented in Laubach and Williams (2003). For example, the trough of 1 percent in 1995 has disappeared. Similar results were published in Laubach and Williams (2016) and Holston, Laubach, and Williams (2017).

Krugman (2015) commented in his influential *New York Times* blog, "The low natural rate is as solid a result as anything in real

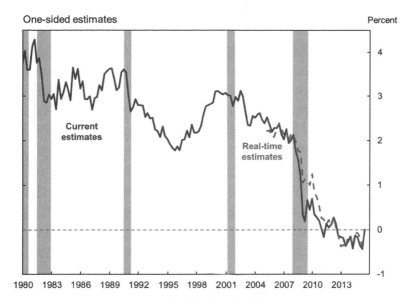

FIGURE 2.1.3. R-star estimates of Laubach and Williams 2016

time can be," referring to the Laubach-Williams estimates. In the same year as well as more recently, FOMC chair Janet Yellen made use of the Laubach-Williams r-star estimates together with the Taylor rule (Yellen 2015, 2017). Substituting the 0 percent natural rate estimate in the rule, she stated, "Under assumptions that I consider more realistic under present circumstances, the Taylor Rule calls for the federal funds rate to be close to zero." Yet neither Lawrence Summers nor Paul Krugman nor Janet Yellen took note of Laubach and Williams's original request: to account for uncertainty about the time-varying (medium-run) r-star estimate.

INSTABILITY, IMPRECISION, AND INCONSISTENT USE OF (MEDIUM-RUN) R-STAR ESTIMATES

Recently, Beyer and Wieland (2017) replicated the Laubach and Williams analysis, subjected it to sensitivity analysis, including

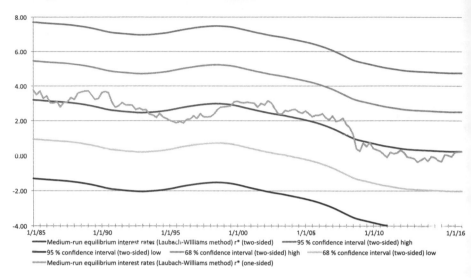

FIGURE 2.1.4. Uncertainty about Laubach and Williams estimates. Source: Beyer and Wieland 2017.

the specification detailed by Garnier and Wilhelmsen (2009), and applied the methodology to the euro area and to Germany. They document a large degree of uncertainty, much like Laubach and Williams (2003). Figure 2.1.4 indicates 66 percent and 95 percent confidence intervals for the smoothed or two-sided r-star estimates. Most recently, the 95 percent confidence interval spans the range between about +5.5 percent and −4.5 percent. So from this perspective, the observed variation in the Laubach-Williams medium-run r-star estimates is not statistically significant.

Furthermore, Beyer and Wieland show that these estimates remain sensitive to seemingly innocuous changes in technical assumptions concerning the underlying atheoretical time-series model. If one plugs in different technical assumptions, one gets very different estimates. The degree of imprecision and instability of these estimates is not a new finding per se but has unfortunately not been appreciated in the above-mentioned policy contributions.

A second concern regards how the estimates of r-star have been used. Laubach and Williams emphasize the joint estimation of the natural interest rate with the natural rate of output. Thus, it would

FIGURE 2.1.5. Inconsistent use of r-star estimates. Source: Beyer and Wieland 2017.

be consistent to use them together in a Taylor rule. By contrast, Yellen uses the Laubach-Williams medium-run r-star estimate of 0 percent together with an estimate of long-run potential output derived from a long-run non-accelerating inflation rate of unemployment (NAIRU) estimate. As a result, she obtains a Taylor rule prescription for the federal funds rate near 0 percent. But if one uses instead the consistent output gap estimate obtained with the Laubach-Williams methodology, the federal funds rate prescriptions from the Taylor rule shift up substantially, as shown by Beyer and Wieland (see Figure 2.1.5).

The Taylor rule calculations in Figure 2.1.5 make use of personal consumption expenditures inflation. The line labeled "Standard Taylor rule" employs a (long-run) r-star estimate of 2 percent together with the (long-run) output gap proposed by Yellen (2017). Her output gap estimate is based on the unemployment rate using Okun's law with an estimate of the long-run NAIRU. This measurement of output gap declines following the start of the global financial crisis, reaching a trough of −8 percent in 2010. The gap has closed in 2016. The line labeled "Yellen-Taylor rule" instead uses estimates of the medium-run r-star obtained with the Laubach-Williams method together with the long-run output gap from Yellen (2017). Finally, the darkest line uses the jointly estimated r-star and natural output level obtained with the Laubach-Williams method. The latter is quite different from the Yellen estimate. Because of low estimated trend growth, the output gap closes much earlier and registers near +2 percent in 2016 and 2017. As a consequence, there is much less disagreement between the standard Taylor rule and the consistent Yellen-Taylor rule in 2016 and 2017 with levels for the federal funds rate near 2 percent.

A third concern is omitted variable bias—a point made by Taylor and Wieland (2016) and Cukierman (2016). For example, r-star estimates based on simple models consisting of an aggregate demand curve and a Phillips curve omit factors such as regulatory, fiscal, and monetary policy. If the output gap in equation (1) is lower than predicted, the method adjusts the estimate of r^* downward. Similarly, if inflation is higher than predicted by a simple Phillips curve that relates inflation to the output gap, then the estimate of y^* is adjusted downward. Yet there may be other reasons for low GDP, such as regulation reducing investment demand or tax policy reducing consumption. In equation (1) these factors are denoted by the variable x, but they are not included in the type of models estimated by Laubach and Williams and many others. Also, they omit a financial sector and a central bank reaction function, which creates another relationship that makes nominal and real interest rates endogenous (see equation [3]). If the federal funds rate is not equal to the prediction from the reaction function, one can adjust the r^*. However, the source of low interest rates may instead be a persistent deviation on the part of the central bank from past policy practice, as suggested by the evidence in Shin (2016) and Hofmann and Bogdanova (2012), among others.

ESTIMATES OF LONG-RUN R-STAR HAVE
NOT DECLINED SIGNIFICANTLY

Given that frequently used estimates of a time-varying medium-run r-star suffer from great imprecision, instability, and omitted variable bias, it would be helpful for monetary policy to consider more structural modeling and focus on the longer run. Thus Wieland and Wolters (2017) employ two recent estimated models for the US economy in the vein of the influential modeling approach of Christiano, Eichenbaum, and Evans (2005): the model of Smets and Wouters (2007), which provides a complete estimation using Bayesian methods on US data, and the model of Del Negro and Schorfheide (2015), which includes frictions and accelerator effects in the financial sector and provides postfinancial crisis estimates.

In these two models, the long-run equilibrium real interest rate—that is, the steady-state interest rate (r^*)—is a function of trend GDP growth in steady state (Y), consumer time preference (β), and intertemporal elasticity of substitution (σ_c):

$$r^* = \frac{\gamma^{\sigma_c}}{\beta} \tag{4}$$

Wieland and Wolters proceed to estimate these steady-state quantities using the two structural models. Here r^* and Y are functions of other structural parameters. Estimates are influenced by empirical averages as well as priors for other structural parameters. Furthermore, these models show why average real interest rates might deviate from the long-run equilibrium rate over a sustained period of time.

Of course, the assumption of a constant steady state may be unrealistic. There may well be changes in long-term trends and structural breaks. Thus Wieland and Wolters estimate the models for different time periods (1966:1–2016:4, 1966:1–1979:1, 1966:1–2004:4, 1984:1–2016:4). Furthermore, they address the issue of structural breaks through rolling estimation. In this case, the model is based on historical data vintages, essentially every quarter, keeping the window of estimation fixed at twenty years.

The original Smets-Wouters estimate of r^* for the sample period 1966:1–2004:1 is 3 percent. This is a bit above the sample mean federal funds rate of 2.65 percent for that period. Trend GDP growth per capita is 1.72 percent for that period. For a shorter sample, up to 1979:1, the estimate of the equilibrium rate is a bit smaller at 2.4 percent. Extending the sample to 2016:1 gives 2.2 percent. Just using data starting 1984:1 results in an estimate of 2.18 percent.

All these estimates are positive and significantly different from 0. Typical 95 percent confidence intervals are +/– 1 percent or at most +/– 1.5 percent wide. They are substantially smaller than the confidence intervals for the medium-run time-varying r-star estimates.

The Del Negro and Schorfheide model typically gives slightly smaller estimates. For example, r^* is 1.75 percent for the 1966:1–2016:1 sample. Yet 95 percent confidence intervals are a bit narrower for this model. The estimation of the Del Negro and Schorfheide model incorporates additional data on corporate risk premiums.

Given these findings, a natural conclusion would be to stick to the more precisely estimated long-run concept of the equilibrium real rate as a reference point for monetary policy. Policy rules such as the Taylor rule then prescribe higher or lower rates in response to developments in observable data such as inflation, GDP, and GDP growth rather than an unobserved concept such as a time-varying medium-run natural real interest rate.

The real-time rolling-window estimates of Wieland and Wolters (2017) shown in Figure 2.1.6 indicate that long-run r-star estimates change a bit over time once the sample period is limited to twenty years (solid black line). To generate these estimates, the respective model is re-estimated every quarter based on the newly available data vintage while restricting the sample period to twenty years. These estimates have declined below the 3 percent estimate from 2007 but remain above 2 percent in 2016. The decline in the

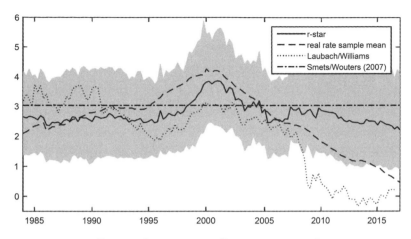

FIGURE 2.1.6. Rolling-window estimates of long-run r-star with Smets-Wouters model. Source: Wieland and Wolters 2017.

estimate of long-run r-star is mostly explained by a decline in the estimated trend GDP growth rate. The shaded area indicates the 95 percent confidence interval. It implies that the estimates are positive and substantially different from the Laubach-Williams estimates of near 0 percent (dotted line).

Figure 2.1.6 also shows the average real federal funds rate over the respective twenty-year periods (dashed line). Since 2009, this average rate has declined substantially. In 2016, it takes on a value of about 0.45 percent. The structural model can be used to analyze sources of the difference between the average real interest rate and the estimated long-run equilibrium real interest rate. Thus, it can answer questions concerning what factors are driving these low real interest rates.

The difference between the twenty-year average of the real funds rate of 0.45 percent and the equilibrium real interest rate in the Smets-Wouters model (in 2016) can largely be attributed to unusually easy monetary policy and unusually high risk premiums. Specifically, 0.83 percent—that is, about one-half of the total difference between the twenty-year average real rate and the long-run equilibrium rate—is attributed to monetary policy shocks. Another 0.48 percent, a bit more than a quarter of the difference, is attributed to risk-premium shocks. The risk-premium shocks lower the real rate of nominally safe assets such as Treasury bills relative to corporate debt, a point recently also made by Del Negro et al. (2017).

CONCLUSIONS

Yellen (2015, 2017) and Draghi (2016) have referred to the decline in estimates of time-varying (medium-run) equilibrium real interest rates obtained with simple IS–Phillips curve time-series models (Laubach and Williams 2003, 2016) as an important argument for keeping policy rates near zero interest-rate levels. Yet these estimates are highly imprecise and unstable. They do not indicate an empirically significant decline and may suffer from omitted variable bias. Thus they are not that helpful for monetary policy practice. In addition, these equilibrium rate estimates are obtained jointly with estimates of potential GDP that have been below actual US GDP for a number of years.

By contrast, estimates of a long-run equilibrium rate obtained with more fully specified structural macroeconomic models have not declined that much. They are positive and statistically quite different from zero. The models attribute lower average real funds rates to unusually easy monetary policy and unusually high risk premiums.

With regard to the use of equilibrium real rate estimates in monetary policy, I would draw the following conclusions. Estimates of time-varying (medium-run) r-star should be treated with great caution. It would seem better to stick to the more precisely estimated long-run concept of the equilibrium real rate as a reference point for monetary policy. Policy rules such as the Taylor rule then prescribe higher or lower rates in response to developments in observable data such as inflation, GDP, and GDP growth rather than some unobserved concept such as a time-varying medium-run natural real interest rate. Interestingly, however, if one uses the jointly estimated (medium-run) y-star (potential GDP) together with the (medium-run) r-star, one obtains federal funds rate prescriptions that are much closer to a rule that uses estimates of long-run equilibrium values for both. Additionally, it would be useful to consider a Taylor-style rule in first differences, which therefore do not include an r-star, as a second reference point.

References

Barsky, Robert, Alejandro Justiniano, and Leonardo Melosi. 2014. "The Natural Rate of Interest and Its Usefulness for Monetary Policy." *American Economic Review* 104 (5): 37–43.

Bernanke, Ben, Mark Gertler, and Simon Gilchrist. 1999. "The Financial Accelerator in a Quantitative Business Cycle Framework." *Handbook of Macroeconomics* 1: 1341–93.

Beyer, Robert, and Volker Wieland. 2017. "Instability, Imprecision and Inconsistent Use of Equilibrium Real Interest Rate Estimates." CEPR Discussion Paper no. 11927, Center for Economic Policy Research, London.

Christiano, Lawrence, Martin Eichenbaum, and Charles L. Evans. 2005. "Nominal Rigidities and the Dynamic Effects of a Shock to Monetary Policy." *Journal of Political Economy* 113 (1): 1–45.

Cukierman, A. 2016. "Reflections on the Natural Rate of Interest, Its Measurement, Monetary Policy and the Zero Bound." CEPR Discussion Paper no. 11467, Center for Economic Policy Research, London.

Curdia, Vasco, Andrea Ferrero, Ging Cee Ng, and Andrea Tambalotti. 2015. "Has U.S. Monetary Policy Tracked the Efficient Interest Rate?" *Journal of Monetary Economics* 70:72–83.

Del Negro, Marco, Domenico Giannone, Marc Giannoni, and Andrea Tambalotti. 2017. "Safety, Liquidity, and the Natural Rate of Interest." Federal Reserve Bank of New York, Staff Reports 812.

Del Negro, Marco, and Frank Schorfheide. 2015. "Inflation in the Great Recession and New Keynesian Models." *American Economic Journal: Macroeconomics* 7 (1): 168–96.

Draghi, M. 2016. "The International Dimension of Monetary Policy." Presented to the ECB Forum on Central Banking, Sintra, June 28.

Garnier, J., and B.-R. Wilhelmsen. 2009. "The Natural Rate of Interest and the Output Gap in the Euro Area: A Joint Estimation." *Empirical Economics* 36:297–319.

German Council of Economic Experts (GCEE). 2015. "Focus on Future Viability." Annual Economic Report for 2015/16.

Hofmann, Boris, and Bilyana Bogdanova. 2012. "Taylor Rules and Monetary Policy: A Global Great Deviation?" *BIS Quarterly Review* (September).

Holston, K., T. Laubach, and J. C. Williams. 2017. "Measuring the Natural Rate of Interest: International Trends and Determinants." *Journal of International Economics*, forthcoming.

Krugman, Paul. 2015. "Check Out Our Low, Low (Natural) Rates." *New York Times*, October 28.

Laubach, T., and J. C. Williams. 2003. "Measuring the Natural Rate of Interest." *Review of Economics and Statistics* 85 (4): 1063–70.

Laubach, T., and J. C. Williams. 2016. "Measuring the Natural Rate of Interest Redux." *Business Economics* 51:257–67.

Neiss, K., and E. Nelson. 2003. "The Real Interest Rate Gap as an Inflation Indicator." *Macroeconomic Dynamics* 7 (2): 239–62.

Shin, Hyun-Song. 2016. "Macroprudential Tools, Their Limits, and Their Connection with Monetary Policy." In *Progress and Confusion: The State of Macroeconomic Policy*, edited by Olivier Blanchard, Raghuram Rajan, Kenneth Rogoff, and Lawrence H. Summers. Cambridge, MA: MIT Press.

Smets, F., and Wouters, R. 2007. "Shocks and Frictions in US Business Cycles: A Bayesian DSGE Approach." *American Economic Review* 97 (3): 586–606.

Summers, Lawrence. 2014. "U.S. Economic Prospects: Secular Stagnation, Hysteresis, and the Zero Lower Bound." *Business Economics* 49 (2): 65–73.

Taylor, John B. 1993. "Discretion versus Policy Rules in Practice." *Carnegie-Rochester Conference Series on Public Policy* 39:195–214.

Taylor, John B., and Volker Wieland. 2016. "Finding the Equilibrium Real Interest Rate in a Fog of Policy Deviations." *Business Economics* 51 (3): 147–54.

Wieland, Volker, and Maik Wolters. 2017. "Little Decline in Model-Based Estimates of the Long-Run Equilibrium Interest Rate." Working paper, IMFS.

Woodford, Michael. 2003. *Interest and Prices: Foundations of a Theory of Monetary Policy*. Princeton, NJ: Princeton University Press.

Yellen, J. 2015. "Normalizing Monetary Policy: Prospects and Perspectives." Remarks at the New Normal Monetary Policy conference, Federal Reserve Bank of San Francisco.

Yellen, J. 2017. "The Economic Outlook and Conduct of Monetary Policy." Remarks at Stanford Institute for Economic Policy Research, Stanford University, January 19.

• •

SECTION TWO

Should Policy Makers Worry about R-Star?

Reconsidering Interest Rate Policies as a Stabilization Tool

Lee E. Ohanian

Policy makers in the Federal Reserve and other central banks have expressed concern that the long-run equilibrium interest rate, referred to as "r-star" in the literature on monetary policy, has declined considerably since the Great Recession, and that this will affect central bank interest rate policies for business cycle stabilization. Specifically, policy makers worry that a low r-star will either constrain or limit the usefulness of traditional monetary (interest rate) policies during economic downturns, given the zero lower bound (ZLB) on nominal interest rates. There is additional concern about monetary policies and the possible effect of r-star through secular stagnation arguments, in which low nominal demand is constraining long-run economic growth.

This chapter presents a very different view of r-star and central bank policies. I argue that the level of r-star is not particularly important, because several of the assumptions underlying the centrality of r-star in policy-making circles, including the importance of short-run monetary policies as an economic stabilizer and the assumed importance of secular stagnation arguments, have limited or in some cases no empirical support. This suggests that policy makers are placing too much emphasis on short-run monetary policies aimed at either stimulating an economy that's perceived to be operating below trend or preventing an economy from rising above trend. I propose an alternative channel for policy makers, which is aimed at improving the efficiency of the allocation of capital through financial markets.

The text is organized as follows. The first section describes the standard view of r-star, delineating how it may affect monetary policies, as well as presenting evidence that the Phillips curve has little if any empirical support in recent US data. The following section presents band-passed filtered data on macroeconomic variables to show that aggregate fluctuations for over thirty years have been driven primarily by very long-run components that are typically considered to be beyond the scope of monetary policies. The final section presents data on asset returns to show that the secular stagnation view on economic growth and returns to investment has no empirical support among business assets.

THE STANDARD VIEW ON R-STAR AND ITS IMPACT ON MONETARY POLICY

R-star is defined by the Federal Reserve Board of Governors (2016) as "the short-term real rate such that policy is neither accommodative nor contractionary." To see how the level of r-star impacts short-run monetary policies, consider the standard Fisher equation, in which the nominal interest rate includes two components, expected inflation, which is denoted as π^e_{t+1}, and the expected real return of the asset, which is denoted as r^e_{t+1}:

$$i_t = \pi^e_{t+1} + r^e_{t+1} \qquad (1)$$

In our current low-inflation environment, the nominal interest rate will be low when the real return (r-star) is low. This affects the Federal Reserve's ability to pursue interest rate policies during a period of perceived economic weakness because of the ZLB.

Note that the level of r-star matters for central bank interest rate policies, which are tools widely used by central banks for business cycle stabilization. The assumed importance of short-run interest policies as a stabilization tool is based on three perceptions. One is the Phillips curve, which I define as a systematic empirical relationship between unemployment—or other measures of economic slack—and inflation, which can be exploited by interest rate policies. The second perception is that business cycle fluctuations are assumed to be primarily due to temporary demand shocks. These two perceptions are key assumptions for policy makers because they provide the foundations of the application of interest policies for the purpose of macroeconomic stabilization.

A third, more recent perception, secular stagnation, is complementary to the first two perceptions. This is the view that chronically low aggregate demand is depressing trend economic growth, and as a result the US economy and some other advanced economies are stuck in a low real rate of return environment. This view further suggests that policy makers may need to significantly increase inflation to avoid the ZLB associated with a low r-star in future policy situations.

There is little evidence, however, to support the perceptions that underlie the importance of short-term monetary policies and the importance of the level of r-star. In 2001, Andy Atkeson and I wrote a paper for the Federal Reserve Bank of Minneapolis on the accuracy of inflation forecasting within the Federal Reserve System (Atkeson and Ohanian 2001). At that time, the Fed and many other inflation forecasters based forecasts of future inflation on the Phillips curve or related relationships. The idea behind this forecasting approach is that future inflation would be low if unemployment was high and, alternatively, that future inflation would be high if unemployment was currently low.

Atkeson and Ohanian (2001) compared different inflation forecasting models to determine their relative accuracy. We judged the accuracy of the forecasts using a standard criterion, which is the root mean square error (RMSE) of the forecast. This statistic measures the average error of the forecast. The forecasts analyzed include those made by the Federal Reserve Board as presented in the Fed's Green Book, which is the material that forms the basis of the discussion by the Fed's Federal Open Market Committee (FOMC), as well as statistical forecasts of inflation developed by James Stock and Mark Watson (2007, 2009).

The accuracy of these forecasts was compared to a "naive" inflation forecast, which is similar to a random walk forecast. The naive forecast predicts that inflation over any four-quarter period would be equal to inflation from the previous four-quarter period. We, as well as other forecasters inside and outside the Fed, were very surprised to find that the naive forecast performed considerably better than either the Board of Governors' Green Book forecast or the Stock-Watson forecasts. In particular, the RMSE, which is a standard measure of forecasting accuracy of professional forecasts, was as much as 94 percent higher than that of the naive forecasting model.

These results raise an important question: Why did such a simple forecasting approach, which made no use of any information other than the previous inflation rate, produce much more accurate forecasts than those using far greater information and the considerable expertise of top professional forecasters and economists?

The answer is that the Board of Governors forecasts and the Stock-Watson forecasts reflected a view that economic slack, as expressed in the unemployment rate, predicts future inflation. However, there is no systematic empirical relationship between future inflation and unemployment or other measures of economic slack. This lack of a systematic empirical basis thus induces significant error into these forecasts.

This surprising finding regarding the relative accuracy of these forecasts led to a number of follow-up studies, including several by Stock and Watson (2007, 2009). After considerable analysis of the failure of the Phillips curve to forecast inflation, Stock and Watson

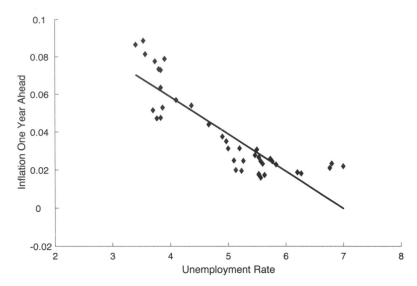

FIGURE 2.2.1. 1959–69: the Phillips curve appears

wrote in 2009, "Suppose you're told the next quarter the economy would plunge into recession, with the unemployment rate jumping by two percentage points. Would that lead you to change your inflation forecast? The literature is now full of formal, statistical evidence suggesting that this information should be ignored."

Figures 2.2.1–2.2.5 demonstrate how the relationship between unemployment and inflation has evolved over time. These figures clearly show the lack of a systematic relationship between these variables. Figure 2.2.1 shows the relationship between the level of unemployment and inflation one year later, between 1959 and 1969, along with a least squares regression line between these variables. This figure shows a negative relationship between these variables and clearly suggests the possibility of using unemployment as a predictor of future inflation based on data at this time.

However, this relationship disappears after 1969. Figure 2.2.2 shows the relationship between the same variables between 1970 and 1999, along with the least squares regression line. Figure 2.2.2

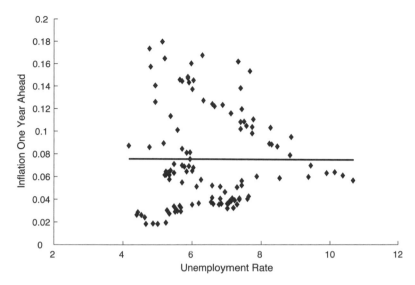

FIGURE 2.2.2. 1970–99: the Phillips curve disappears

shows that the negative relationship is gone, with a regression coefficient that is roughly zero. Figure 2.2.3 shows the Phillips curve from 2008, which is the beginning of the financial crisis, through 2016. The figure shows that the Phillips is now sloping upward. These figures show that the stable, downward-sloping Phillips curve relationships that motivate the forecasting approaches used by the Fed and other forecasters have not been in the data for more than forty years.

The breakdown of the 1959–69 Phillips curve led some economists to reformulate the Phillips curve. This reformulation of the Phillips curve was known as the non-accelerating inflation rate of unemployment (NAIRU) Phillips curve. The NAIRU specification of the Phillips curve fits a relationship between the change in the inflation rate and unemployment, rather than the level of inflation and unemployment, as used in Figure 2.2.1.

Figure 2.2.4 shows the NAIRU Phillips curve for the 1970–83 period for unemployment, and the change in inflation one year

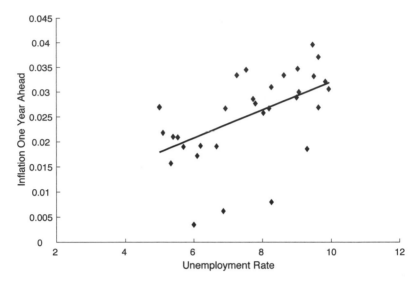

FIGURE 2.2.3. 2008–16: the Phillips curve is gone

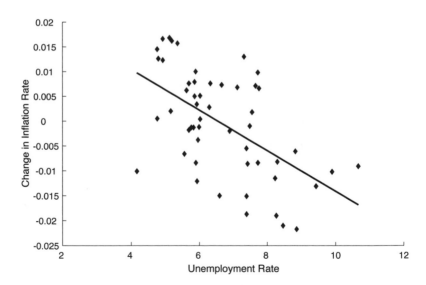

FIGURE 2.2.4. 1970–83: the expectation Phillips curve appears

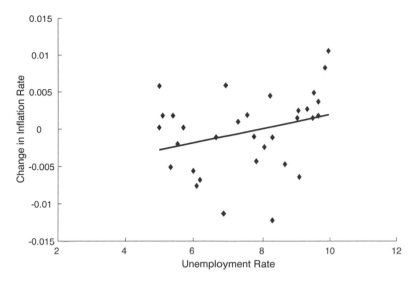

FIGURE 2.2.5. 2008–2016: the expectation Phillips curve is gone

later. Note that a negative relationship appears in this graph, which led forecasters to believe they had found a reliable specification to forecast inflation based on the Phillips curve. However, this reformulated specification also broke down over time. Figure 2.2.5 shows the NAIRU Phillips curve between 2008 and 2016, and as in the case of the standard Phillips curve, the regression line is upward sloping, indicating the exact opposite relationship between unemployment and future inflation relative to forecaster beliefs. These data highlight why Stock and Watson indicate that unemployment and other measures of economic slack should not be used to forecast inflation.

These figures show that both formulations of the Phillips curve broke down over time and raise questions as to why it has changed so much. Since Lucas (1976), economists have known that the Phillips curve is probably not a structural relationship and therefore may exhibit temporal instability that reflects individual and business expectations. However, the breakdown in the Phillips curve probably goes much deeper than that. The premise behind the Phillips curve is that nominal wages and nominal prices are both inflexible and can take quite some time to change in response to monetary policy changes. However, there are a number of good reasons for why these nominal price and wage inflexibilities have changed over time. In fact, there is considerable evidence to suggest that impediments to changing nominal prices and wages, as well as incentives to change nominal prices and wages, have changed considerably.

One important factor is that unionization is much different today than in the past. In the 1950s and 1960s, which is the period in which the Phillips curve was present in the data, the private-sector unionization rate peaked at about 35 percent. Moreover, union collective bargaining contracts specified wages for periods as long as five years into the future. Today, the private-sector unionization rate has declined from a peak of 35 percent to about 6 percent. Moreover, the duration and rigidity of nominal wages within collective bargaining contracts have changed. Thus, a large and important source of wage stickiness has changed considerably over time.

The incentives to change nominal wages have also changed. The implicit view underlying nominal wage stickiness is that the benefit of modifying the employment terms is fairly small, amounting to less than the cost of making these changes. But a growing body of literature shows that workers who lose a job during a recession experience a very large drop in long-term future wages. This research dates back to work by Jacobson, Lalonde, and Sullivan (1993) and more recently includes research by Davis and Von Wachter (2011). These analyses show that workers who lose a job during a recession suffer future wage declines of as much as 25 percent far into the future. This evidence suggests that workers will be highly motivated to renegotiate their wages with their current employer should the value of their labor services decline, rather than accept a layoff, experience potentially long-term unemployment, and ultimately accept future compensation that is 25 percent lower than their previous compensation.

In terms of price stickiness, enormous technological change has affected many aspects of consumer and business transactions, including pricing technologies and information about prices, as well as marketing and distribution technologies. This has been accompanied by tremendous growth in online purchases and imports, both of which suggest considerably more competitive pressure today relative to the economy of the 1950s and 1960s. These developments suggest that the cost of changing prices has declined significantly, and the incentives to change prices have increased, as the failure to do so may substantially affect a firm's ability to compete. In addition, deregulation in transportation, telecommunications, finance, and other areas indicates more price competition.

While much more research is required to gain a better understanding of these important issues, these points suggest that nominal wage and price stickiness, as well as the distortionary allocative effects of this inefficiency, may have declined considerably over time. This indicates that the disappearance of the Phillips curve from recent US data is not at all surprising, and that this disappearance may indeed be a permanent feature of the US economy.

MACROECONOMIC FLUCTUATIONS ARE DRIVEN BY EXTREMELY PERSISTENT SHOCKS

The second perception underlying the importance of r-star is that transitory demand shocks are the dominant component driving US cyclical fluctuations. This perception is key, because it is a long-standing foundation of the use of traditional central bank interest rate policies as a tool for macroeconomic stabilization. Figures 2.2.6–2.2.12 show that this view has limited empirical support, particularly for fluctuations since the early 1980s. These figures, which are updated from recent research I conducted with Gary

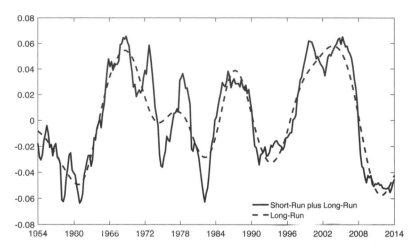

FIGURE 2.2.6. The relative importance of long- and short-run components in a log of real GDP

Hansen (Hansen and Ohanian 2016), decompose a number of macroeconomic variables into two components. One component is the traditional business cycle, with cycles of no more than eight years in length. The other component involves very long-run fluctuations, which have cycles between eight and fifty years. Monetary policy is traditionally presumed to be potentially important for the short-run cycles, but not for the very long-run cycles.

These components are constructed using the band pass filter (see Hansen and Ohanian 2016). The sum of the two components is roughly equal to all deviations from a straight trend line. Figure 2.2.6 shows the log of real GDP in the United States from 1954 through 2016. The solid line represents the sum of the two components, and the dashed line represents only long-run fluctuations of more than eight years. There are two notable patterns. In the 1960s and 1970s, there's a large difference between the dashed line and the solid line, which means that the short-run transitory component is quantitatively important. This pattern, however, changes after the early 1980s. After this time, the dashed and solid

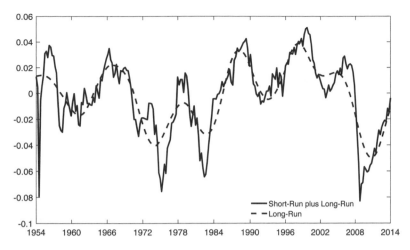

FIGURE 2.2.7. The relative importance of long- and short-run components in a
log of total hours worked

lines are almost the same. This means that the transitory movements in real GDP for most of the last thirty-five years are negligible, indicating that the potential for monetary policy either
depressing the economy or promoting economic growth in this
period was negligible. In contrast, almost all of the deviations from
trend most likely reflect very long-run factors, such as technological change, and long-run policy changes, rather than monetary
policy. Figures 2.2.7–2.2.9 present analogous graphs for US hours
worked, consumption, and total factor productivity. These graphs
present similar patterns, with a significant short-run component
in the earlier years but very long-run fluctuations being by far the
most important after the early 1980s.

The short-run component is also quantitatively unimportant in
other countries. Figures 2.2.10–2.2.12 show real GDP from three
European countries: France, Germany, and Spain. Note that the
dashed and solid lines are almost identical, indicating that almost
all the deviation from a linear trend is due to very long-run changes
and not short-run, demand-induced changes. As discussed above,

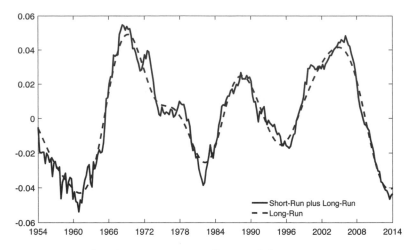

FIGURE 2.2.8. The relative importance of long- and short-run components in a log of consumption

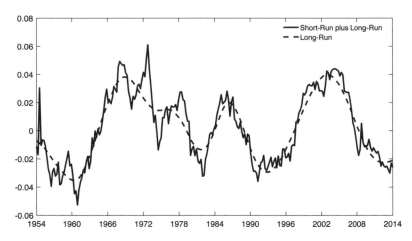

FIGURE 2.2.9. The relative importance of long- and short-run components in a log of total factor productivity

these long-run changes more plausibly reflect long-run changes in technologies, demographics, and regulatory, tax, or other long-run policies, rather than monetary policy. These data provide substantial evidence against the view that monetary policy is an effective stabilization tool in today's economy, irrespective of the level of r-star.

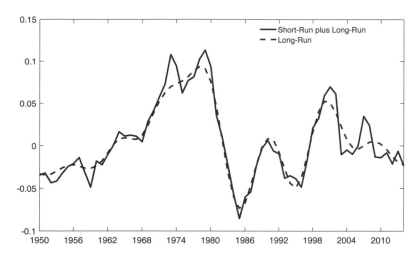

FIGURE 2.2.10. The relative importance of long- and short-run components in a log of real GDP: France

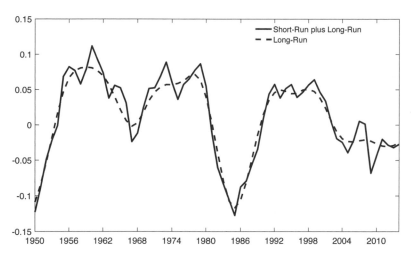

FIGURE 2.2.11. The relative importance of long- and short-run components in a log of real GDP: Germany

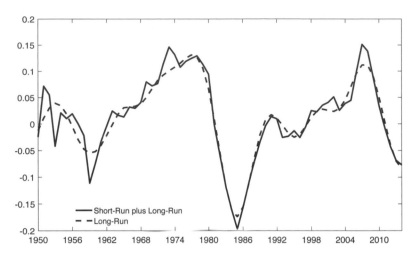

FIGURE 2.2.12. The relative importance of long- and short-run components in a log of real GDP: Spain

SECULAR STAGNATION? THE RETURN TO PRIVATE-SECTOR CAPITAL IS HISTORICALLY HIGH

Concern about the level of r-star is also associated with secular stagnation, which is the perception that the combination of high savings and low demand keeps returns to saving low, which in turn depresses economic growth. This section presents data on returns and shows that returns to business capital—which is the stock of assets that are directly relevant for economic growth—are historically high, not low, and that low returns only exist for safe government assets. The data presented here are updated from that presented in Gomme, Ravikumar, and Rupert (2011), which constructed returns on a number of assets, both government assets and private assets.

Figure 2.2.13 shows the return for the ninety-day real Treasury rate. Today's real Treasury rate is clearly low compared to historical performance. Recently the real rate has been around twenty-five basis points or even less, whereas it fluctuated from fifty basis

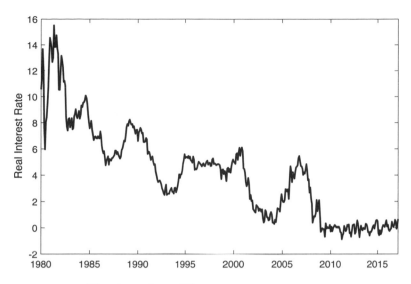

FIGURE 2.2.13. The ninety-day real Treasury rate

points all the way up to nearly 6 percent between the early 1990s
and 2005. Today's low returns on government debt are the foundation of the secular stagnation view. However, these assets are
government assets, and they are not the capital used by private business to produce goods and services. Figures 2.2.14 and 2.2.15 show
both before- and after-tax returns to private business capital. Figure
2.2.14 shows the raw returns, and Figure 2.2.15 shows the same
returns smoothed using a moving average. These data indicate that
both pre- and post-tax returns to investment are historically high.
Over the last five years, the pre-tax return has been about 11.8 percent per year, which is about 110 basis points above its historical
average, and the post-tax return has been about 7.6 percent, which
is about 160 basis points above its historical average.

These data do not support the secular stagnation view that
returns to business assets are low.

Despite these high returns to business capital, business investment has been remarkably low. To demonstrate, I first note that in

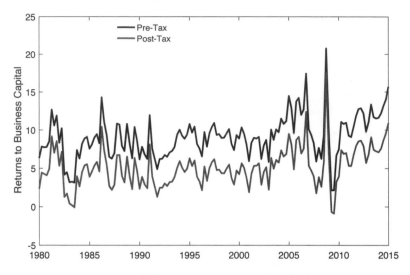

FIGURE 2.2.14. Pre-tax and post-tax returns to capital are high: raw returns

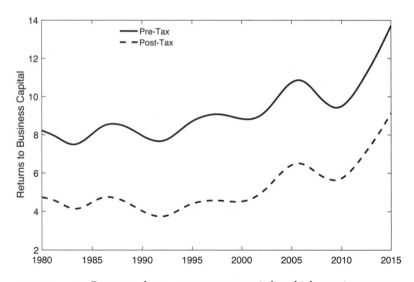

FIGURE 2.2.15. Pre-tax and post-tax returns to capital are high: moving average

the 1960s and 1970s real gross domestic investment growth averaged over 5 percent per year. This declined to just under 4 percent for the 1980s, but then rebounded to nearly 6 percent in the 1990s. Since 2000, however, the business investment growth rate is just 1.1 percent. This long-run decay in business investment is incredibly troubling for future economic growth. Future research should consider why investment is so low, despite historically high current real returns. One possibility is that expectations of future productivity growth will be low. Another possibility is that the perception of future risk is very high, and this is constraining investment. Both of these factors, however, are well beyond the scope of being addressed by monetary policy.

CONCLUSION

The data presented here shows little evidence for policy-maker concerns about the level of r-star. In fact, these data refute the view that traditional monetary policies can be potent stabilizers of the US economy, independent of the level of r-star. These data show that there is little evidence supporting the Phillips curve and that most economic fluctuations appear to be due to very long-lived components and not short-run demand factors. Moreover, the data show that returns to business capital are high, which challenges the secular stagnation view.

Taken together, these data suggest that monetary policy makers should consider placing less emphasis on short-run demand management through monetary policy. As an alternative, monetary policy makers could work on developing policies that promote long-run growth and investment. Much of the job creation, innovation, and productivity growth in the United States comes from rapidly growing start-ups. Those running start-ups frequently remark how difficult it is to obtain financing for their organizations, particularly in recent years. This suggests that policies which advance the efficient allocation of capital investment, such as reforming banking and financial system regulatory policies, could have sizable growth and welfare benefits for the United States.

References

Atkeson, Andrew, and Lee E. Ohanian. 2001. "Are Phillips Curves Useful for Forecasting Inflation?" *Federal Reserve Bank of Minneapolis Quarterly Review* 25 (1): 2–11.

Davis, Steve, and Till Von Wachter. 2011. "Recessions and the Costs of Job Loss." *Brookings Papers on Economic Activity*, no. 2 (Fall): 1–72.

Federal Reserve Board of Governors. 2016. "FRB U.S. Model Technical Questions and Answers." Federal Reserve Board, https://www.federalreserve.gov/econres/us- technical-qas.htm.

Gomme, Paul, B. Ravikumar, and Peter Rupert. 2011. "The Return to Capital and the Business Cycle." *Review of Economic Dynamics* 14 (2): 262–78.

Hansen, Gary D., and Lee E. Ohanian. 2016. "Neoclassical Models in Macroeconomics." In *Handbook of Macroeconomics*, edited by John B. Taylor and Harald Uhlig. Amsterdam: Elsevier.

Jacobson, Louis S., Robert J. LaLonde, and Daniel G. Sullivan. 1993. "Earnings Losses of Displaced Workers." *American Economic Review* 83 (4): 685–709.

Lucas, Robert E., Jr. 1976. "Econometric Policy Evaluation: A Critique." *Carnegie-Rochester Series on Public Policy* 1 (1): 19–46.

Stock, James, and Mark Watson. 2007. "Why Has U.S. Inflation Become Harder to Forecast?" *Journal of Money, Banking and Credit* 39 (1).

———. 2009. "Phillips Curve Inflation Forecasts." In *Understanding Inflation and the Implications for Monetary Policy: A Phillips Curve Retrospective*, edited by Jeff Fuhrer, Yolands K. Kodrzycki, Jane Sneddon Little, and Giovanni P. Olivei, 101–86. Cambridge, MA: MIT Press, 2009.

GENERAL DISCUSSION

AMIT SERU: Let me just quickly summarize the issues, and then we can open up the discussion. I think essentially there is a debate on measurement. Over what horizon should we be measuring r-star? Long run? Short run? If we agree r-star is relevant, which model do we think r-star is relevant in? Because that then means we've got to worry about measuring demand shocks versus supply shocks, because they could have different implications for how we will think about r-star. And finally, if we agree r-star is important, what should the Fed do? What's the right level? Is 2 percent the right number? Three percent? Zero? We should debate that. And potentially, what should it target? The long-run interest rate, the nominal interest rate, or the inflation rate?

MICHAEL DOTSEY: This question is for Volker. I think there are lots of interesting questions regarding why we might care about long-run interest rates or twenty-year moving averages of real rates. But in the monetary policy context, I just don't see it. You're using these New Keynesian models to look at stuff, but if I remember my textbook New Keynesian models, what we respond to is some output level relative to its flexible-price benchmark, and some real interest rate relative to its flexible benchmark. Those are high-frequency things that have nothing to do with twenty-year averages of real rates. In fact, Carl Walsh has demonstrated that if you respond to these long-run statistical type of trends instead of the theoretical constructs, you can make tremendous mistakes. It's a mistake to do that. So I was wondering why you chose to do monetary policy rather than some other type of policy?

VOLKER WIELAND: First of all, you mentioned New Keynesian models. These models include a construct that is the short-run natural rate, that is, the flexible-price interest rate or output level. Ed

Nelson was one of the first to compute them but they were extremely variable, which is precisely why we've had trouble getting policy makers to even focus on them. Based on a particular model, you can think of this highly variable natural short rate as a policy prescription. If the price level were fully flexible, this is where the economy would be. However, it depends on all the shocks in the model, all the parameters in the model. It's highly model and shock dependent. If we all agreed on what's the right model, and if that model actually delivered good real-world policy outcomes, then we'd be in an ideal world. But we're not in that world. So I don't share your view that this is the agreement in the field, that that's the way to do it. I also don't think that's how policy makers have acted, because typically we've had a hard time getting them interested in such model-based short-run natural rates.

The long-run equilibrium rate concept, as I've showed, is a pretty standard one. It was already in the 1993 Taylor rule, for example. What the New Keynesian models can add is model-based estimates of this long-run equilibrium. More important, the models can tell you something about what factors are driving the potential deviations of the average interest rate from the long-run equilibrium. For example, is such a deviation driven by monetary policy or by something else? So I think that's where they can be helpful. In terms of policy recommendations, I would certainly argue against a policy that is driven entirely by an unobservable short-run natural rate, which requires a model to estimate it and then that model to be right, because if the economy is closer to a different model, then policy would be totally off track.

MICHAEL DOTSEY: I agree with what you've just said, but I totally disagree with your solution. Methodologically, we have this problem about uncertainty of parameters, uncertainty of models. We have tool kits to think about that. I mean, John Williams has done a tremendous amount of work in this area looking at robust rules. And often he says, "Well, if these level things are really tough to measure, go to some first-difference rule," which he finds works well in a number of contexts. So his answer is to just throw the damn things out.

VOLKER WIELAND: Yes, that is what I mentioned, right? This is one of the options. I said, "Why not focus on strategies where you don't need an equilibrium rate such as a first-difference rule?" Actually, I've looked at that jointly with John Williams and with John Taylor in different papers. You can see from our research that a first-difference rule does pretty well under many circumstances in the models we've studied. In terms of tool kit, we've been putting up a database of models, where you can compare the performance of rules across models. This provides a strong case for simple rules. And a difference rule may be one of the rules that should be given much weight. However, when you try to figure out past policy mistakes, then the difference rules are not very helpful, because every quarter, they re-normalize to the most recent level of the interest rate. So whether policy has been off for a while is very hard to assess with those.

And if you have the view that monetary policy may not have been optimal before the financial crisis, then the Taylor rule, which actually gave a signal before the crisis that interest rates were unusually low, is one that shouldn't be ignored.

JOHN COCHRANE: I want to address this "who cares?" issue. Who cares about the long-run real rate of interest? If this were a conference about government debt sustainability or the present value of social security, we would care a lot, directly, about the long-run real rate of interest. But it's not. It's a monetary policy conference. So why do we care?

I think Janet Yellen made one answer really clear in the speech she gave here in January. If the long-run real rate of interest is not 2 percent but 1 percent, she says, then when we tack on our

2 percent inflation target, that means the current sequence of interest rate rises will go up to 3 percent, not 4 percent. And if r-star is zero, then we're going to top out at 2 percent. So it's about the long-run glide path of nominal interest rates. It's not really about short-run policy; it's about our long-run nominal interest rate targets and Fed communication about where interest rates will end up.

But the question I'd like to ask is, Who wrote that procedure in stone? Why do we take some guess at the real rate, add a 2 percent inflation target, and that's where interest rates have to go?

We mentioned headroom. The number one thing that comes up is that we need to get nominal rates up so we have room to lower them when the next recession comes. As opposed to, say, Milton Friedman, who might say, based on his optimal quantity of money essay, the right nominal interest rate target is zero. Well, now we say not zero, because then the Fed doesn't have any headroom to lower interest rates.

But both of those considerations—either just zero, for the optimal quantity of money, or headroom to lower in the next recession—just say the *nominal* interest rate target ought to be whatever it is. If you need 4 percent headroom at r-star 3 percent, you need 4 percent headroom at an r-star of 0 percent. So just ignore r-star. R-star is irrelevant if you're thinking about headroom arguments or optimal quantity money arguments.

The procedure Ms. Yellen described, which everyone seems to take for granted, must mean that we really think the inflation target itself matters, that pi-star has a definite life, that we really need to start with 2 percent inflation, then add our r-star, and *that* tells us where nominal interest rates go.

But why 2 percent inflation? Who wrote that in stone, anyway? I mean, the Federal Reserve Act says "price stability." It doesn't say 2 percent inflation forever. Why not a price-level target? Why not zero? Why not negative? Perhaps there is something about sticky prices and 2 percent being the optimal amount to unstick them, but I'm just making that up.

The differences comment is interesting in this context. Why bother with any of this? Let's just talk about how the Fed adjusts interest rates in response to events and not talk about a long-run target. But I think the Fed wants to "anchor expectations" more than that.

MARTIN EICHENBAUM: This may be the last time today that I agree with John. But I want to point out that Irving Fisher is still alive. The nominal interest rate is still equal to the real interest rate plus the inflation rate. It's clear that the real interest rate—whether you call it r-star or something else—has fallen. So unless we raise the inflation target, the normal nominal interest rate will go down.

Two points on Lee's discussion. The first concerns his view that wage rigidities are becoming less important. That view is premised on his enormous confidence about the rationality of union-led workers. I suggest that he talk to union officials at Alitalia, where workers just voted themselves out of a job rather than take a wage cut. I'm not sure we understand why wages aren't the flexible objects that we put in real business cycle models. But that doesn't mean they aren't nominal wage rigidities.

Second, Lee argued that monetary policy isn't particularly important. I have no problem with the view that total factor productivity growth is immensely important. But when the next big recession or financial crisis comes, it just won't do for the Fed to say, "Dodd-Frank put us out of business. And we can't cut interest rates. But that's okay. TFP growth in the long run is important."

LEE OHANIAN: The key is understanding why we're in an economy that has such a high equity premium. That's what really jumps out from the data. Returns to private capital are very high. The low rates that people refer to are relevant only for a very small set of securities, primarily government bonds. Understanding how to make useful policies requires understanding why the equity premium is currently so high. Virtually all of the discussion about r-star seems to me to completely omit this important issue. We need to understand the very high equity premium and why investment remains so low despite very high returns to private capital. We do not yet understand these important issues.

In terms of wage stability and Marty's comment about the Italians, I am not sure that the Italian workers are representative of the behavior of US workers. Italy's economic performance has been remarkably different than ours; Italian economic performance is among the worst among the advanced countries. Their per capita GDP is actually lower today than it was twenty years ago. In the United States, there is now incredible competitive pressure on wages.

ANDREW LEVIN: So just a few thoughts. The intersection I saw between Volker and Lee is that there used to be a lot of confidence in models and economic forecasts, so the idea of inflation forecast targeting seemed like a natural approach for setting the course of monetary policy. But it seems that one thing we've learned over the last ten years, and certainly Volker has multiple papers about this, is the extent to which the forecasts have been persistently wrong, with little or no ability to understand why they're going wrong so that the forecast errors can be avoided in the following year. The alternative approach is to follow what John Taylor has been advocating for many years, which is the use of simple policy benchmarks.

One potential benchmark for assessing r-star would be to use the average of professional forecasters' longer-term projections of real interest rates. After all, those forecasters are using lots of different kinds of models. Some of them talk to Stock and Watson. Some of them may talk to Lee. That might be a reasonable benchmark. If you wanted to use the Taylor rule, or a variant of the Taylor rule that's in levels, using an estimate of r-star based on the consensus of professional forecasters seems reasonable to me.

An alternative would be to switch to a difference rule, like Volker has mentioned. How does a difference rule work? Well, it's like getting in a shower in the morning. You have no idea what the appropriate setting of hot and cold is. So you start twisting the knobs, and if it's too hot, you start dialing back the hot and dialing up the cold a bit. That's a difference rule. The difference rule says, if inflation's a little bit too high, above the target, that means our interest rate is probably too low. So let's dial up. But here we are in 2017. Inflation is pretty close to the Fed's 2 percent target. GDP growth is roughly 2 percent, not much different from its potential. So, as of today, a difference rule might imply that this is pretty comfortable, without any need to adjust the dial much. I can't see how any difference rule would call for moving the federal funds rate all the way up to 3 or 4 percent. I'm curious what each of you have to say about that.

VOLKER WIELAND: First, regarding what John said, he highlighted the concern about the headroom for easing, which has been very important in policy practice, both before and after the crisis. For example, the Fed used the argument to explain why it kept interest rates low in the years before the financial crisis. The idea was that we can't lower interest rates below zero, and if there is deflation, real interest rates will rise, and that will drag the economy farther down. According to this view, there should be an asymmetric response. Interest rates should stay lower for longer. And a higher inflation objective would provide more headroom. That's a valid argument. I've contributed to research developing this argument. Except that the experience of the financial crisis shows there are also opposite risks. Keeping interest rates too low for too long may create financial instability. Negative effects on bank profitability are another concern that people have worked on. Accordingly, interest rate policy is not quite as effective when rates are kept lower and lower. Hence, I think there is something to say for symmetry in terms of policy responses.

Andy explained again the difference rule, I think very intuitively. So that's one way to go. I think that's one benchmark I would use. You know there is a legislative process in the United States where the idea is to let the Fed pick a rule. I think it would be major progress if the Fed would say, "Under such and such a scenario, the difference rule is the one we focus on." Then, maybe the Taylor rule would be another one to be compared— it's even in the legislation. This would help motivate a discussion about when and why the Fed deviates from the particular rule it picked. The Fed could deviate from it for particular reasons, but it would then explain the differences. I wouldn't want to argue that much about which rule the Fed should pick, because I think the format itself would be a big step forward. At the moment, we're still far from that.

LEE OHANIAN: There's an interesting and important tension in inflation forecasts versus inflation outcomes. You've got monetary policy makers and monetary policy being made in conjunction with private markets and nominal spending, and this has produced a remarkably stable record of inflation. And at the same time, we have people forecasting inflation who are way, way off in terms of accuracy, and who are systematically making the same forecast errors time and again. So at some level, it's like when we're making monetary policy and we see how the private markets are working; we're generating perfectly stable, low inflation, but when we predict inflation, we make these large mistakes. It is hard to rationalize those two points of view, though I think it would be interesting and important to figure out why policy makers are able to produce stable inflation but aren't able to forecast what they ultimately accomplish.

CHAPTER THREE

LESSONS FROM THE QUIET ZERO LOWER BOUND

. . . .

SECTION ONE

The Radical Implications of Stable Quiet Inflation at the Zero Bound

John H. Cochrane

For nearly a decade in the United States, United Kingdom, and Europe, and for three decades in Japan, short-term interest rates have been stuck near zero, known as the "zero bound," because central banks can't lower interest rates substantially below zero. Central banks also embarked on immense open market operations. The US Federal Reserve bought nearly $3 trillion of bonds and mortgage-backed securities in return for newly created money. Bank reserves—essentially checking accounts that banks hold at the Fed—rose from $10 billion on the eve of the crisis in August 2008 to $2,759 billion in August 2014. Figure 3.1.1 summarizes the US experience.

The response to this important experiment in monetary policy has been surprising silence. Inflation is stable and if anything less volatile than before. Similar plots of GDP growth and

This essay summarizes "Michelson-Morley, Fisher, and Occam: The Radical Implications of Stable Quiet Inflation at the Zero Bound," *NBER Macroeconomics Annual*, 2017, and available at http://faculty.chicagobooth.edu/john.cochrane. I thank Lars Hansen for helpful comments.

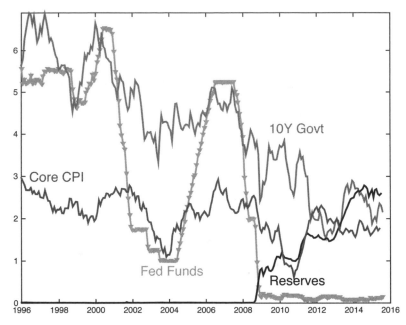

FIGURE 3.1.1. Recent US experience

unemployment show no large difference in the behavior of the economy during the time when interest rates were stuck near zero and not responding to economic conditions. The zero bound is not an obvious "state variable" for economic dynamics. Unemployment came down if anything a little quicker than in previous recessions. GDP growth, while too low in many opinions, has been if anything a little less volatile than before.

Existing theories of inflation make sharp predictions about the zero bound. Old Keynesian models, in use throughout the policy world, predict that inflation is unstable at the zero bound and, more generally, when interest rates cannot or do not move in response to inflation. These models predict a deflation spiral: Inflation goes down, so the real cost of borrowing money rises. That depresses the economy, inflation goes down more, the real cost of borrowing money rises more, and so on ad infinitum. Think of the Fed as a seal balancing a ball (inflation) on its nose. If the seal does not or cannot quickly move its nose (interest rates), then the ball will fall off. It did not happen.

Monetarist theory that inflation fundamentally comes from increases in the quantity of money predicts that a massive increase in reserves must lead to galloping inflation. It did not happen.

Since the late 1980s, most academic work on monetary policy has been conducted in the framework of New Keynesian models. These models recognize that people make their decisions about what to do today thinking about the future, not the past. In economicspeak, they are "intertemporal" and feature "rational expectations." They also are fully specified economic models, obeying all the rules that well-posed models should obey. For example, they impose that people's plans to work, save, and spend are consistent. They impose budget constraints and market-clearing conditions.

Simple New Keynesian models predict that inflation is stable when interest rates do not move, and they predict that quantitative easing operations are irrelevant. The intuition is fairly straightforward. If a driver looks only in the rearview mirror, forming his expectations of the road ahead based on what lies behind, he will soon veer off the road. He needs a prescient Federal Reserve in the backseat to induce stability. If the driver looks forward, the car will return to the center of the road on its own, even if the Federal Reserve does no backseat driving. Likewise, from the perspective of modern finance, reserves at the Fed are indistinguishable from government debt. An exchange of short-term debt for reserves is like exchanging a $20 bill for two $10 bills. Without lots of extra "frictions," such an operation does not change overall spending.

Thus, the observed stability of inflation and apparent ineffectiveness of quantitative easing are big feathers in the New Keynesian cap. But they fail on quiet. Standard New Keynesian models predict that at the zero bound or when interest rates do not move, inflation jumps around randomly. The models have "multiple self-confirming equilibriums" or "sunspots" when interest rates do not move. If people expect inflation, inflation happens. These models tie down expected inflation but not actual inflation. Think of a coin being flipped. Interest rate targets tie down the fact that on average half the flips will be heads. But the actual flips are a volatile mixture of heads and tails. In these models, when interest rates can move, the Fed can guarantee all heads or all tails and eliminate the random volatility.

This prediction that inflation is more volatile at the zero bound is a central component of the New Keynesian paradigm. The central empirical success of these models was explaining the greater volatility of inflation in the 1970s relative to the 1980s by such "sunspots," resulting from interest rates that did not move enough in response to inflation in the 1970s but did so in the 1980s. Two decades of New Keynesian research starting in the 1990s was devoted to devising means to escape the "zero bound" or "liquidity trap" of zero interest rates, precisely to avoid the reemergence of such "sunspots." Well, here we are, and the long-feared volatility did not happen. As Figure 3.1.1 emphasizes, instead of extra "sunspot" volatility, inflation is if anything quieter than before.

New Keynesian models also predict a menagerie of policy paradoxes when interest rates are stuck at zero: productivity improvements are bad, promises farther in the future have larger effects today, and reducing price stickiness makes matters worse, without limit.

One last theory remains. The fiscal theory of the price level states that inflation is fundamentally anchored by fiscal policy. In the end, the value of money comes from the government's commitment to accept its money, and only its money, for tax payments. If there is more government debt outstanding than people expect to be soaked up by tax payments, the value of that debt falls, and inflation breaks out.

More deeply, the fiscal theory proceeds from the observation that the real value of government debt must equal the present value of the primary budget surpluses that will eventually pay down that debt. If people think surpluses will not be sufficient to pay off the debt, they will try to get rid of that debt by buying goods and services. This will drive up the price level, until the now-lower real value of the debt is equal to the lower value of expected surpluses. Nominal debt is, formally, just like stock in the government, with the price level as the stock price and the discounted value of surpluses as the discounted value of dividends.

This theory can be merged easily with the New Keynesian description of the rest of the economy, including its interest rate targets and sticky prices. The Fed, by setting interest rates, still determines expected inflation. But now fiscal policy determines the actual outcome—whether the coin comes up heads or tails. Each New Keynesian sunspot corresponds to a change in expectations about fiscal policy. With no big changes in fiscal policy (the present discounted value of future primary surpluses), there will be no sunspot volatility.

The resulting theory is consistent with stable quiet inflation at the zero bound. It also resolves the policy paradoxes of the New Keynesian model. This small change in ingredients has a large effect on the models' prediction for what we see and for the effects of policy.

Telling these theories apart was difficult before interest rates hit zero. Each offered a plausible account of the data up to that point. If a seal does a good job of balancing the ball, it's hard to tell if the ball is unstable and the seal is doing a great job, or if the ball is glued to the seal's nose. If someone holds the seal still, it's easier to tell. The zero bound period starting in 2008 offers a genuine and important experiment.

Theories fail sometimes in a dramatic manner. In the 1970s, prevailing Keynesian theory predicted little inflation, and the emergence of stagflation dramatically disproved that theory. In the 1980s, the same theory predicted that inflation would remain intractably high. The sudden disappearance of inflation in 1982–84 again proved it wrong. Theories fail no less when they unambiguously predict a large inflation, deflation, or volatile inflation and nothing happens. It's just a lot less public.

DO HIGHER INTEREST RATES RAISE
OR LOWER INFLATION?

What do this experience and theoretical interpretation imply about monetary policy going forward?

First, if inflation is stable when interest rates are stuck at zero, then it follows that if the central bank were to raise interest rates permanently, inflation must eventually *rise* to meet the higher interest rates. This reversal of the usual sign of monetary policy has become known as the "neo-Fisherian" hypothesis.

However, higher interest rates might still *temporarily* lower inflation before eventually raising it. The traditional belief that raising rates lowers inflation could still be right in the short run, and most evidence is about short-run correlations anyway. Is that possible? What do the models say?

It turns out the standard simple New Keynesian model, with or without fiscal theory, robustly predicts that a rise in interest rates produces a steady rise in inflation, with no temporary decline. It does produce an output decline—our central bankers are half right. Figure 3.1.2 illustrates.

This model produces a temporary inflation decline only if we pair the interest rate rise with a fiscal contraction: the fiscal contraction produces the temporary negative inflation, then the higher interest rates kick in to produce higher inflation.

That mixture may describe historical events—fiscal and monetary policy react to the same events—and therefore account for experience and econometric estimates. But if we define "monetary policy" as an increase in interest rates that does not come with a fiscal contraction, then our model still predicts that a future pure monetary policy interest rate rise will lead only to inflation.

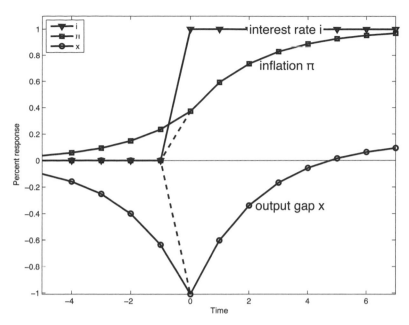

FIGURE 3.1.2. Response of inflation and output to a step function interest rate change in the standard IS-Phillips curve New Keynesian model. The solid lines show the response to an expected change. The dashed lines show the response to an unexpected change. Parameters $\beta = 0.97$, $\kappa = 0.2$, $\sigma = 1$.

I investigate what minimal set of ingredients it takes to produce a negative short-run impact of interest rates on inflation. The obvious candidates do not work: pricing frictions, adding money and monetary frictions to the model, even adapting classic backward-looking Phillips curves. With any forward-looking behavior, higher interest rates mean higher inflation. It is simply not true to say, "Sure, in a frictionless model higher rates mean higher inflation, but since prices are sticky / the real world has money in it / price setting seems to look backward, higher rates temporarily lower inflation." They don't.

One ingredient can robustly and simply produce the desired temporary negative sign. If we add long-term debt, a rise in interest rates can produce a temporary decline in inflation. In brief, when the Fed raises interest rates and communicates that interest rates will be higher for some time in the future, long-term bond prices fall. In that case, the total market value of the debt falls. But if the Treasury does not make any change in fiscal policy, then the real value of debt has not changed. We have an imbalance. Treasuries are worth more than their market price. People try to buy more Treasuries and buy less goods and services to get them. But with the supply of Treasuries fixed and their price (interest rate) fixed, the lower aggregate demand for goods and services pushes the price level down. Once the price level has fallen, the higher inflation corresponding to higher interest rates can take over.

Figure 3.1.3 illustrates this mechanism. Here I plot the response to a permanent one percentage point increase in interest rates,

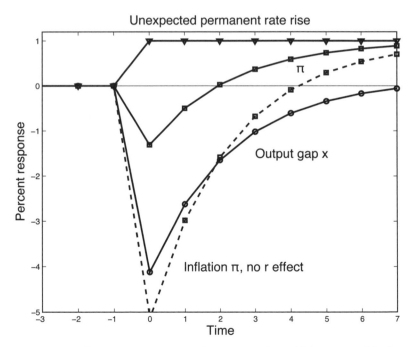

FIGURE 3.1.3. Response to permanent interest rate rises with long-term debt. I use the 2014 maturity structure of the debt. The dotted line ignores the effect of rising real rates in devaluing future surpluses.

using the same economic model as in Figure 3.1.2, but with long-term debt calibrated to the US maturity structure. The main "inflation" line shows the temporary decline and later rise. The output gap line shows that this temporary tightening still produces a substantial recession.

This theory works even in a completely frictionless model—no price stickiness, no money, no frictions at all. It allows the analysis of monetary policy to (finally) start with simple supply and demand, like the rest of economics, and then add frictions to better match the economic dynamics in the data, rather than requiring monetary, financial, pricing, or other frictions just to get the basic determination of the price level and basic signs and stability properties of monetary policy right. And it describes interest rate policy, quantitative easing, and forward guidance in one breath. The interest rate rise involves bond sales that look just like quantitative easing. Forward guidance of future interest rate declines lowers bond prices; in fact, the expectation of future high interest rates is the key mechanism.

However, this mechanism does not restore classic beliefs. First, it only works for unexpected interest rate increases. If people know the interest rate increase will happen, they are not surprised by lower bond prices, and the inflation happens immediately without a temporary dip. Second, in part for this reason, it does not rescue policy advice that relies on expected interest rates lowering inflation. Central banks cannot plan to systematically raise and lower interest rates in response, say, to inflation by this mechanism. Third, the mechanism works entirely via fiscal policy. If this is "monetary policy," it has nothing at all to do with money, credit, lending, price stickiness, or anything else. In turn, whether it works or not depends entirely on the Treasury. When the Fed raises rates, and thus future inflation, the Treasury could say, "Great, now we don't have to raise taxes as much to pay off the debt. The Fed is inflating it away for us." If it does so, the inflation dip disappears.

We are left with a logical conundrum: either (1) the world really is Fisherian, and higher interest rates raise inflation in both the short and long run; (2) more complex ingredients, including frictions or irrationalities, are *necessary* as well as sufficient to deliver the negative sign, so this hallowed belief relies on those complex ingredients; or (3) the negative sign ultimately relies on the fiscal theory story involving long-term debt—and has nothing to do with any of the mechanisms commonly blamed for it.

The first view is not as crazy as it seems. The empirical evidence for the traditional sign is weak. Estimates for years confronted the "price puzzle" of the data indicating that higher interest rates led to higher inflation. This finding was only tempered with lots and lots of effort. Perhaps the price puzzle has been trying to tell us something for all these decades.

OCCAM'S RAZOR

Proof is rare in economics, and one can imagine many patches to rescue existing theories. Perhaps inflation really is unstable at the zero bound, but clever central bankers around the world offset a pending deflationary spiral with just enough hyperinflationary quantitative easing, helped by fiscal stimulus, that all we see is quiet. Even in Japan. Perhaps. Or perhaps the stability we observe is just what it seems—stability. Occam's razor—accept the simplest explanation—suggests the latter.

Similarly, one might rescue the long-standing prediction that interest rates at the zero bound would result in additional sunspot volatility by supposing that sunspots just didn't happen. But taking that path, one would have to throw out the theory's central empirical success and ask why the literature made such clear and loud predictions. And we're not here for cocktail party ex post explanations; we're here for theories with predictive content. Just why were there no sunspots this time, yet there were lots of them in the 1970s in this theory's reading? Are our central bankers that much better at making speeches? In any case, choosing what's on the menu, this possibility remains in the realm of future possibilities, as no New Keynesian research has offered a serious explanation. And again, Occam's razor speaks loudly. Perhaps there are no sunspots now *or* in the 1970s. Perhaps the whole sunspot theory is wrong. Perhaps the very simple fiscal theory that has no sunspots at any time describes now and the 1970s.

Perhaps the long zero bound represents the proverbial seven years of bad luck—twenty-five in Japan—and not a true zero bound. Perhaps people, like many professional forecasters, expected a swift recovery and interest rates rising above zero within a year, allowing conventional "active" (moving quickly with inflation) interest rate policy to emerge. Perhaps this wasn't really a period of passive monetary policy (interest rates not moving enough with inflation) like the 1970s. That would explain the absence of sunspots.

This story is also offered for the 1980s. The 1980s pose a similar challenge to New Keynesian models, because they predict that persistent interest rate increases eventually raise inflation. The Fed can only generate a decline in inflation from a quite temporary increase in interest rates. But the conventional view of the 1980s is that persistent, indeed dogged, high interest rates were required to squeeze out inflation. Well, maybe the 1980–2000 experience was twenty years of good luck. Maybe people continually expected inflation to return and were surprised that it did not. I call these the "springtime in Chicago" expectations, as it seems every week the weather forecast reads, "Snow and ice this week, returning to the seventies next week."

Well, perhaps. We should not be religious about rational expectations. Perhaps the 1980s and 2008 were unique events, and people had no way of preparing for them or knowing what would happen. Perhaps the time series we observe are a fundamentally misleading measure of the structural response functions, the former stable but the latter really unstable.

Or perhaps not. At some point, after many decades, perhaps we should take the very simple model sitting on the plate before us, which describes these episodes with simple supply and demand economics, without requiring people to be fundamentally wrong in how they perceive the world and to ignore the ample historical precedents of financial crises, inflations, deflations, and near-zero interest rates. Perhaps every day is not a new stochastic process, but just a day like the last.

Furthermore, a stable quiet zero bound does not require extreme rational expectations. Small amounts of forward-looking behavior will do. The stable quiet zero bound still obtains if one of the consumption or pricing decisions is irrationally backward looking. To rescue classic beliefs, one needs all expectations to be mechanically adaptive.

To generate the long-standing belief that higher interest rates produce at least temporarily lower inflation, one might naturally start adding complications to the very simple models I outline here, such as extensive borrowing or collateral constraints, hand-to-mouth consumers, a lending channel or other financial frictions, habits, durable goods, housing, multiple goods and other non-separabilities, novel preferences, labor and leisure choices, production, capital, variable capital utilization, adjustment costs, alternative models of price stickiness, informational frictions, market frictions, payments frictions, more complex monetary frictions, timing lags, individual or firm heterogeneity, and so forth. Going farther, perhaps we can add fundamentally different views of expectations formation and equilibrium concepts.

Even this is not so easy. One must face the twin challenges of producing a negative temporary effect of interest rates on inflation, together with the observed long-run stability of inflation at the zero bound. "Let's just go back to adaptive expectations" will not do. That course produces a negative sign, but it also produces instability and the prediction of a deflation spiral, which we did not see.

One can, and many papers do, add complex ingredients to the New Keynesian framework, which is consistent with stability. If we must go down this path, however, we then accept that there is no simple economic model that produces the hallowed belief that higher interest rates reduce inflation. The extra complexities become *necessary* rather than just *sufficient*. Imagine a Fed chair trying to explain to Congress that monetary policy *necessarily* relies on such ingredients for the basic sign of its effect. In the absence of the Fed's technocratic understanding of such ingredients, the Fed would steer the ship the other way, raising interest rates to raise inflation, not the other way around.

If so, that circumstance radically changes the nature of monetary policy. And one must admit that the scientific basis on which we analyze policy and offer advice to public officials and the public at large becomes more tenuous.

I do not mean to disdain frictions, including the above list of ingredients. Such frictions surely are important to understand the details of real-world dynamics. Ideally, we add such frictions to simple models that get the basic sign and stability right. The trouble comes when frictions are necessary to the basic sign and stability.

Again, proof is rare in economics. But ex post patches, in the face of clear predictive failures, are always suspect. Sometimes it is right to patch a theory. Planetary orbits are elliptical, not circular. More often, ex post patches are epicycles, and the Occam's razor advice is right.

That advice is not easy. The theoretical interpretation of the long quiet zero bound I have offered is indeed strikingly simple. But it asserts that long-standing classic doctrines of monetary economics—that interest-rate pegs must be unstable or that "money" creation must inevitably lead to inflation—were simply wrong. That pill should be hard to swallow.

POLICY

What are the implications of this experience, and its theoretical interpretation, for policy going forward?

First, we should not unduly fear the zero bound. Much current policy discussion regards the past zero bound as a narrow scrape with the deflation spiral and argues for a higher inflation target or dry powder in the arsenal of unconventional monetary policy and large fiscal stimulus to prevent the spiral from breaking out should we return to the zero bound in the next recession or crisis.

Second, we should not unduly fear large interest-paying reserves. We have discovered that abundant, safe, government-provided, interest-paying electronic money will not cause inflation, any more than government-provided banknotes necessarily did in the nineteenth century. (That proposition, regarding the inflationary consequences of paper money, was also hugely contentious.) Much current policy discussion, by contrast, sees large reserves as permanently stimulative, in urgent need of reduction.

Third, we can live with permanently low and steady interest rates, if we wish, so long as people trust fiscal policy. If the real interest rate needs to rise and fall, inflation will eventually fall and rise, respectively, to accommodate that change.

However, the Fed may wish to vary nominal interest rates according to its best guess of needed real interest rates. Such policy can further reduce inflation volatility, and given that prices are somewhat sticky, it will also reduce output volatility. So actual day-to-day policy need not change radically. The Fed will still raise rates when the economy is doing well and lower them when it is doing poorly.

FISCAL FOUNDATIONS

Shoals remain ahead. The fiscal foundations that theory needs to understand the stable quiet zero bound could easily fall apart.

It would be easy to misinterpret these results to say that all a country like Brazil or Turkey, which wishes to lower its inflation rate, needs to do is to lower its interest rate.

First, such an interest rate move must be persistent and credible. You can't just try the waters. Second, it must wait out a potential move in the other direction, via the long-term debt effect, or the many real-world complications discussed above. Most important, the fiscal backing and fiscal coordination must be there, especially for disinflation. Lowering nominal rates cannot cure a fundamentally fiscal inflation.

Successful stabilizations, such as the 1980s in the United States and Europe, involved joint monetary and fiscal reform. Conversely, many countries have seen all sorts of monetary stabilization plans fall apart when fiscal cooperation was lacking. Just lowering interest rates will not work with fiscal trouble brewing.

Likewise, it does not follow from the analysis here that the United States, Europe, and Japan can just peg low interest rates and sleep soundly. The fiscal foundations of our quiet inflation could evaporate quickly as well.

The fiscal theory says that inflation is determined by demand for government bonds, which in turn comes from the expected discounted value of future surpluses. This is an identity—the only question is which one is in investors' minds at the moment. Are investors holding lots of government bonds and not trying to buy goods and services or real assets instead because they think surpluses will be strong or because they are willing to hold government debt at very low rates of return? The answer seems pretty clear: the value of government debt is high now because discount rates—expected real returns on government bonds—are very low right now.

But low discount rates can evaporate quickly, especially when government debt is largely short term and frequently rolled over. A change in discount rate provokes exactly the same sort of unexpected inflation as a change in fiscal surpluses. And like such a change, there is nothing a central bank can do about it.

Concretely, if in the next moment of economic trouble, when our governments try to borrow another several percent of GDP to bail out troubled financial institutions, or fight a war or a recession, or all at the same time, while simultaneously rolling over a large stock of debt, bond market investors may decide our governments are not serious about long-run fiscal solvency. Investors will demand higher real interest rates to hold government debt, putting more strain on budgets. Investors may abandon government debt, driving up inflation. Such an event feels like a "speculative attack," a "bubble," or a "run" to central bankers.

Inflation's resurgence can happen without Phillips curve tightness. It can surprise central bankers of the 2020s just as it did in the 1970s—just as the decline in inflation surprised them in the 1980s, and just as its stability surprised them in the 2010s.

· ·

SECTION TWO

Comments on the Zero Lower Bound

Martin Eichenbaum

This essay focuses on two distinct but related points. The first is a critique of John Cochrane's claim that the Great Recession is a Michelson-Morley moment for New Keynesian (NK) models. Since this argument is based on Cochrane (2017), I will reference that paper throughout my comments. The second point builds on the empirical argument made in my first point that the private sector and policy makers systematically underestimated the gravity and duration of the zero lower bound (ZLB) episode and the Great Recession. At a minimum, this fact suggests that economists and policy makers should not depend on analyses that rely critically on a strong form of rational expectations. This view has particular force when we are dealing with rare events like the financial crisis, the Great Recession, or the so-called "quiet ZLB." We should take seriously only model implications that are robust to at least small deviations from rational expectations. I illustrate the usefulness of this "robustness principal" by applying it to three properties of the standard NK model.

DID WE SEE A MICHELSON-MORLEY MOMENT?

A central claim in Cochrane (2017) and the preceding chapter builds on the observation that the federal funds rate was constant for a long period after early 2009. According to John, we can think of that experience as an interest-rate peg. The standard NK model predicts that under a peg, the rational expectations equilibrium is indeterminate and gives rise to the possibility of sunspot volatility. Since inflation has actually been smooth, John infers that we've experienced a Michelson-Morley moment. In his view that moment has invalidated the standard NK model. Since monetarism has also been discredited, we need a new standard model. That model, according to John, is the fiscal theory of the price level coupled with nominal rigidities.

I agree with John about monetarism. The monetarists have been precisely wrong about everything that's happened since the financial crisis ("A tsunami of inflation is coming!"). For this we should thank them. Being exactly wrong exactly all of the time is socially useful because of the guidance it gives to the rest of us. So thanks to the "MV = PQ, V is kind of constant" crowd.

That said, I fundamentally disagree with the premise of John's argument about the NK model and the so-called quiet ZLB. The Fed was not in any sense on an interest-rate peg. What matters for determinacy in the NK model is agents' expectations about the length of the ZLB. In reality no one expected the ZLB to last very long. So determinacy wasn't an issue in the NK model given realistic assumptions about what people were expecting. The experiment that John appeals to just didn't happen. Claiming that we had a Michelson-Morley moment is a clever analogy to the physical sciences. But it doesn't mean that we actually had such a moment.

To substantiate my claims about agents' expectations, consider the evidence in Swanson and Williams (2014). These authors estimate the time-varying sensitivity of the yields on intermediate and long-term bonds to macro announcements using high-frequency data taken from the period when the ZLB was binding. They compare that sensitivity to a benchmark period in which the ZLB wasn't an issue. The idea is that if a given yield is about as sensitive to news in the benchmark period, then the ZLB wasn't a binding constraint on the relevant yield. When a yield responds very little to news, they infer that policy was largely constrained by the ZLB. Based on their analysis, they conclude that until August 2011, market participants expected the ZLB to constrain policy for only a few quarters.

Next consider evidence from the federal funds futures market. The dotted lines in Figure 3.2.1 show what risk-neutral market participants would have thought, at different points in time, the federal funds rate was going to be in the future. The solid line in Figure 3.2.2 shows what the actual federal funds rate was at various points in time. Note that the market consistently overestimated how quickly the federal funds rate would return to normal levels. That's a serially correlated error if I ever saw one. Granted, one could appeal to the last refuge of scoundrels, unobserved time-varying risk premiums. But trying to correct for risk premiums, as

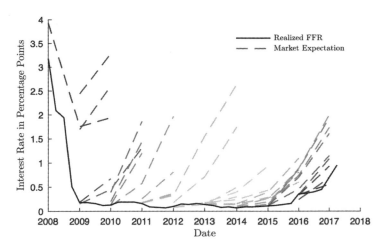

FIGURE 3.2.1. Federal funds rate: level and futures market rate. Source: Federal Reserve Economic Data, Bloomberg.

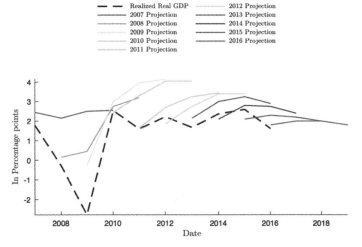

FIGURE 3.2.2. Growth rate of real GDP: level and Board of Governors' forecast. Source: Federal Reserve Economic Data, Board of Governors of the Federal Reserve System.

in Kim and Wright (2005), does little to change your mind: market participants were overly optimistic for a very long time.

What about policy makers? Unfortunately the Green Book forecasts for the federal funds rate aren't available over the relevant sample period. But the Board of Governors' real GDP forecasts are available. The various lines in Figure 3.2.2 display the annualized projections of the Board of Governors, made at various points in time, for future annualized growth rates of real GDP. The dashed line depicts the actual annualized growth rate of real GDP over time. Notice that the board systematically overestimated the growth rate of real GDP. Again the evidence of serially correlated errors is painfully clear.

Figures 3.2.1 and 3.2.2 provide clear evidence that policy makers and market participants thought the economy would recover much more quickly from the financial crisis and the Great Recession than it did. They certainly didn't expect a long-lasting interest-rate peg. Critically, in NK models, how long agents think the interest will be constant is the key determinant of whether the multiplicity issue that Cochrane emphasizes will arise. Given the empirical evidence about agents' expectations, I conclude that the experiment John describes didn't happen. So any conclusions stemming from the alleged episode are unwarranted.

What about John's broader claim that NK models can't explain the postcrisis behavior of inflation? It's true that toy NK models can't do the job. But non-toy NK models do reasonably well at this task. Christiano, Eichenbaum, and Trabandt (2015) show that once you allow for the fact that the growth rate of total factor productivity fell during the Great Recession and the cost of working capital went up, a full-scale NK model does a reasonably good job of accounting for the observed rate of inflation. It's true that the Christiano et al. model isn't simple, but it has the virtue of being able to account for the facts in a plausible way.

THE ROBUSTNESS PRINCIPLE

Figures 3.2.1 and 3.2.2 make clear that people didn't understand in real time the causes of the Great Recession or how long it would last. This evidence motivates what I call the robustness principle. By this I mean that we shouldn't trust model implications that rely on a strict version of rational expectations, certainly not for rare episodes like the Great Recession.

This raises a question: What are the robust implications of the NK model? It is well known that the NK model has multiple equilibriums. But is multiplicity a substantive issue? By this I mean, can we appeal to an interesting selection criterion to rule out alternative equilibriums as empirically uninteresting? The stakes involved in the answer to this question are high. If the answer is no, then the NK model doesn't have any robust properties, and it should be dismissed as pretty much useless for either normative or positive purposes.

Whether you can rule out various equilibriums in the NK model depends on why you think the rational expectations model is an interesting hypothesis to begin with. So let's go back to the distant past, before this model ossified into a religion. At the dawn of creation, it was widely understood by the creators that you should take rational expectations seriously *only* if they were the outcome of some plausible learning process.

Consider the following quote from Lucas (1978): "The model described above 'assumes' that agents know a great deal about the structure of the economy, and perform some non-routine computations. It is in order to ask, then: will an economy with agents armed with 'sensible' rules of thumb, revising these rules from time to time . . . tend as time passes to behave as described in the rational expectations equilibrium?" Lucas took this view so seriously that he devoted an entire section of the paper to a derivation of the rational expectations equilibrium as the limiting outcome of a learning equilibrium.

Now fast-forward to a time when modelers were becoming more familiar with the properties of rational expectations models. Lucas (1986) suggests using stability-under-learning as an equilibrium selection criterion. He writes, "Recent theoretical work is making it increasingly clear that multiplicity . . . can arise in a wide variety of situations involving sequential trading, in competitive as well as finite-agent games. All but a few of these equilibriums are, I believe, behaviorally uninteresting: They do not describe behavior that collections of adoptively behaving people would ever hit on. I think an appropriate stability theory can be useful in weeding out these uninteresting equilibriums."

Multiple Equilibriums in Benhabib, Schmitt-Grohé, and Uribe (2001)

Let's take Lucas at his word. Suppose that agents make a small error in forming expectations about a set of variables relative to their values in a particular rational expectations equilibrium. Would the economy converge back to the rational expectations equilibrium under some plausible learning rule? If the answer is yes, we call the equilibrium stable or learnable. If the answer is no, we say the equilibrium isn't stable or learnable. Like Lucas, I take the view that if an equilibrium isn't learnable, it's uninteresting, and we should just disregard it as a theoretical curiosum. If the equilibrium is learnable, it is empirically interesting. It's even more interesting if we can construct explicit, behaviorally sensible near alternatives to the rational expectations model with unique equilibriums that look like the learnable one.

Consider the classic analysis of multiplicity by Benhabib, Schmitt-Grohé, and Uribe (2001) that is often cited by proponents of the so-called neo-Fisherian view of monetary policy. The basic model is an endowment economy populated by a large number of identical infinitely lived households with additively separable preferences defined over consumption and real balances. The representative household receives a constant endowment of the consumption good and faces the budget constraint

$$C(t) + \tau(t) + B(t)/P(t) + M(t)/P(t) \leq$$

$$(1 + R(t-1))(B(t-1)/P(t)) + Y + M(t-1)/P(t). \quad (1)$$

Here $P(t)$, $C(t)$, $\tau(t)$, and Y denote the price level, consumption, lump-sum taxes, and endowment at time t. The variables $B(t)$ and $M(t)$ denote the end of time t holdings of one-period nominal bonds and money, respectively. The variable $R(t-1)$ is the nominal interest rate on a bond held at the end of time $t-1$. Monetary policy is given by a Taylor rule, subject to a ZLB constraint on the nominal interest rate:

$$R(t) = \max\{1, \pi^*/\beta + \alpha(\pi(t) - \pi^*)\}. \quad (2)$$

Here π^* is the monetary authority's target rate of inflation, which we suppose is 1. We assume $\alpha > 1$ so that the Taylor principle is satisfied. The presence of the max operator reflects the ZLB constraint.

In this model there are two steady-state equilibriums. Optimality and market clearing imply the Fisher equation

$$1 = \beta R(t)/\pi(t+1). \quad (3)$$

In Figure 3.2.3 the lower line depicts the Taylor rule, while the upper line depicts the Fisher equation. Equations (2) and (3) summarize the equations whose solutions characterize the equilibriums of the model. The first steady-state equilibrium of the model

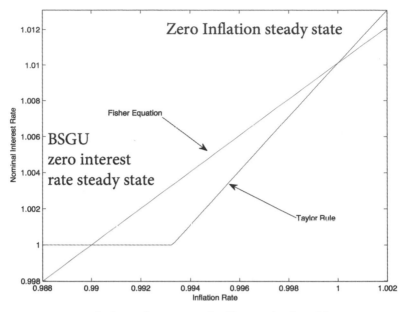

FIGURE 3.2.3. Multiple steady states in a flexible price-level model

economy is deflationary, that is, the steady-state rate of inflation is negative. The other "normal" steady-state equilibrium has the property that inflation is zero (recall π^* is equal to 1).

Is there some reason to take one of the steady states more seriously than the other? Suppose we begin from a particular steady state. Under rational expectations, agents would know what rate of inflation to expect in the future. But suppose that agents made an arbitrarily small mistake about expected inflation. Next period agents would realize that they had made a mistake. Suppose they have some rule for changing their expectations. For simplicity, assume that they set their new expectation as a linear combination of current data and past expectations, that is, they use a constant gain filter. In my experiment agents don't need to know that monetary policy is determined by a Taylor rule (never mind the parameters of that rule). They just revise expectations according to the constant gain filter. So the identification issues stressed by Cochrane (2011) are irrelevant in our context. It is well known that the economy would always *diverge* from the deflationary steady state. If there's an interior equilibrium, the economy will always converge to the zero-inflation steady-state equilibrium (see Christiano, Eichenbaum, and Johansen 2016 and the references therein).

So the deflationary steady-state equilibrium isn't learnable, and the zero-inflation steady-state equilibrium is learnable. Why would you ever want to use the nonlearnable deflationary steady state as a description of the data? The so-called neo-Fisherians sometimes talk about Japan as being caught in a low-deflation steady state. It's certainly true that Japan has low interest rates and low inflation. And I'm not entirely sure I understand why. But the idea that the cause is a nonlearnable rational expectations equilibrium where for twenty years no one has ever made the tiniest expectation error is wildly implausible.

Applying the Robustness Principal to the NK Model

Christiano, Eichenbaum, and Johansen (2016) analyze the nonlinear version of the standard NK model, both with Rotemberg-style and Calvo-style nominal price rigidities. They find that the model has a unique, learnable minimum-state rational expectations equilibrium.[1] The properties of that equilibrium correspond to the standard equilibrium emphasized in the literature. On that basis they infer that multiplicity is not a substantive problem in the NK model. But learnability isn't the same as robustness in the sense that I am using that term. To illustrate this distinction, I now apply the robustness principle to assess some implications of the NK model.

---

1. We are currently extending the analysis to consider non-minimum state variable equilibriums.

The Response of Inflation and the Nominal Interest Rate to a Monetary Policy Shock

Here I consider the response of inflation and the nominal interest rate to a monetary policy shock in two models: the log-linearized version of the standard NK model and Gabaix's (2017) behavioral NK model, in which agents are partially myopic to unusual events. The Gabaix model is an interesting near alternative to a rational expectations model with strong implications for determinacy issues. For example, the Taylor principle is strongly modified, so that even with an interest-rate peg there's a unique bounded equilibrium. With Gabaix-style behavioralism, the determinacy issue raised by John is a nonissue.

For convenience I assume that the period utility function of the representative consumer is separable over consumption and hours worked, with logarithmic preferences over c_t. The equations defining the log-linearized NK model are given by

$$-\hat{c}_t = \hat{R}_t - E_t\hat{c}_{t+1} - E_t\hat{\pi}_{t+1}$$

$$\hat{\pi}_t = \frac{(1 - \beta\theta)(1 - \theta)}{\beta}[(\varphi(1 - \eta_g) + 1)\hat{c}_t + \varphi\eta_g\hat{g}_t] + \beta E_t\hat{\pi}_{t+1}$$

$$\hat{R}_t = \phi_\pi\hat{\pi}_t + \varepsilon_{R,t}.$$

The first equation corresponds to the representative consumer's Euler equation, while the second equation is the NK Phillips curve. The third equation is a Taylor rule for setting the interest rate. A ^ over a variable denotes the percentage deviation of a variable from its steady-state value. In addition ϕ_π is the coefficient on $\hat{\pi}_t$ in the Taylor governing monetary policy, η_g is the proportion of steady-state output that goes to government spending, φ is the inverse Frisch elasticity of labor supply, β is the time discount factor, and θ is the Calvo parameter. We assume that $\varepsilon_{R,t}$ with AR coefficients

ρ_x. I set $\beta = 1$, $\theta = 0.75$, $\varphi = 1$, $\eta_g = 0.2$, $\theta_\pi = 1.5$. Steady-state output is normalized to 1 by setting $\chi = 1.25$.

The Gabaix NK model is defined by the set of equations

$$-\hat{c}_t = \hat{R}_t - ME_t\hat{c}_{t+1} - E_t\hat{\pi}_{t+1}$$

$$\hat{\pi}_t = \frac{(1 - \beta\theta)(1 - \theta)}{\beta}[(\varphi(1 - \eta_g) + 1)\hat{c}_t + \varphi\eta_g\hat{g}_t] + M^f\beta E_t\hat{\pi}_{t+1}$$

$$\hat{R}_t = \phi_\pi\hat{\pi}_t + \varepsilon_{R,t}. \tag{4}$$

The parameters M and M^f quantify how poorly agents understand future policy and its impact on them. When M and M^f are equal to 1, agents have rational expectations. The closer these parameters are to zero, the more myopic agents are. In what follows we assume that M and M^f are equal to 0.9.

Figure 3.2.4 displays the response of inflation and the nominal interest rate in the learnable equilibrium of the standard NK model

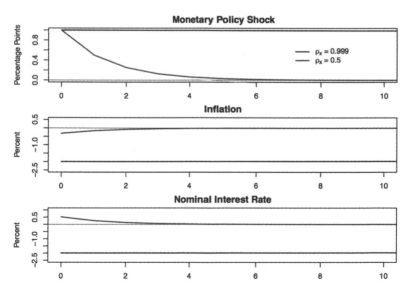

FIGURE 3.2.4. The response of the interest rate and inflation to a monetary policy shock in the NK model

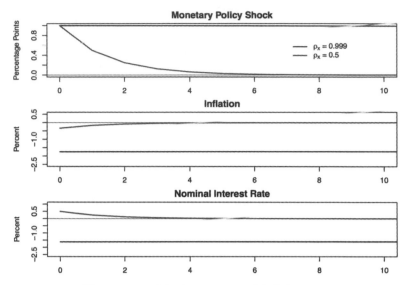

FIGURE 3.2.5. The response of the interest rate and inflation to a monetary policy shock in the Gabaix model

to a monetary policy shock of one hundred basis points when ρ_x = 0.999 and when ρ_x = 0.5. Figure 3.2.5 presents the corresponding impulse response functions in the Gabaix model.[2] The impulse response functions in Figures 3.2.4 and 3.2.5 are very similar and have what I call a modified-Fisherian property. In particular, a transitory increase in the federal funds rate is associated with a decrease in inflation. But a very persistent decrease in the federal funds rate is associated with a decrease in inflation.

The claims made in Cochrane (2017) that we don't have a model in which transitory increases in the nominal interest rate are robustly associated with decreases in inflation is simply wrong. That pattern is a generic feature of the learnable equilibrium of the standard NK model. It is a virtue of the NK model consistent with the Fisherian view that very persistent increases in the nominal interest

---

2. The impulse response functions in the Gabaix model don't depend sensitively on the value of M in the area of 0.9.

rate are associated with increases in inflation. No one should be surprised that the model has this property. After all, the limit of a persistent monetary policy shock is a permanent change in π^*, the target rate of inflation in the Taylor rule. In the NK model, a credible change in π^* is associated with a one-to-one change in the nominal interest rate.

Based on the previous results, I conclude that the neo-Fisherian relationship between interest rates and inflation is a robust feature of the standard NK model.

The Fiscal Multiplier When the ZLB Is Binding

We now consider the implications of the standard and Gabaix NK models for the effects of an increase in government purchases when the ZLB is binding. For comparison I also consider a version of the NK model where agents update expectations according to the rule

$$E_t x_{t+1} = x_{t-1}.$$

The timing in this rule reflects the fact that agents don't see the time t aggregate value of variables that their collective decisions determine at time t.[3] Monetary policy is given by (4) subject to the constraint that the net interest rate cannot be negative.

$$R_t = \max\left\{1, \frac{1}{\beta} + \theta_\pi(\pi_t - 1)\right\}.$$

A representative household maximizes

$$E_0 \sum_{t=0}^{\infty} d_t \left[\log(C_t) - \frac{\chi}{2} h_t^2\right],$$

where C_t denotes consumption, h_t denotes hours work, and

---

3. See Christiano, Eichenbaum, and Johansen (2016) for a more detailed discussion of this point.

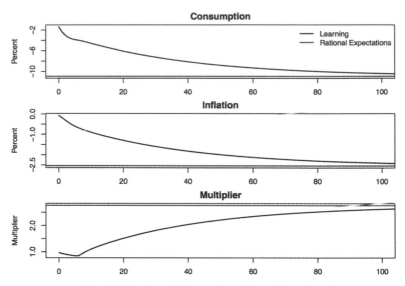

FIGURE 3.2.6. The ZLB fiscal multiplier in the NK model and in a learning model

$$d_t = \prod_{j=0}^{t} \left(\frac{1}{1 + r_{j-1}} \right).$$

The variable r_t can take on two values: r and r^ℓ, where $r^\ell < 0$. The stochastic process for r_t is given by

$$\Pr[r_{t+1} = r^\ell \,|\, r_t = r^\ell] = p, \Pr[r_{t+1} = r \,|\, r_t = r^\ell]$$
$$= 1 - p, \Pr[r_{t+1} = r^\ell \,|\, r_t = r] = 0,$$

where $r^\ell = -0.02/4$ and $p = 0.775$. I assume that G is equal to 1.05 percent of its steady value for as long as $r = r^l$. Here I work with a log-linearized version of the standard NK model in the ZLB discussed in Christiano, Eichenbaum, and Rebelo (2011).[4]

Figure 3.2.6 displays the value of the constant linear multiplier in the learnable rational expectations equilibrium of the NK model

---

4. See Christiano, Eichenbaum, and Johansen (2016) for a comparison of the multiplier in the linear and nonlinear learnable equilibriums of the standard NK model.

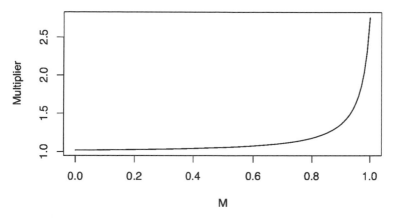

FIGURE 3.2.7. The ZLB fiscal multiplier in the Gabaix model

as well as the multiplier in the learning version of the NK model. Two features are worth noting. First, the multiplier in the standard NK model is very large. Second, while not as large, the multiplier in the learning model soon climbs above 1 and converges to the value in the rational expectations model.

Figure 3.2.7 displays the multiplier in the Gabaix model for different values of the inattention parameter, M. Recall that when M is 1, the model is the same as the standard rational expectations model. As we move to the left, agents are increasingly inattentive. Note that the multiplier substantially exceeds 1 for even substantial deviations of M from 1.

It's worth noting that large fiscal mutipliers emerge even in models that assume the fiscal theory of the price level. Leeper, Traum, and Walker (2017) develop and estimate a full-scale NK model that embeds the fiscal theory of the price level in it. Evaluated at the mean of the posterior distribution of the estimated parameter values, their model implies that, when the ZLB is binding, the fiscal multiplier is approximately equal to 1.5.

Based on the previous results, I infer that the large fiscal multiplier when the ZLB binds is a robust feature of the NK model, even if we embrace John Cochrane's preferred version, namely one that assumes the fiscal theory of the price level.

Forward Guidance

In standard simple NK models, news about shocks to future interest rates are powerful. It turns out that this result is very sensitive to deviations from rational expectations. For example, in Gabaix's NK model, forward guidance is much less powerful because agents discount the future more heavily than in the standard NK model.

A related form of non-robustness pertains to the assumption of complete markets in the standard NK model. McKay, Nakamura, and Steinsson (2016) consider a modified NK model in which agents face uninsurable idiosyncratic income risks and borrowing constraints. Agents' motive for precautionary savings is much stronger than in the standard model, and consumption is much less responsive to news about future interest rates. So forward guidance is much less powerful than in the standard model.

Based on these observations, I infer that the NK model's implication about the efficacy of forward guidance when the ZLB is a binding constraint is not robust. Thus, it shouldn't be taken very seriously.

CONCLUDING REMARKS

In this text I have challenged the central idea in Cochrane (2017). His argument is premised on a counterfactual assumption: we did *not* have a Michelson-Morley moment. That's because private-sector agents and policy makers systematically underestimated how long we would be in a ZLB environment. More generally, I have challenged his claim that multiple equilibriums are an important issue in NK models. In my view, they aren't. Going back to the roots of the rational expectations revolution virtually compels us to insist that equilibriums be learnable as a condition for taking them seriously. Nonlearnable equilibriums are simply (interesting) intellectual curiosa. They should not distract us from the task of using models to understand how the actual economy behaves and giving robust guidance to policy makers.

References

Benhabib, Jess, Stephanie Schmitt-Grohé, and Martin Uribe. 2001. "The Perils of Taylor Rules." *Journal of Economic Theory* 96 (1): 40–69.

Christiano, Lawrence, Martin Eichenbaum, and Benjamin Johansen. 2016. "Does the New Keynesian Model Have a Uniqueness Problem?" Unpublished manuscript.

Christiano, Lawrence, Martin Eichenbaum, and Sergio Rebelo. 2011. "When Is the Government Spending Multiplier Large?" *Journal of Political Economy* 119, no. 2.

Christiano, Lawrence, Martin Eichenbaum, and Mathias Trabandt. 2015. "Understanding the Great Recession." *American Economic Journal: Macroeconomics* 7 (1): 110–67.

Cochrane, John. 2011. "Determinacy and Identification with Taylor Rules." *Journal of Political Economy* 119 (3): 565–615.

———. 2017. "Michelson-Morley, Fisher, and Occam: The Radical Implications of Stable Quiet Inflation at the Zero Bound." *NBER Macroeconomics Annual.*

Gabaix, Xavier. 2017. "A Behavioral New Keynesian Model." Unpublished manuscript.

Kiley, Michael T., and John M. Roberds. "Monetary Policy in a Low Interest Real World." Brookings Papers.

Kim, Don H., and Jonathan Wright. 2005. "An Arbitrage-Free Three-Factor Term Structure Model and the Recent Behavior of Long-Term Yields and Distant-Horizon Forward Rates." Federal Reserve Board Finance and Economics Discussion Series.

Leeper, E. M., N. Traum, and T. B. Walker. 2017. "Clearing Up the Fiscal Multiplier Morass." *American Economic Review.*

Lucas, Robert E., Jr. 1978. "Asset Prices in an Exchange Economy." *Econometrica* 46 (6): 1429–45.

———. 1986. "Adaptive Behavior and Economic Theory." *Journal of Business* 59 (4): 401–26.

McKay, Alisdair, Emi Nakamura, and Jon Steinsson. 2016. "The Power of Forward Guidance Revisited." *American Economic Review* 106: 3133–58.

Swanson, Eric T., and John C. Williams. 2014. "Measuring the Effect of the Zero Lower Bound on Medium- and Longer-Term Interest Rates." *American Economic Review* 104 (10): 3154–85.

GENERAL DISCUSSION

ANDREW LEVIN: I'm reading from the English version of equation 1. Unexpected inflation equals news about present value of surpluses or debt. So let me describe two more Michelson-Morley experiments for you apropos of equation 1.

Experiment 1: We're in a situation where the Congressional Budget Office is projecting that the entire government debt's going to be paid off, and I'm actually going into positive government holdings of assets. And then that outlook suddenly changes, and we're now in a situation where the ratio of government debt to GDP stabilizes. So, according to equation 1, I sort of think of that as a surprise, at least to many people in the public. Experiment 2 is a situation where the government debt-to-GDP ratio is stable at 20 to 30 percent of GDP. And it suddenly jumps up to 80 percent of GDP. And I would think of that Michelson-Morley style as, wow, that's going to create a big jump in unexpected inflation.

Well, these two scenarios are not just hypothetical. The first scenario is similar to the CBO's October 2000 outlook, which was then followed by substantial fiscal adjustments in 2001 and subsequent years. As for the second scenario, in 2008–12 the ratio of government debt to GDP jumped from 30 percent to 80 percent, but inflation remained very subdued. So I'm trying to challenge you here a bit with the fiscal theory of the price level, pushing back against your arguments here. Wouldn't those kind of huge fiscal surprises, if the fiscal theory of the price level is right, cause huge changes in unexpected inflation?

JOHN COCHRANE: Thanks for that softball. This equation is an identity. It's a present value relationship, just like price is the present value of dividends. Why can't you go out and measure expectations of dividends, discount them back, and predict stock prices?

Well, we've been trying to do that for forty years. It's not easy! It doesn't mean that price equals present value of dividends is a good place to start when you're thinking about how asset prices work. The fiscal theory works the same way. No, you can't take easily available surplus projections, discount them back, and nail inflation. That doesn't mean it isn't just as useful a framework as price equals present value of dividends.

Those CBO projections are largely, "Dear Congress, here is how the economy explodes if you don't do something," not a conditional mean of what will happen. If the CBO forecasts come true, we have a debt crisis. I think markets rightly believe that America will, once again, after she's tried everything else, do the right thing, which is the point of the CBO projections. I'll remind you that every war has huge deficits and huge debts, and markets understand that you guys are eventually going to pay this stuff off, and there is not huge inflation.

There's nothing as simple in the fiscal theory of the price level as a testable prediction that large debts give you big inflation, or large deficits give you big inflation. That's a good thing too, because the data scream that large debts and deficits are not highly correlated with inflation. Come on, I would not have spent twenty-five years with this if it could be dismissed that easily.

ANDREW LEVIN: But that sounds a little bit like your description of the captain steering between the two sea monsters. You know, the reason inflation didn't jump in either 2001 or 2008–9 is that the markets were already expecting everything that actually happened.

JOHN COCHRANE: It's on my last slide. As you understand, stock price moves largely with changes in discount rates, not with visible expectations of dividends. Likewise, changes in the valuation of government debt are far more important to understand changes in inflation. The amazing feature of the world right now is that the interest rate on government debt is so low. Low discount rates make government debt valuable, so if there is a puzzle, it is that with r very close to g, that we don't have *deflation*.

MARKUS BRUNNERMEIER: I would like to come back to John's last point. In his earlier research, especially in his presidential address to the American Finance Association, John Cochrane stressed the importance of time variation of the stochastic discount factor.[5] In other words, asset prices are primarily driven by movements in the stochastic discount factor rather than by cash flow news. In my work with Yuliy Sannikov, "The I Theory of Money," monetary policy is primarily driving the stochastic discount factor and the risk premium rather than primary surpluses.[6] Hence, it is not the expectations about future primary surpluses (the analog to cash flows) that matter most for the current price level (and inflation) but the projection of stochastic discount factor movements. In your presentation, you didn't stress this component much, and I was wondering whether you can you elaborate on that further.

JOHN COCHRANE: Yes! I didn't want to show endless models and equations, but yes, when you have price stickiness, then changes in the real interest rate have an effect on the present value of surpluses. So there is an interesting mix between fiscal and monetary policy there.

EDWARD NELSON: Just as a matter of clarification, I think there are a couple of respects in which the models John was criticizing were more defensible than he was suggesting. In the case of the New Keynesian model, obviously one of the absolutely crucial papers in that literature is the Julio Rotemberg and Mike Woodford paper from twenty years ago, which had the standard New Keynesian equations but modified them with some fairly minor

5. John Cochrane, "2011 Presidential Address," American Finance Association, January 6, 2011, http://www.afajof.org/details/video/2870771/2011-Presidential-Address.html.

6. Markus K. Brunnermeier and Yuliy Sannikov, "The I Theory of Money," NBER Working Paper no. 22533, August 2016.

and transparent timing conventions about spending decisions.[7] And certainly their Figure 1 has an impulse response of the "correct sign" in which a tightening of monetary policy reduces inflation. So I think only a fairly minor modification of the standard New Keynesian model might be needed to get you that result.

On the matter of monetarism, you have to remember that Friedman and Schwartz's *Monetary History* certainly looked at periods in which M2 and the monetary base behaved differently, and whenever those occurred, they regarded money as M2, not the monetary base. And it's basically elementary textbook stuff that reserves aren't money and don't count in the money stock. Certainly big issues have been raised in the last few years about the relationship between the monetary base and M2. But I think there are important elements of the Great Recession period that make looking at M2 of interest. We didn't have a great depression, and in the Great Depression, M2 fell by a third, but it didn't this time. The Bank of England was very explicit in its QE policy, that holding up the money stock was one of the criteria of QE, and there are ways you can do that without relying on the money multiplier mechanism. So I don't think monetarism is going to be dismissed just by saying that the expansion of reserves didn't cause inflation. Remember, Friedman and Schwartz eventually wrote a whole book, *Monetary Statistics*, defending M2 as the definition of money. The variable that John quite rightly says did rise enormously and didn't lead to inflation is the quantity of reserves; and that variable doesn't appear in the money stock, according to the core monetarist literature.

JOHN COCHRANE: Let me briefly address both points, and Marty may want to respond too. The standard New Keynesian model, including Rotenberg and Woodford, generates a negative response to a transitory interest rate. Rotenberg and Woodford

---

7. Julio J. Rotemberg and Michael Woodford, "An Optimization-Based Econometric Framework for the Evaluation of Monetary Policy," *NBER Macroeconomics Annual* 12 (1997).

do not look at permanent interest rate changes. The standard model also needs to pair a monetary policy shock with a change in fiscal policy, so that you get that jump-down in inflation. If that "passive" change in fiscal policy doesn't happen, the deflation is not going to happen either.

The issue at hand is not whether M2 times V equals PY. The issue at hand is, Are we in a liquidity trap? Can the Fed accomplish anything by running open market operations and increasing reserves? If your view is that we didn't get inflation because reserves didn't leak out into M2, that's exactly my point. The reserves don't leak out into M2, so open market operations don't do anything when you're paying interest on money.

MARTIN EICHENBAUM: I'll repeat that the standard New Keynesian model has no problem getting the nominal interest rate and inflation to move in opposite directions after relatively transitory policy shocks. For persistent shocks, you get exactly what you'd expect. The nominal interest rate and inflation move in the same direction. After all, a permanent shock is the same as a rise in the nominal interest rate target that appears in the Taylor rule. And that kind of change moves the nominal interest rate and inflation by the same amount and in the same direction.

JOHN COCHRANE: But Marty, this does cause a bit of a problem for the standard interpretation of the 1980s, where the standard story is that persistently high interest rates drove inflation down.

MARTIN EICHENBAUM: Larry Christiano points out in his discussion of your *Macroeconomics Annual* paper that Andy Levin has a brilliant paper with Chris Erceg in the 2003 *JME*, which argues that if it took time for agents to believe that the Volcker disinflation was credible, then nominal interest rates and inflation would move in opposite directions during the transition period.[8] This seems plausible in light of the historical record.

---

8. Christopher Erceg and Andrew Levin, "Imperfect Credibility and Inflation Persistence," *Monetary Economics* 50 (May 2003): 915–44.

JOHN COCHRANE: So you're saying that monetary policy inherently relies on people being systematically irrational. I'd love to see Janet Yellen go to Congress and say, "Look, this is all a confidence game; we cleverly exploit the irrationality of the American people."

MARTIN EICHENBAUM: No, I'm saying that the Volcker disinflation wasn't instantly credible. A wise agent would not have instantly assumed that it was.

JOHN COCHRANE: The only way this thing works is if people are too dumb to know what's happening.

MARTIN EICHENBAUM: Let's be clear. The Erceg-Levin paper assumes that agents have rational expectations.

RICHARD CLARIDA: I enjoyed this session a lot. I actually learned from both. I'm glad you did the point-counterpoint, because I learned a lot. I want to piggyback off something Marty said and reinforce. One thing I've noticed is if you take the Laubach and Williams estimate of r-star, which is done without any reference to financial asset prices, and plot the forward Treasury inflation-protected securities yields, which I've done, it's striking how they come together. I'm not saying the TIPS market's right or Laubach and Williams are right, but I think it is revealing that you had this break in the TIPS implied forward yields at about the same time and the same magnitude as Laubach and Williams.

The second point, which I think is relevant to this discussion, is that it's always convenient to work in silos, but in fact there is a global dimension to real rates, both theoretically and empirically. And we can go back and forth as to whether it's the US factor or a global factor, but empirically, it's a very robust effect. So we don't have 180 countries with a 180 real rates. We've got one factor that's 90 percent of it. But I think that's relevant to stabilization policy, because we've essentially had a global decline in real rates now, and that impacts how much you get in currencies and how much other policies can do.

And the third thing, which is a bit more cynical but relevant to the policy discussion, is that even though I'm in the camp that thinks time-varying r-star is important for policy, it does open up a communications challenge for central banks compared to the world where r-star is a constant, because you get into this potential issue of a central bank that wants to run a very, very gradual, behind-the-curve policy, say, "Well, r-star is low, and we're just following r-star up." And since it's unobservable, or at least poorly measurable, it can complicate communication. But as a practical matter, I think time-variation r-star is very relevant, and there's a global piece as well.

KENNETH JUDD: First, I must say that I'm sure Michelson, Morley, and Einstein are all spinning in their graves. Second, to Marty. You talk about uniquely learnable equilibriums in these dynamic models. I remember Sargent some years ago had some work on learning, where the learning process, I think, created novel dynamics that were more complex than the simple rational expectations equilibrium. I also know that there are many, many learning rules you can use. Are you saying there exists a learning rule that gives you uniqueness, or is this true for all learning rules? Anyway, the claim struck me as surprising.

MARTIN EICHENBAUM: Let me clarify very briefly. I'm not making a global claim with respect to all possible learning rules. I am considering a particular class of learning rules. Within that class, the learning equilibriums converge to a particular rational expectations equilibrium.

JOHN COCHRANE: I have a paper that shows the opposite: the standard New Keynesian model is not learnable, and the fiscal theory model is learnable.

MARTIN EICHENBAUM: That's a different definition of learning. Agents are learning about something entirely different in your paper.

JOHN COCHRANE: There are other learning criteria in which it goes the other way.

MARTIN EICHENBAUM: Nope. The word is the same, but it refers to a different thing.

JAMES BULLARD: Marty's right: you should take learning very seriously. But I just wanted to get a clarification, because this is a little different discussion of neo-Fisherian effects. You're saying you agree that if there's a temporary move in the policy rate, all the other impulse responses we have looked at over the years are right. But if there's a permanent move, then I guess you agree with this, Marty, that you will get higher or lower inflation, depending on which way it goes?

MARTIN EICHENBAUM: Of course. Absolutely.

JAMES BULLARD: So would you say that in Japan, according to our models, what dragged inflation lower is the move from a high to a persistently low nominal interest rate?

MARTIN EICHENBAUM: I'm not an expert on Japan, and I don't pretend to understand all that's going on there. But there are lots of real models that can generate low real interest rates in Japan. Those models rely on low fertility rates, an aging population, and low growth rates of total factor productivity. Granted there's a tension about open economy versus closed economy issues that Rich Clarida points out. But if r-star permanently fell by a lot, the New Keynesian model wouldn't have a problem in generating low inflation and low nominal interest rates for Japan.

CHAPTER FOUR

MONETARY POLICY AND PAYMENTS

. . . .

SECTION ONE

Payment Systems and the Distributed Ledger Technology

Laurie Simon Hodrick

An essential function of the Federal Reserve is to manage the central payment system. The distributed ledger technology is a digital innovation with the potential to transform payments, clearing, and settlement processes. In my brief remarks, I will introduce the Federal Reserve's management of payment systems, emphasize how the distributed ledger technology could reduce operational and financial inefficiencies for payment systems, and highlight some potential challenges to the distributed ledger technology's broad implementation.

In "Strategies for Improving the U.S. Payment System," the Federal Reserve pronounces, "A U.S. payment system that is safe, efficient, and broadly accessible is vital to the U.S. economy, and the Federal Reserve plays an important role in promoting these qualities as a leader, catalyst for change, and provider of payment services to financial institutions and the U.S. Treasury."[1] This includes keeping

---

1. Federal Reserve System, "Strategies for Improving the U.S. Payments System," January 2015, 1. Available at https://fedpaymentsimprovement.org/wp-content/uploads/strategies-improving-us-payment-system.pdf.

sufficient currency in circulation, providing check collection services to depository institutions, operating electronic payment systems, and providing financial services to the US government. In aggregate, US payment, clearing, and settlement systems process approximately 600 million transactions per day, valued in excess of $12.6 trillion.[2]

The Federal Reserve's approach to improving US payment systems has been to encourage the private sector to innovate real-time payment solutions for both the Federal Reserve payment systems and private sector payment systems. As new payment technologies develop, the Federal Reserve has summarized its effectiveness criterion to be "a ubiquitous, safe, faster electronic solution(s) for making a broad variety of business and personal payments, supported by a flexible and cost-effective means for payment, clearing, and settlement groups to settle their positions rapidly and with finality."[3] That is the payment system criterion I focus on here. I then apply it specifically to the distributed ledger technology, which is being piloted and utilized in many applications worldwide to enhance and even replace existing transaction infrastructures.

Within this criterion are the following considerations:

Ubiquity: A system that is accessible and applicable to all relevant parties with multiple use cases, ideally with cross-border functionality.

Safety: Providing a trusted secure system of record with cryptographic integrity, no fraud, and direct legal enforcement.

Speed: Rapid clearing and settlement, moving toward real-time "immediate payments" systems. For example, stock trades currently

---

2. Federal Reserve Board, "Distributed Ledger Technology in Payments, Clearing, and Settlement," 2016. Available at https://www.federalreserve.gov/econresdata/feds/2016/files/2016095pap.pdf.

3. Federal Reserve Banks, "Federal Reserve System Faster Payments Task Force Charter Established 2015," FedPayments Improvement website, 2015. Available at https://fedpaymentsimprovement.org/wp-content/uploads/faster-tf-charter.pdf.

settle in T+3 days, moving to T+2 settlement in September. Why not T+0, same day settlement of stocks?[4]

Efficiency: Lower costs and increased convenience, achieved in part through scalability.

Payment finality: A process for handling and resolving disputed claims for prompt resolution.

I use "distributed ledger" as a collective term that encapsulates the continuously growing decentralized consensus databases secured by cryptography that authenticate ownership provenance by recording transactions. Blockchain, so named because it gathers and orders data into blocks of encrypted information and then chains them together, was originally developed in 2009 as the permissionless underlying ledger platform for the digital currency bitcoin. This technology is now being levered beyond the currency bitcoin to support a wide range of applications. Other distributed ledgers have emerged as well, the second largest being Etherium, which is associated with the cryptocurrency ether. There is also a collaborative public effort, Hyperledger, which is an open-source initiative hosted by the Linux Foundation.[5]

The distributed ledger, with its decentralized trust, is a striking alternative to classic double-entry bookkeeping maintained by a central authority. This difference is at the heart of its significant potential benefits, like enhanced speed and efficiency, but also its many challenges.

---

4. As of September 5, 2017, compliance with the amendment of Rule 15c6-1(a) of the Securities Exchange Act of 1934 will shorten the "regular way" settlement cycle for most stock transactions from three business days after the trade date (T+3) to two business days after the trade date (T+2). With the ledger technology, almost instantaneous (T+0) stock settlement could be possible.

5. The Bank of England is one of over 140 members of Hyperledger, which has no crypto assets built into it.

Let me focus first on the benefits of the distributed ledger technology for payment systems. It offers greater transparency of ownership and hence the ability to safely transfer more quickly, at lower cost, without the need for an intermediary.[6] In terms of ubiquity, it has the potential for broad application and accessibility if it is standardized. In terms of safety and security, it has non-falsifiable cryptographic integrity without a central authority or "trusted third party." In terms of speed, settlement can be nearly instantaneous. In terms of cost efficiency, it could eliminate intermediaries and infrastructure costs, allowing direct settlement. In terms of finality, it provides an immutable record that cannot be altered retrospectively.

The other side of the cryptocoin, if you'll forgive the pun, involves the ledger's potential challenges. In addition to the risks already inherent in payment activities, these challenges include operational, technological, legal, regulatory, and other hurdles. In terms of ubiquity, there is currently a lack of standardization and interoperability, both across applications as well as across jurisdictions. In terms of safety and security, there are issues of privacy and transparency. Currently, there is a full spectrum of networks, from open and public and permissionless, to consortium, to fully private and permissioned. There are key questions of who has permission to update the code and to legally enforce transactions. There are FINRA rule requirements, including compulsory anti–money laundering compliance (FINRA Rule 3310) and know-your-customer (FINRA Rule 2090) processes.[7] There has been a history of hacks

---

6. The ledger could also provide an additional monetary policy instrument in the form of a central-bank-issued digital currency, like that being considered by Norway's Norges Bank.

7. Silk Road, a website founded in 2011 that allowed the transaction of narcotics and other illicit goods, used bitcoin to mask the identities of merchants and customers. Some 600,000 bitcoins changed hands on the site, worth over $1.5 billion at current exchange rates. The Justice Department successfully prosecuted founder Ross Ulbricht.

in some of the ledgers.[8] In terms of speed, as transaction volume has approached a distributed ledger network's capacity limit, transaction processing speed has slowed.[9] In terms of cost efficiency, one growing challenge to scalability is that transaction fees have risen. The fee necessary to foster transaction processing has risen in response to a growing transaction backlog. In terms of finality, unresolved ambiguities include how to satisfy the regulatory requirements and how to handle disputed claims, with a possible solution being to have regulated authorities as observer nodes.

While not included in the Federal Reserve's criterion, other overarching questions emerge. These include who will pay for progress and whether central banks should form their own consortium.

In summary, while the distributed ledger is not yet ready for wide-scale adoption, it may become a transformative technology that provides ubiquitous, safe, faster electronic solution(s) for making a broad variety of business and personal payments, supported by flexible and cost-effective means for paying, clearing, and settling positions rapidly and with finality. While there are significant implementation challenges ahead, there are also huge benefits to their resolution.

Although I have focused today specifically on payment systems, the distributed ledger technology can be used to transfer any asset that can be presented in digital form. There is an important

---

8. In 2014, the Tokyo-based exchange Mt. Gox collapsed after a yearlong series of attacks resulted in the theft of $460 million in bitcoins, about one-fourth of which were later recovered. In 2016, a hacker used the Decentralized Autonomous Organization code to withdraw $60 million of ether. A hack on the Hong Kong–based digital currency exchange Bitfinex resulted in the theft of $65 million in bitcoin. In 2017, Bitcoin was attacked by WannaCry ransomware, which locked down over 200,000 computers in at least 150 countries, demanding a ransom payment of $300 each in bitcoin.

9. For the past two years, there has been contentious debate between segregated witnesses (SegWit) and Bitcoin Unlimited about whether to conduct a hard fork or use lightning networks and side chains to raise the block limit (currently 1MB for the Bitcoin network, as compared to 8MB for the Litecoin network). On August 1, 2017, the Bitcoin Cash hard fork increased block size to 8MB.

parallel between what is emerging at the Federal Reserve for payment systems, and what is emerging, for example, with regulators for securities markets. As my own research explores, this gives the distributed ledger technology the potential to disrupt not only payments and money transfers, but also the execution, clearing, and settlement of securities transactions.

In "The Blockchain and Its Implications for Corporate and Securities Law and Practice," David J. Berger, a litigation partner at Wilson Sonsini Goodrich & Rosati, Joseph A. Grundfest, my colleague at Stanford Law School, and I explore the requirements for the distributed ledger technology's adoption by US securities markets; the emergent role of this technology in those markets; the implications for corporate and securities trading, law, and practice; and how the SEC should prepare for and respond to these technological developments.

· ·

SECTION TWO

Cryptocurrencies

Some Lessons from Monetary Economics

Jesús Fernández-Villaverde and Daniel Sanches

In 1976, F. A. Hayek published a short pamphlet, "The Denationalization of Money." Worried that the high inflation of the 1970s in Western countries would not be tackled by central banks because of political constraints, Hayek argued that money issuing should be opened to market forces and that the government monopoly on the provision of means of exchange should be abolished. He envisioned a system of private monies where the forces of competition would induce banks to provide a stable means of exchange (Hayek 1999). Despite some attention from a group of market-oriented economists (see, for example, Salin 1984), Hayek's proposal languished for decades as more a curiosity than a workable idea.

Technological developments over the last few years have made Hayek's proposal a reality, but as the result of many individual decisions and not the outcome of a planned policy change (a process Hayek would have appreciated). Nowadays it is straightforward to create a cryptocurrency, a privately issued money.[10] Thanks to fascinating advances in cryptography and computer science, cryptocurrencies are robust to overissuing, the double-spending problem—the holder of the currency should not be able to spend the same token twice—and counterfeiting (see Narayanan et al. 2016 for details).[11] These cryptocurrencies are different from the notes issued by financial institutions during the era of free banking (Dowd 1992) for three reasons. First, most cryptocurrencies are fully fiduciary, while notes in the free banking era usually represented claims against deposits in gold or other assets. Second, cryptocurrencies are not directly related to credit but are issued

---

10. The views expressed in this paper are those of the authors and do not necessarily reflect those of the Federal Reserve Bank of Philadelphia or the Federal Reserve System. This paper summarizes the main results in Fernández-Villaverde and Sanches (2016), from which we borrow heavily .

We are not referring here to possible electronic monies issued by governments (even if relying on the same set of cryptographic techniques as private cryptocurrencies). Moving from government-issued paper money to government-issued e-money is not very different from the moves in past decades from paper Treasury bonds to electronic Treasury bonds (except, perhaps, the ability of e-money to impose negative nominal interest rates and therefore provide further flexibility to central banks in implementing their monetary policy).

11. Not all problems are eliminated by cryptography. An example is a "Goldfinger" attack. In the famous 007 movie, Auric Goldfinger plans to break into Fort Knox, not to steal the gold as in the original Ian Fleming novel (a logistic nightmare quickly pointed out by reviewers of the novel), but to detonate a small, particularly dirty nuclear bomb inside the bullion depository and radiate the US gold stock out of circulation, thus causing Goldfinger's stock of gold to appreciate considerably. Similarly, the owner of a rival cryptocurrency or a foreign power may install enough computing power to achieve "false" consensus in Bitcoin, not to profit directly from it but to destroy the payment system and benefit indirectly.

by computer networks according to some predetermined criteria (such as a "proof-of-work," i.e., the solution of a complex mathematical problem). Third, cryptocurrencies such as Etherium can also work as a sophisticated automatic escrow account. It is effortless to add to the code that controls the cryptocurrency a condition that states, "Peter will pay Mary ten ethers if, tomorrow at noon, the weather in Philadelphia according to weatherunderground.com is over eighty degrees." Once we have that piece of code in place, the verification of the condition and the payment, if the condition is satisfied, are automatically implemented.

Today, any person with Internet access can use a bewildering array of cryptocurrencies as means of exchange. Everyone has heard about Bitcoin, whose market capitalization (the price per unit times the circulating supply) as of July 6, 2017, exceeds $42 billion, only slightly below the market capitalization of Ford Motor Company. But six other cryptocurrencies (Etherium, Ripple, Litecoin, Etherium Classic, NEM, and Dash) have market capitalizations over $1 billion, and another thirty-seven have between $100 and $999.99 million. While it is true that cryptocurrencies represent only a trivial fraction of all payments in the world economy, it is not inconceivable that such shares may exponentially increase over the next few years and even become widespread in emerging economies with dysfunctional government monies.

This observation opens many positive and normative questions about how currency competition may work that Hayek did not address using modern economic theory (he admitted that his idea was more a springboard for further discussion than a thorough analysis). Among the positive questions: Will currency competition among private monies yield a stable price level? Will we have a "winner-take-all" situation where one currency dominates the market? Or will we observe a landscape of several currencies, each with a significant market share? How important are network effects? Can we have in the long run fully fiduciary private monies or will commodity-backed currencies dominate? Will we have the "right" amount of money in equilibrium? Can private monies and a government-issued money coexist? Among the normative questions: How should governments react to private monies? Should governments have an "industrial policy" regarding private cryptocurrencies? Should they favor one cryptocurrency over others? Or should they follow a policy of "benign neglect"? There are even questions relevant for would-be entrepreneurs: What is the best strategy to issue currency? What are the competitive advantages that a new cryptocurrency requires to flourish? A formal theory of currency competition is surely needed.

In Fernández-Villaverde and Sanches (2016), we take a first pass at this problem. We build a model of competition between privately issued fiduciary currencies by extending Lagos and Wright's (2005) environment, a workhorse of modern monetary economics. The standard Lagos and Wright model is augmented by including entrepreneurs who can issue their own currencies to maximize profits or by automata following a predetermined algorithm (as in Bitcoin). Otherwise, the model is standard. In our framework, competition is perfect: all private currencies have the same ability to settle payments, and each entrepreneur behaves parametrically with respect to prices.

Despite its simplicity, our analysis offers several valuable insights. In the interest of space, we highlight only a few of them. First, in general, a monetary equilibrium with private monies will not deliver price stability. When money is issued by a profit-maximizing entrepreneur, she will try to maximize the real value of seigniorage. With many cost functions of minting money, this maximization does not imply that the entrepreneur delivers a stable currency. For example, if the cost function is strictly convex, entrepreneurs will always have an incentive to mint additional units of the currency. Hayek's conjecture that a system of private monies competing among themselves would provide a stable means of exchange is, in general, wrong. When money is issued by an automaton, there is no particular reason why the quantity of money would be compatible with price stability (except, perhaps, by "divine coincidence"). Bitcoin has already decided how many new units of currency will be issued in 2022 even though nobody knows what the demand for currency will be in that year.

Second, even when the cost function of minting money is such that we have an equilibrium with price stability, there is a continuum of equilibrium trajectories where the value of private monies monotonically converges to zero. In other words, the self-fulfilling inflationary episodes construed by Obstfeld and Rogoff (1983) and Lagos and Wright (2003) in economies with government-issued money and a money-growth rule are not an exclusive feature of public monies. Self-fulfilling inflationary episodes are, instead, the consequence of using intrinsically useless tokens (even if electronic and issued by private profit-maximizing, long-lived entrepreneurs) whose valuation can change depending on expectations about the future.

But, as economists, we do not care about price stability per se. The goal of a well-behaved monetary system must be to achieve some efficiency goal. Our third, and perhaps most important, result is that a purely private monetary system does not provide the socially optimum quantity of money even in the equilibrium with stable prices. Despite having entrepreneurs that take prices parametrically, competition cannot provide an optimal outcome because entrepreneurs do not internalize, by minting additional tokens, the pecuniary externalities they create in the market with trading frictions at the core of all essential models of money (Wallace 2001). These pecuniary externalities mean that, at a fundamental level, the market for currencies is very different from the market for goods such as wheat, and the forces that drive optimal outcomes under perfect competition in the latter fail in the former. The "price" of money itself does not play a fully allocative role:

if one believes that money is used because there are frictions in transactions, one should not believe that the market can provide the right amount of money.[12]

These three results cast serious doubts on Hayek's proposal of currency competition. In most cases, a system of private monies will not deliver price stability, and even when it does, it will always be subject to self-fulfilling inflationary episodes, and it will supply a suboptimal amount of money. Currency competition works only sometimes and partially.

How can Hayek be vindicated? A simple possibility is to think about the existence of productive capital. If entrepreneurs use the seigniorage to purchase productive capital and this capital is sufficiently productive, then there is an equilibrium in which a system of private monies may achieve social efficiency. Other possibilities would include the presence of market power (different currencies are slightly different from each other in their ability to make payments) and, thus, a franchise value that a private entrepreneur may want to preserve (allegedly, this environment may be closer to what Hayek envisioned than our perfect competition world). However, we also know that long-run market power does not necessarily deliver the right outcomes and that incentives to "cheat" always exist (Mailath and Samuelson, 2006).

Finally, what are the effects of cryptocurrencies on government monetary policy? (Government-issued money is different from private money because it has fiscal backing.) How is monetary policy changed by the presence of alternative means of exchange? The first case of interest is when the government follows a rather standard money-growth rule. Under this policy, profit-maximizing entrepreneurs will frustrate the government's attempt to implement a positive real return on money through deflation when the public is willing to hold private currencies. There are, fortunately,

---

12. This argument restates, in a slightly modified form, the ideas in Friedman (1960). In comparison with Hayek, Friedman was skeptical of the role of markets in monetary supply.

alternative policies that can promote stability and efficiency simultaneously. For example, the government may peg the real value of its money. Under this rule, the government can implement an efficient allocation (i.e., supply the amount of money that maximizes social welfare) as the unique equilibrium outcome, although it requires driving private money out of the economy.

There is an important lesson here: the threat of competition from private monies imposes some market discipline on any government involved in issuing currency. If a central bank, for example, does not provide a sufficiently "good" money, then it will have difficulties in the implementation of allocations. This may be the best feature of cryptocurrencies: in a world where we can switch to Bitcoin or Etherium, central banks need to provide, paraphrasing Adam Smith, a tolerable administration of money. Currency competition may have, after all, a large upside for human welfare.

References

Dowd, K. 1992. *The Experience of Free Banking*. New York: Routledge.

Fernández-Villaverde, J., and D. Sanches. 2016. "Can Currency Competition Work?" CEPR Discussion Paper no. 11095.

Friedman, M. 1960. *A Program for Monetary Stability*. Bronx: Fordham University Press.

Hayek, F. 1999. "The Denationalization of Money: An Analysis of the Theory and Practice of Concurrent Currencies." In *The Collected Works of F. A. Hayek: Good Money, Part 2*, edited by S. Kresge. Chicago: University of Chicago Press.

Lagos, R., and R. Wright. 2003. "Dynamics, Cycles, and Sunspot Equilibria in 'Genuinely Dynamic, Fundamentally Disaggregative' Models of Money." *Journal of Economic Theory* 109 (2): 156–71.

———. 2005. "A Unified Framework for Monetary Theory and Policy Analysis." *Journal of Political Economy* 113 (3): 463–84.

Mailath, G., and L. Samuelson. 2006. *Repeated Games and Reputation*. Oxford: Oxford University Press.

Narayanan, A., J. Bonneau, E. Felten, A. Miller, and S. Goldfeder. 2016. *Bitcoin and Cryptocurrency Technologies*. Princeton, NJ: Princeton University Press.

Obstfeld, M., and K. Rogoff. 1983. "Speculative Hyperinflations in Maximizing Models: Can We Rule Them Out?" *Journal of Political Economy* 91 (4): 675–87.

Salin, P. 1984. *Currency Competition and Monetary Union.* Leiden: Martinus Nijhoff.

Wallace, N. 2001. "Whither Monetary Economics?" *International Economic Review* 42 (4): 847–69.

• •

SECTION THREE

Central Bank Digital Currency and the Future of Monetary Policy

Michael D. Bordo and Andrew T. Levin

For there was once a time when no such thing as money existed. . . . [A] material was selected which, being given a stable value by the state, avoided the problems of barter by providing a constant medium of exchange. That material, struck in due form by the mint, demonstrates its utility and title not by its substance as such but by its quantity, so that no longer are the things exchanged both called wares but one of them is termed the price. And today it is a matter for doubt whether one can talk of sale when no money passes.
—Julius Paulus Prudentissimus, circa 230 CE[13]

In ancient Rome, the emperor's chief legal adviser described the fundamental rationale for a government-issued currency using terms familiar to modern monetary economists: (1) a *unit of account* for the pricing of goods and services; (2) a *method of storing*

---

13. Paulus served as chief legal adviser to the Roman emperor Severus Alexander (222–235 CE), during a period of multiple revisions to the designated purity and weight in silver of the Roman denarius. He was granted the honorific "prudentissimus," and his commentaries were later included in the *Digest*, a legal compendium produced by the Byzantine emperor Justinian. The excerpt shown here is taken from section 18.1 of the *Digest*; the translation from the original Latin is that of Watson (2010, 55).

value; and (3) a *medium of exchange* that facilitates economic and financial transactions. Moreover, the Roman jurist recognized that the utility of currency depends not on its material substance but on its nominal quantity—that is, the efficacy of the currency hinges on public confidence in the authorities' management of the monetary system.[14]

Nearly two millennia later, as electronic devices and high-speed networks have become practically ubiquitous, central banks around the globe are actively exploring the possibility of establishing sovereign digital currencies.[15] Just like paper currency and coins, central bank digital currency (CBDC) would be fixed in nominal terms, universally accessible, and valid as legal tender for all public and private transactions. Consequently, CBDC is essentially different from the various forms of virtual currency (such as Bitcoin, Etherium, and Ripple) that have been created by private entities and whose market prices have exhibited sharp fluctuations in recent years.[16]

In this text, we analyze the key features of CBDC, focusing on basic design characteristics rather than technical details. In particular, we consider the following issues: (1) Should CBDC payments involve transfers between accounts held at the central bank or digital "tokens" that can be transferred directly from payer to payee? (2) Should cash be abolished or should the central bank establish

---

14. Schumpeter (1954, 67) interpreted Paulus's text as indicating that "people, in handling money in everyday transactions, usually take a coin at its nominal value without any conscious thought of the commodity value of its materials."

15. For example, the Sveriges Riksbank has an accelerated time frame for deciding whether to launch a CBDC (Boel 2016; Skingsley 2016), the People's Bank of China is experimenting with technical specifications (Fan 2016), and the Bank of England is conducting a multiyear investigation (Broadbent 2016). See also recent perspectives from officials at the European Central Bank (Mersch 2017) and Norges Bank (Nicolaisen 2017).

16. See McCallum (2015) and Weber (2016). As of July 2017, the market capitalizations for Bitcoin, Etherium, and Ripple were about $42 billion, $25 billion, and $9 billion, respectively, and the year-to-date changes in their unit prices were roughly 250 percent, 3,000 percent, and 4,000 percent, respectively (http://coinmarketcap.com).

a schedule of fees for transferring funds between CBDC and paper currency? (3) Should CBDC be interest bearing or indexed to an aggregate price index rather than having a constant nominal value like cash and coins? (4) What are the implications of CBDC for the central bank's monetary policy strategy and operating procedures? (5) How will CBDC affect the interactions between the central bank and the fiscal authorities?

In considering these issues, we assume that the central bank's objective is to maximize the effectiveness of CBDC in fulfilling the basic functions of any public currency, namely, its efficiency as a medium of exchange, its security as a store of value, and its stability as the unit of account for economic and financial transactions. Using those criteria, we identify the following characteristics of a well-designed CBDC:

- An *account-based* CBDC could serve as a practically costless medium of exchange. Such accounts could be held directly at the central bank itself or made available via public-private partnerships with commercial banks.
- An *interest-bearing* CBDC could provide a secure store of value, with a rate of return in line with other risk-free assets such as short-term government securities. The CBDC interest rate could serve as the main tool for conducting monetary policy.
- To facilitate the *gradual obsolescence of paper currency*, CBDC could be made widely available to the public, with a graduated schedule of fees on transfers between cash and CBDC. Consequently, adjustments to the CBDC interest rate would not be constrained by any effective lower bound.
- The monetary policy framework could foster *true price stability*; that is, the real value of CBDC would remain stable over time in terms of a broad consumer price index. Such a framework would facilitate the systematic and transparent conduct of monetary policy.

This analysis draws on a very long strand of literature in monetary economics. The quest for a stable unit of account was pursued by luminaries like Jevons (1875), Marshall (1877), Wicksell (1898), Fisher (1913), Buchanan (1962), and Hayek (1978).[17] The rationale for an efficient medium of exchange was highlighted by Friedman (1960), who argued that government-issued money should bear the same rate of return as other risk-free assets. These two goals—that is, a stable unit of account and an efficient medium of exchange—seemed to be irreconcilable due to the impracticalities of paying interest on paper currency, and hence Friedman advocated a steady deflation rather than price stability. But the achievement of both goals has now become feasible via a well-designed CBDC.[18]

As a practically costless medium of exchange, CBDC would significantly enhance the efficiency of the payments system. For example, a recent IMF study has pointed out that the introduction of CBDC would facilitate more rapid and secure settlement of cross-border financial transactions.[19] CBDC would be particularly beneficial for lower-income households, which tend to rely heavily on cash, and for small businesses, which incur substantial costs for handling cash or substantial interchange fees for taking payments via debit and credit cards. At a macroeconomic level, researchers at the Bank of England have estimated that the productivity gains from adopting CBDC would be similar to those of a substantial reduction in distortionary taxes.[20]

The interest-bearing design of CBDC and the obsolescence of paper currency would also contribute to greater macroeconomic stability, because interest rate adjustments would no longer be con-

17. See also Bordo (1984), Black (1987), Cagan (1987), Patinkin (1993), and the papers collected in Dorn and Schwartz (1987) and Dorn (2017).

18. True price stability was *not* achieved during the classical gold standard era; rather, the general price level exhibited substantial fluctuations and persistent drift due to shifts in the relative supply and demand for gold. For further analysis and discussion, see Bordo (1984) and Bordo, Dittmar, and Gavin (2007).

19. See He et al. (2017).

20. See Barrdear and Kumhof (2016).

strained by any effective lower bound in response to severe adverse shocks.[21] That lower bound has been a key reason why many central banks currently aim at positive inflation rates of 2 percent or more, whereas CBDC will essentially eliminate the need to maintain such an "inflation buffer" or to deploy alternative monetary policy tools such as quantitative easing or credit subsidies. Moreover, in the event of a severe economic downturn, CBDC would facilitate the provision of money-financed fiscal stimulus.[22] Indeed, Friedman (1948) highlighted the complementarities between monetary and fiscal expansion under such circumstances.

The initiation of CBDC would represent a fairly natural progression in light of current trends in monetary operations. For example, most central banks already pay interest on the reserves of commercial banks, which comprise a substantial portion of the total monetary base. The Federal Reserve has expanded its capacity to pay interest to an even wider range of counterparties by borrowing funds in the US Treasury repo market.[23] Moreover, the Federal Reserve Banks now maintain segregated deposit accounts for systemically important financial market utilities (FMUs), so that the customers of those FMUs may rest assured that their funds are secure, liquid, and interest bearing.[24]

---

21. Goodfriend (2000, 2016), Buiter (2009), Agarwal and Kimball (2015), and Pfister and Valla (2017) discuss the merits of eliminating the effective lower bound on nominal interest rates.

22. For example, as noted by Dyson and Hodgson (2017), funds could be deposited directly into the CBDC accounts of lower-income households, thereby cushioning their purchasing power from the effects of the downturn as well as from the temporarily negative level of the CBDC interest rate.

23. As of mid-July 2017, the Federal Reserve's reverse repurchase agreements stood at around $400 billion, comprising about one-sixth of its interest-bearing liabilities and roughly one-tenth of its total liabilities. Information about the design of the Federal Reserve's reverse repo facility and the expanded range of counterparties is available at "FAQs: Reverse Repurchase Agreement Operations," Federal Reserve Bank of New York, December 16, 2005, https://www.newyorkfed.org/markets/rrp_faq.html.

24. For example, segregated reserve accounts at the Federal Reserve Bank of Chicago have been created to hold the funds of customers of the Chicago Mercantile Exchange ("Change in Interest Rate on House, Customer Segregated and Customer Cleared Swaps Performance Bond USD Cash Balances," CME Group, March 15, 2017, www.cmegroup

As for monetary policy strategy, aiming at true price stability would be substantively different from the current practice of inflation forecast targeting. As noted above, most central banks have a positive inflation target (typically 2 percent or higher) and place no weight on previous deviations of inflation from target ("Let bygones be bygones"), so that the aggregate price level follows a random walk with upward drift. By contrast, under a price-level target, consumer prices would still exhibit transitory fluctuations while monetary policy ensures that the aggregate price level returns to its target over time. Thus, households and businesses would be able to formulate their plans with confidence that the cost of a representative basket of consumer items (as measured in terms of the CBDC) would be reasonably stable over the medium run and roughly constant at planning horizons of five, ten, twenty, and even fifty years into the future. Such stability could be particularly beneficial for lower-income households and small businesses, which typically have little or no access to sophisticated financial planning advice or complex financial instruments that can help insure against such risks.

The widespread use of CBDC and the obsolescence of paper currency would be helpful in discouraging tax evasion, money laundering, and other illegal activities.[25] This benefit is significant for advanced economies but likely to be even more pertinent for developing economies, where a large fraction of economic activity is conducted using cash and hence the incidence of tax evasion is very high. The feasibility of CBDC has been demonstrated in Ecuador, where CBDC has become widely available through a simple and secure platform (i.e., two-step verification with cell phones and

.com/notices/clearing/2017/03/Chadv17-107.html) and the initial margin accounts of customers of ICE Clear Credit ("Circular 2017/015: ICE Clear Credit Client Federal Reserve Account," ICE Clear Credit, February 16, 2017, https://www.theice.com/publicdocs/clear _credit/circulars/Circular_2017_015_FINAL.pdf).

25. Rogoff (2016) considers how large-denomination bills facilitate various forms of illegal activity.

text messages).[26] Likewise, Kenya's government has been a pioneer in establishing a public-private partnership for providing low-cost digital payments.[27]

Finally, given the rapid pace of recent and prospective innovations in payment technology, it might not be prudent for central banks to take a passive and inertial approach to CBDC. Scenarios in which the central bank does not produce any form of digital currency may be associated with a number of salient risks, including loss of monetary control and greater susceptibility to severe economic downturns. Indeed, in light of such considerations, many central banks are moving expeditiously in considering the adoption of CBDC.

EFFICIENT MEDIUM OF EXCHANGE

In this section we focus on the design elements of CBDC that pertain to its role as an efficient medium of exchange. Some characteristics are intrinsic to any government-issued currency: namely, it can be held by anyone and serves as legal tender for all public and private payments.[28] However, a crucial issue is whether CBDC should more closely parallel cash or a debit card. Our analysis indicates that the former approach would have significant drawbacks, whereas the latter design would provide a simple and practically costless medium of exchange that could be provided directly by the central bank or via public-private partnerships with commercial banks. Moreover, the initiation of CBDC would likely facilitate the obsolescence of paper currency and coins.

---

26. See "Electronic Money," Central Bank of Ecuador, https://www.bce.fin.ec/en/index .php/electronic-money-system.

27. Safaricom Ltd. currently provides digital payments (using the M-Pesa platform) to about 25 million Kenyan customers ("Safaricom Annual Report 2016," Safaricom, https:// www.safaricom.co.ke/annualreport_2016). Its two largest shareholders are Vodafone (50 percent) and the Kenya Treasury Department (25 percent).

28. Fung and Halaburda (2016) identify these intrinsic features as distinct from other design elements of CBDC.

Tokens versus Accounts

In particular, one potential design (analogous to cash) would be for the central bank to issue *CBDC tokens*, which would circulate electronically among private individuals and firms and might only rarely be redeposited at the central bank.[29] Like bitcoin, this approach would use some form of distributed ledger technology (DLT) for verifying the chain of ownership of each token and validating payment transactions without requiring the direct involvement of the central bank or any other clearinghouse.[30] In contrast to bitcoin and other virtual currencies, however, the central bank would determine the supply of CBDC tokens, which would be fixed in nominal terms and serve as legal tender. Moreover, the central bank could establish transparent procedures for incorporating appropriate updates to the DLT software—a challenge that has proven difficult in the case of virtual currencies.[31]

Under the alternative design (analogous to debit cards), individuals and firms would hold funds electronically in *CBDC accounts* at the central bank or in specially designated accounts at supervised depository institutions.[32] Under this approach, the central bank would process each payment transaction by simply debiting the payer's CBDC account and crediting the payee's CBDC account.

---

29. Motamedi (2014) and Koning (2014) each proposed a token-based CBDC using the nicknames "bitdollar" and "fedcoin," respectively. For further discussion, see Andalfatto (2015) and Raskin and Yermack (2016a).

30. Danezis and Meiklejohn (2016) formulate a design for a token-based CBDC in which verification would be performed by a limited number of authorized institutions and hence would be substantially more efficient than the design of bitcoin.

31. For example, in mid-2016 the Etherium user community was divided on the appropriate response to a major security breach, and hence there was a "hard fork" into two distinct currencies (now referred to as "ethereum" and "ethereum classic"). In mid-2017, the Bitcoin user community seemed headed toward a similar outcome due to concerns about scalability, but at present it appears that situation will be resolved by a "soft fork."

32. Scorer (2017) provides a lucid and insightful discussion of these alternatives and concludes that central banks should implement digital currency using accounts rather than tokens.

One crucial advantage of an account-based system is that CBDC payments could be practically instantaneous and costless. Of course, during the initial creation of each CBDC account, the identity of the account holder would need to be verified using procedures like those followed in obtaining a driver's license or opening an account at a commercial bank. From that point onward, however, payment transactions could be conducted rapidly and securely (e.g., using two-step verification with a cell phone and digital pin), and the central bank would be able to monitor any unusual activity and implement additional antifraud safeguards as needed.

By contrast, the cost of verification for a token-based system would be inherently expensive. The entire chain of ownership of every token must be stored in an encrypted ledger (the blockchain), and a copy of that ledger must be stored on each node of the payment network. New payment transactions are collected into blocks that must be verified before being added permanently to the ledger. This verification process—referred to as mining—involves computational procedures that are highly complex and energy intensive.[33] For example, in the case of bitcoin, miners' revenue is equal to about 0.8 percent of the total value of payment transactions.[34] In effect, a token-based CBDC might be preferable to existing forms of payment but would be far less efficient than an account-based CBDC.[35]

---

33. In the case of bitcoin, the difficulty threshold is adjusted automatically every two weeks in response to changes in the computational capacity of the network, thereby ensuring that new blocks are added to the blockchain about once every ten minutes. For example, during the twelve months ending in July 2017, that difficulty threshold grew by a factor of about four ("Bitcoin Stats," Blockchain, http://blockchain.info/stats).

34. Bitcoin costs are very transparent because miners' revenue is denominated in bitcoin and recorded in the blockchain ("Cost % of Transaction Volume," Blockchain, https://blockchain.info/charts/cost-per-transaction-percent). These costs mostly reflect electricity: miners are currently processing about 520 trillion gigahash per hour, and each gigash requires about 0.75 watts of electricity, so total usage is about 40 terawatt-hours per year—roughly similar to the electricity consumption of a large US city of about 2.5 million people.

35. Researchers are actively investigating alternative forms of DLT that would involve much lower verification costs, such as algorithms involving "proof of stake" instead of "proof of work"; see Zamfir (2015) and Buterin (2016). However, such algorithms may allow some

The efficiency gains from establishing an account-based CBDC would be substantial. Consumers typically pay substantial fees (2 to 5 percent or more) for withdrawing cash from automated teller machines, while retail businesses incur substantial costs for sorting, cleaning, and verification of cash as well as interchange fees for taking payments via debit and credit cards. To gauge these effects at an aggregate level, Barrdear and Kumhof (2016) analyzed a dynamic stochastic general equilibrium (DSGE) model of the US economy; in their benchmark scenario, the adoption of CBDC permanently raises the level of real GDP by about 3 percent.

Alternative Forms of Accounts

As noted above, an account-based CBDC could be implemented via accounts held directly at the central bank.[36] Such an approach would be reminiscent of the early years of central banking, when individuals and nonfinancial firms held accounts at the Bank of England and the Sveriges Riksbank; during that era of paper bookkeeping, however, maintaining a large number of private accounts became increasingly impractical, and hence such accounts were eventually discontinued. By contrast, in the current environment of immense data storage and high-speed network capacities, providing CBDC via accounts at the central bank is now eminently feasible, as evident from the recent experience of Ecuador.

Alternatively, following the approach of Dyson and Hodgson (2017), CBDC could be provided to the public via specially designated accounts at supervised commercial banks, which would hold the corresponding amount of funds in segregated reserve accounts at the central bank. This approach may be particularly beneficial to

---

imperfections in the accuracy of the blockchain—a property that might be plausible for a virtual currency but probably not acceptable for the design of CBDC.

36. Under this approach, legal safeguards would be essential for protecting the privacy of all CBDC transactions, similar to the regulations for protecting personal and proprietary information obtained by government agencies.

smaller banks that have a strong orientation toward "relationship banking." In many communities, such banks play a crucial role in providing financial services to disadvantaged households, small businesses, and entrepreneurs.

The feasibility and potential benefits of such public-private partnerships are apparent from the recent experience of Kenya. Moreover, the US Federal Reserve System has recently instituted a roughly similar approach in establishing segregated accounts for maintaining the funds of customers at systemically important financial market utilities (FMUs).[37]

Finally, CBDC need not be aimed at monopolizing the payments system but could instead be complementary to the payment services provided by private entities. Indeed, individuals and businesses would remain free to hold funds at private institutions and to make payments using private networks and virtual currencies.[38] In fact, a number of financial institutions are actively engaged in developing new payment networks using DLT and other innovative approaches.[39] In the absence of competition from CBDC, however, such private networks might exhibit increasing returns to scale and become quasi-monopolistic, which might in turn result in complex and opaque government regulations aimed at mitigating systemic risk and preventing price gouging of consumers and small businesses. Consequently, moving forward with public-private CBDC partnerships might seem appealing even to many large multinational banks.[40]

---

37. The Commodity Futures Trading Commission has issued regulations pertaining to the use of such Federal Reserve accounts ("CFTC Announces Enhancements to Protect Customer Funds," US Commodity Futures Trading Commission, press release, August 8, 2016, www.cftc.gov/PressRoom/PressReleases/pr7421-16).

38. See Selgin (2008).

39. See Arnold (2016) and Powell (2017).

40. As noted above, Paulus specifically referred to the role of the government in providing currency to facilitate market competition and efficiency. See also Smith ([1776] 2003) and Friedman and Schwartz (1986).

Paper Currency

In many countries around the globe, the demand for paper currency has been diminishing rapidly as consumers have turned increasingly to using credit and debit cards as well as cell phones and online payment methods. For example, Swedish households used cash for about 15 percent of their retail transactions last year—only half the usage rate observed four years earlier.[41] Indeed, a prominent global payments firm recently launched a campaign aimed at incentivizing small businesses to stop accepting cash at all.[42]

Nonetheless, these trends are not uniform across countries or types of households. The amount of cash in circulation is about 10 percent of GDP in the eurozone and in Switzerland and exceeds 20 percent of GDP in Japan.[43] Even in Sweden, about one-third of the households in a recent Riksbank survey indicated that they would not be able to cope with the disappearance of cash.[44] Those survey results also point to significant variations across demographic groups, with the greatest use of cash by the elderly and by individuals with relatively low levels of education and income.

Such considerations weigh strongly against abruptly abolishing the use of cash. Rather, the central bank could facilitate the gradual obsolescence of cash by making CBDC widely available to the public and initiating a graduated schedule of fees for transfers between cash and CBDC. To avoid imposing a burden on lower-income households, the fee could be minimal (or perhaps none at

---

41. "Payment Statistics," Sveriges Riksbank, www.riksbank.se/en/Statistics/Payment -statistics/.

42. "Visa to Help U.S. Small Businesses Go Cashless," Visa, July 12, 2017, http://investor .visa.com/news/news-details/2017/Visa-to-Help-US-Small-Businesses-Go-Cashless/default .aspx.

43. See figure 1 of Segendorf and Wretman (2015) and the commentary of Wheatley (2017).

44. The tabulation of the Riksbank report "The Payment Behavior of the Swedish Population" is posted at www.riksbank.se/en/Statistics/Payment-statistics/."

all) for making small and infrequent transfers (e.g., a small weekly cash deposit or withdrawal), whereas the fees would be substantial for larger and more frequent transfers. In effect, such a fee structure would be the inverse of the typical ATM, which charges a fixed fee regardless of the amount of cash withdrawn. Moreover, as discussed below, this fee structure would be crucial for ensuring that the continued existence of paper currency did not constrain the central bank's ability to reduce nominal interest rates to negative levels in response to a severe adverse shock.

Such arrangements would also foster individual freedom of choice while discouraging tax evasion, money laundering, and other illegal activities. If desired, individuals would still be able to preserve their anonymity by engaging in small transactions using cash, or alternatively, virtual currencies or other private payments. But the graduated fee schedule described above would serve as a significant tax on black-market transactions, and such activities would be increasingly difficult with the accelerating obsolescence of cash. Moreover, with the widespread availability of CBDC, it would be reasonable to phase out the issuance of large-denomination paper currency bills.[45]

SECURE STORE OF VALUE

Now we turn to the aspects of CBDC that can enhance its role as a secure store of value. In particular, if funds are deposited and retained in a CBDC account over some time period, what happens to the value of such funds? Should the nominal amount of CBDC remain constant (as with paper currency and coins), be indexed to the general price level (thereby preserving its real value), or earn interest like that paid on short-term government securities?

---

45. See the analysis and recommendations in Rogoff (2016).

Here we briefly consider each of these approaches in terms of the benefits to CBDC holders as well as potential spillover effects to the broader financial system.

Option #1: Constant Nominal Value. Funds in CBDC accounts could have a constant nominal value, just like paper currency.[46] In effect, the CBDC accounts of the general public would be treated distinctly from the reserves of commercial banks held at the central bank, which are generally interest bearing. Consequently, during periods of positive nominal interest rates, households and businesses would be incentivized to minimize the amount of funds held in CBDC accounts, and hence the total value of CBDC might remain fairly modest.

As in current practice, the central bank could conduct monetary policy by adjusting short-term nominal interest rates. However, its ability to push nominal interest rates below zero would be tightly constrained, because depositors could readily move their funds into CBDC earning zero interest. Consequently, in a protracted period of weak aggregate demand and deflation, the central bank would likely need to rely on other tools, such as quantitative easing; alternatively, the government would need to engage in fiscal stimulus to boost aggregate demand and thereby push the price level back up to its target.

With such constraints on the conduct of monetary policy, it would be reasonable to maintain—or perhaps even expand—the inflation buffer to mitigate the severity of the lower bound on nominal interest rates. Alternatively, if the central bank specified a target for the price level (rather than the inflation rate), it might be sensible for that target to have a positive trend—that is, the trajectory of prices would be stabilized around an upward-sloping path rather than a constant target.[47]

---

46. As discussed in Boel (2016), the Sveriges Riksbank has been actively considering this approach.
47. See King (1999) and Svensson (1999a, 1999b).

Option #2: Stable Real Value. The real value of funds in CBDC accounts could be preserved by indexing these funds to past changes in the general price level. Such an approach would essentially encapsulate the "tabular standard" proposed by Jevons (1875) and Marshall (1887) and the "compensated dollar" of Fisher (1913). The rationale for indexing currency and other financial contracts was compelling under the gold standard, because the general price level was subject to large and persistent fluctuations.[48] By contrast, the rationale for indexing CBDC might be much less clear, as long as the monetary policy framework ensures that the price level remains reasonably stable (as discussed below).

Of course, the practical obstacles to indexation were daunting during the gold standard era, whereas indexing CBDC would now be fairly straightforward from a technical perspective. In particular, the nominal value of CBDC funds would increase temporarily during periods when the price level was rising above target and then diminish as the price level subsided back to target.

Nonetheless, indexation of CBDC would be highly problematic whenever aggregate demand is depressed and hence real interest rates drop below zero. During such episodes, financial market participants would be incentivized to shift the bulk of their assets into CBDC bearing a zero real interest rate. In effect, such indexation would induce a *zero lower bound on real interest rates*, which would pose a much more severe constraint on monetary policy than a zero lower bound on nominal rates. Consequently, the central bank would likely need to rely heavily on other monetary policy tools such as quantitative easing; alternatively, fiscal policy could end up bearing primary responsibility for fostering economic recovery and restoring price stability.[49]

---

48. See Bordo (1984) and Bordo, Dittmar, and Gavin (2007).

49. A variant of this approach would be to provide asymmetric indexation analogous to that of US Treasury Inflation-Protected Securities (TIPS), i.e., the nominal value of digital currency funds would be increased if the price level exceeded its target but not reduced if

Option #3: Interest-Bearing CBDC. From a technical perspective, the central bank could easily pay interest on CBDC. In effect, all funds held at the central bank would bear the same nominal interest rate, regardless of whether those funds belonged to an individual, a firm, or a financial institution. This approach would encapsulate the analysis of Friedman (1960), who argued that in an efficient monetary system, government-issued money should bear the same return as other risk-free assets. That reasoning underpins the arrangements of many central banks around the world, which pay interest on the reserves of commercial banks held electronically at the central bank. In fact, the Federal Reserve now pays interest to an even wider range of financial counterparties through its reverse repo facility.[50]

Paying interest on CBDC might well enhance the competitiveness of the banking system. Depository institutions that engage in customer-focused "relationship banking" would not be affected, whereas depositors in other less-competitive institutions would have the option of shifting funds into CBDC accounts.

In a growing economy with a stable price level, the interest rate paid on CBDC would typically be positive. However, if the economy encountered a severe adverse disturbance that exerted downward pressure on the general price level, it should be feasible for the central bank to reduce interest rates as needed to foster economic recovery and price stability.[51]

At present, paper currency puts a significant constraint on the central bank's ability to cut its policy rate in response to severe adverse shocks. Cash accrues zero interest and hence becomes

---

the price level dropped below target. Such a scheme would impose a constraint like that of cash, namely, a zero lower bound on nominal rates instead of real rates.

50. The design of the Federal Reserve's reverse repo facility and its range of counterparties is available at "FAQs: Reverse Repurchase Agreement Operations," Federal Reserve Bank of New York, December 16, 2005, https://www.newyorkfed.org/markets/rrp_faq.html.

51. In recent years, a number of major central banks (including the European Central Bank and the Bank of Japan) have paid negative rates on bank reserves.

increasingly attractive as a store of value when nominal interest rates are negative. In effect, if rates on bank deposits and other short-term assets were pushed too far below zero, the financial system could undergo a severe disintermediation into cash, similar to what transpired during the bank panics of the early 1930s.

That constraint on monetary policy could be eliminated by establishing a graduated schedule of fees on transfers between cash and CBDC. In particular, imposing substantial fees on relatively large or frequent transfers would serve as a "wedge" that would make it unprofitable for investors to disintermediate into cash during a period of negative nominal interest rates. With such arrangements in place, monetary policy would no longer be constrained by an effective lower bound on nominal interest rates.

Thus, the interest rate on CBDC could serve as the primary tool of monetary policy, thereby mitigating the need to deploy alternative monetary tools such as quantitative easing or to rely on fiscal interventions to restore price stability. Moreover, the lower bound on nominal interest rates has been a primary motivation for maintaining a positive inflation buffer. Major central banks currently have inflation targets of 2 percent, and in the wake of the financial crisis some economists have advocated raising those targets.[52] With interest-bearing CBDC, there would no longer be a compelling need to maintain any inflation buffer.

STABLE UNIT OF ACCOUNT

Providing a stable unit of account facilitates the economic and financial decisions of individuals and businesses, including the determination of wages and prices, the spending and saving decisions of consumers, and the specification of financial contracts. It should be noted, however, that stabilizing the value of the currency

52. Blanchard, Dell'Ariccia, and Mauro (2010) and Ball (2014) analyze the merits of expanding the inflation buffer.

in terms of a broad price index (rather than a single commodity) cannot be achieved merely by issuing a legal edict. Indeed, in a market economy, it is logically impossible to define the value of the currency in terms of the general price level, because the prices of individual goods and services are set by businesses operating in specific markets rather than determined by a central planner. Consequently, price stability can *only* be accomplished by the appropriate setting of monetary policy.

Of course, even after the introduction of CBDC, the central bank could continue to maintain a positive inflation target. But with the elimination of the effective lower bound on nominal interest rates, it would become feasible to foster true price stability. In particular, the monetary policy framework could ensure that the value of CBDC remains stable over time in terms of a general index of consumer prices.

Apart from mitigating the effective lower bound, previous analysis has cited two other factors that would potentially warrant the continued targeting of a positive inflation rate: (1) systematic measurement bias and (2) downward nominal wage rigidity (DNWR).[53] However, recent analysis using individual price records indicates that the magnitude of measurement bias is very small for an appropriately chain-weighted price index.[54] As for DNWR, the Japanese experience is informative: DNWR was prevalent until the mid-1990s but essentially vanished during the era in which consumer inflation was persistently close to zero; moreover, the level

---

53. Concerns about systematic measurement bias in the US CPI were raised by the Boskin Commission in 1996 ("The Boskin Commission Report," December 4, 1996, https://www.ssa.gov/history/reports/boskinrpt.html). Akerlof, Dickens, and Perry (1996) documented the low incidence of nominal wage cuts for US and Canadian employers and formulated a macro model with DNWR in which reducing the steady-state inflation rate to zero could induce a substantial increase in the equilibrium unemployment rate.

54. Handbury, Watanabe, and Weinstein (2013) examine this topic using "the largest price and quantity dataset ever employed in economics" and find that when measured inflation is zero, the measurement bias is about 0.25 percent for a Törnqvist index and about 0.5 percent for the methodology used for the US PCE. See also Johnson, Reed, and Stewart (2006) and Greenlees and McClelland (2011).

of unemployment has not exhibited any marked shifts despite the substantial swings in trend inflation that have occurred over the past several decades.[55] That experience and other recent evidence bolsters the view of Bewley (2005) that wage-setting practices are mainly influenced by perceptions of fairness and reciprocity rather than money illusion. Indeed, a clear and credible commitment to true price stability would enhance the accuracy of those perceptions and thereby facilitate the transparency of wage negotiations.[56]

A large body of literature has analyzed the macroeconomic effects of targeting the price level rather than the inflation rate. These studies have generally concluded that price-level targeting can provide substantial benefits to macroeconomic stability if the policy framework is transparent and the commitment to price stability is credible. Moreover, consistent with analysis of optimal monetary policy and simple benchmark rules, the stance of monetary policy should respond to real economic activity as well as to the price level.[57] Thus, such frameworks are often characterized in the literature as *flexible price-level targeting*, as distinct from the now-conventional practice of flexible inflation targeting.[58]

Finally, it should be noted that an abrupt shift from a positive inflation target to a stable price level could be disruptive to the economy and the financial system. Consequently, the transition process would need to be carefully planned and managed to ensure

---

55. Kuroda and Yamamoto (2014) analyze both micro-level and macro data and find that DNWR was present in Japan thru the early to mid-1990s but disappeared after 1998.

56. Fallick, Lettau, and Wascher (2016) find significant evidence for DNWR in the US labor market and examine alternative hypotheses about its impact, concluding that "the most compelling reason for the lack of macroeconomic consequences from DNWR relates to the possibility that firms take a multiyear view about their labor costs when implementing their compensation practices."

57. For example, see Taylor (1993), Clarida, Gali, and Gertler (1998, 1999), and Woodford (2003).

58. See Svensson (1999a, 1999b), Svensson and Woodford (2003), and Woodford (2003). We do not adopt that particular terminology here because the word "flexible" could be misinterpreted as referring to an opaque and discretionary approach to determining monetary policy.

that this transition is well understood and fully incorporated into the planning of households and firms.

MONETARY POLICY FRAMEWORK

Over the past few decades, monetary economists have reached a broad consensus that the conduct of monetary policy should be systematic and transparent, thereby facilitating the effectiveness of the monetary transmission mechanism as well as the central bank's accountability to elected officials and the general public.[59] The launching of CBDC provides a landmark opportunity to enhance the transparency of the central bank's monetary policy framework, including its nominal anchor, its tools and operations, and its policy strategy.

Nominal Anchor

As noted above, the monetary policy framework should provide a transparent nominal anchor that facilitates the private sector's economic and financial decisions.[60] In recent decades, central banks have made remarkable progress along these lines through the adoption of specific numerical inflation objectives.[61]

---

59. For example, in its "Statement of Longer-Run Goals and Policy Strategy" (adopted in 2012 and unanimously reaffirmed annually since then), the Federal Open Market Committee (FOMC) states, "The Committee seeks to explain its monetary policy decisions to the public as clearly as possible. Such clarity facilitates well-informed decision-making by households and businesses, reduces economic and financial uncertainty, increases the effectiveness of monetary policy, and enhances transparency and accountability, which are essential in a democratic society" (https://www.federalreserve.gov/monetarypolicy/files /FOMC_LongerRunGoals.pdf).

60. For example, the FOMC's "Statement of Longer-Run Goals and Policy Strategy" states, "Communicating this symmetric inflation goal clearly to the public helps keep longer-term inflation expectations firmly anchored, thereby fostering price stability and moderate long-term interest rates and enhancing the Committee's ability to promote maximum employment in the face of significant economic disturbances."

61. See McCallum (1996), Bernanke and Mishkin (1997), and Bernanke et al. (2001). For empirical analysis of the benefits of inflation targets, see Levin, Natalucci, and Piger (2004), Gürkaynak, Levin, and Swanson (2010), and Beechey, Johannsen, and Levin (2011).

In theory, the central bank's inflation target would be permanently and credibly fixed at a specific value. But in practice, the choice of the target has seemed somewhat subjective and arbitrary. Thus, while many central banks currently have a target of 2 percent, some policy makers have expressed a preference for a lower target, and some economists have advocated raising the target to mitigate the effective lower bound on nominal interest rates.[62] Unfortunately, such debates could inadvertently undermine the credibility of the central bank's nominal anchor—especially if the public starts wondering whether the setting of the inflation target may be susceptible to the vagaries of politics and election outcomes.

By contrast, with the adoption of interest-bearing CBDC, the central bank could establish a constant price-level target that would be a natural focal point for expectations and hence serve as an enduring and credible nominal anchor. Of course, as with inflation targeting, the price-level target would need to be specified in terms of a particular price index, but that specification would not be modified subsequently without compelling technical reasons. To facilitate transparency, the index would ideally be constructed from publicly posted prices of final goods using a published methodology that would be reproducible by private-sector analysts. Moreover, to ensure continuity over time, the index would utilize chain-weighting rather than relying on any specific base year.[63]

---

62. For example, at a time when core PCE inflation was running at about 1 percent, Greenspan (2004) stated, "Our goal of price stability was achieved by most analysts' definition by mid-2003. Unstinting and largely preemptive efforts over two decades had finally paid off." From 2009 to 2011, the Federal Reserve published information about FOMC participants' assessments of the appropriate inflation target, which ranged from 1.5 to 2 percent. Warsh (chapter 8 below) has advocated a target range of 1 to 2 percent, whereas Blanchard, Dell'Ariccia, and Mauro (2010) and Ball (2014) have advocated raising the inflation target substantially.

63. For example, the appropriate US price index might be the chain-weighted CPI or the market-based PCE price index. For many other central banks, the price-level target might be specified using the same index that is currently being used to characterize the central bank's inflation target.

Tools and Operations

To facilitate transparency and public accountability, the interest rate on CBDC would serve as the primary tool of monetary policy. In particular, policy makers would be able to push market interest rates below zero in response to a severe adverse shock, and hence the central bank would be able to provide an appropriate degree of monetary accommodation without resorting to measures aimed at modifying the size or composition of its balance sheet—often referred to as quantitative easing or credit easing.

Thus, the central bank's balance sheet could become very transparent. In particular, the central bank would generally hold short-term government securities in the same quantity as its liabilities of digital currency. The central bank's operating procedures would be correspondingly transparent: it would simply engage in purchases and sales of short-term government securities so that the supply of CBDC moves in line with changes in demand for CBDC.

Finally, the central bank would need to retain its capacity to serve as the lender of last resort. In particular, during a financial crisis the central bank would have the ability to expand the quantity of CBDC to provide emergency liquidity to supervised financial institutions. Alternatively, the central bank could provide those funds to another public agency, such as the deposit insurance fund. In either case, appropriate legal safeguards would be essential to ensure that the central bank's role as lender of last resort did not undermine its ability to carry out its commitment to price stability.

Policy Strategy

In characterizing the central bank's monetary policy strategy, one potential approach would be to specify a *price-level targeting rule*.[64]

---

64. See Svensson (1999a, 1999b), Woodford (2003), and Eggertsson and Woodford (2003).

Such a rule could be expressed in terms of the deviation of the price level from target and the deviation of economic activity from its sustainable longer-run path, but the rule would not explicitly involve the CBDC interest rate. In effect, the targeting rule represents an optimal-control strategy for managing the short-run trade-offs between price stability and other aspects of macroeconomic stability. Consequently, this approach may be feasible and effective in a setting where the central bank has a clear understanding of the monetary transmission mechanism (i.e., the dynamic relationship between the setting of the policy rate and the behavior of prices and real economic activity).

Nevertheless, the experience of recent years has clearly underscored the shortcomings and limitations of the current state of knowledge about macroeconomic dynamics. Moreover, given the prospect of continued rapid developments in automation and financial technology, the extent of uncertainty about the monetary transmission mechanism might well heighten further rather than diminishing back toward the relative confidence (or complacency) that prevailed prior to the global financial crisis.[65]

Thus, an alternative approach would be for the central bank to frame its policy strategy in terms of a *simple benchmark rule*. As emphasized by Taylor (1993, 1999), such a benchmark would not be followed in a purely mechanistic fashion but rather would be used to clarify the central bank's overarching strategy and explain its specific policy decisions.

To provide a concrete example, we assume that CBDC is interest bearing so that the stance of policy can be framed in terms of adjustments to the CBDC interest rate. Thus, our benchmark rule is analogous to the Taylor rule but oriented toward stabilizing the price level rather than the inflation rate, and hence can be expressed as follows:

---

65. For example, just before the onset of the global financial crisis, Blanchard (2008) wrote that "the state of macro is good."

$$\tilde{\pi}_t = \tilde{p}_t + r_t^* + \alpha(\tilde{p}_t - p^*) + \beta(p_t - p^*) + \delta(y_t - y_t^*),$$

where i_t denotes the interest rate on CBDC, p_t denotes the price level, p^* denotes the target price level, $\tilde{p}_t$ denotes a "core" measure of the price level (i.e., smoothed to remove transitory fluctuations in volatile components), $\tilde{\pi}_t$ denotes the core inflation rate, r_t^* denotes the equilibrium real interest rate, and $(y_t - y_t^*)$ denotes the output gap (that is, the deviation of real GDP from its potential level). The interest rate should respond more strongly to the core measure than to fluctuations in the overall price index ($\alpha \gg \beta > 0$) and should respond appropriately to movements in the output gap ($\delta > 0$).

As in the Taylor rule, this specification can be interpreted as a benchmark for adjusting the real interest rate in response to fluctuations in economic activity and prices. In particular, when the price level is at its target and output is at potential, then the ex post real interest rate $i_t - \tilde{\pi}_t$ equals its equilibrium value r_t^*. That value could reflect historical average real rates, as in the Taylor rule, or could be specified as the median estimate of professional forecasters, as in Levin (2014). The coefficient values in this benchmark rule (α, β, and δ) could be chosen to generate robust macroeconomic stabilization outcomes based on evaluations of a wide array of alternative macroeconometric models.[66]

This policy strategy echoes various proposals to target the level of nominal GDP.[67] In fact, our benchmark rule would be equivalent to that approach if p_t were specified as the GDP price index and the coefficients β and δ were constrained to be equal. Nonetheless, our analysis indicates that such an approach would be inferior to the framework proposed here. In particular, the GDP price index is a value-added deflator, not an index of final goods prices, and

---

66. See Taylor (1999), Levin, Wieland, and Williams (1999, 2003), and Levin et al. (2006).
67. See Taylor (1985), Hall and Mankiw (1994), and Sumner (2011).

hence not appropriate for anchoring the unit of account. Moreover, the GDP price index exhibits some counterintuitive properties: for example, a fall in the price of imported fuel induces an increase in the GDP price index.

Monetary-Fiscal Interactions

The interest rate spread between CBDC and short-term government securities would generally be negligible, given the practically costless arbitrage between these two assets. Consequently, shifts in the size of the central bank's balance sheet would have no direct fiscal consequences. Furthermore, with the obsolescence of paper currency, the government would no longer receive any substantial seigniorage revenue, and the central bank would simply cover its own expenses by imposing miniscule fees on payment transactions.

Moreover, the maturity composition of the stock of government securities held by the public would be determined by the fiscal authorities, *not* the central bank.[68] Indeed, that division of responsibilities was the standard practice prior to 2008; since that time, a number of central banks—including the Federal Reserve, the Bank of England, the Bank of Japan, and the European Central Bank (ECB)—initiated large-scale purchases of government bonds to exert downward pressure on longer-term yields under circumstances in which conventional monetary policy was constrained by the effective lower bound on nominal interest rates.

Finally, it should be noted that while government spending and taxes can have a significant influence on wages and prices, it would be a grave error to task fiscal policy with stabilizing the price level over time. The prudent approach is for the central bank to maintain primary responsibility for this mission, while the fiscal authorities

---

68. See Greenwood et al. (2014).

only become involved under extraordinary circumstances; this arrangement is broadly consistent with modern practice and echoes the conclusions of Simons (1936).

CONCLUSION

Central banks have generally been renowned as conservative institutions—staid, cautious, and inertial. For example, following the collapse of Bretton Woods and the "Great Inflation" of the 1970s, it took more than a decade before explicit inflation targets were instituted in a few small open economies; another decade had elapsed before the ECB clarified its inflation objective ("close to but below 2 percent"), and yet another decade until numerical inflation goals were finally adopted by the FOMC and the Bank of Japan.[69] By contrast, in recent years many central banks have taken extraordinary lender-of-last-resort actions and have deployed a remarkable array of unconventional monetary policy tools.[70]

In this analysis, we have found that CBDC can serve as a practically costless medium of exchange, secure store of value, and stable unit of account. However, one crucial question is whether central banks should move expeditiously in considering its adoption. In particular, it might seem prudent to defer such consideration while monitoring developments in private payments and experiences of "early adopters" of CBDC, even if such a deferral involves forgone benefits. Nonetheless, policy makers should be aware of several salient risks of taking a relatively passive and inertial approach:

---

69. Levin and Taylor (2013) examine how US longer-term inflation expectations drifted upward from 1965 to 1980 in the absence of an explicit inflation goal. Bordo and Eichengreen (2013) analyze the links between the collapse of Bretton Woods and the onset of the Great Inflation. Bordo and Siklos (2017) consider the evolution of central banking practices and find that the typical pattern involves small open economies as pioneers and larger economies as later movers.

70. See Borio and Zabai (2016) for a recent synopsis and discussion.

Macroeconomic instability. Suppose that paper currency becomes obsolete and the central bank does not produce any form of digital currency, so that all payments are made using privately issued money (including virtual currencies). Under these assumptions, the analysis of Fernández-Villaverde and Sanches (chapter 4) indicates that the economy may be subject to indeterminacy and that there may not be any equilibrium that exhibits stable prices. In contrast, their analysis finds that price stability *can* be ensured by the issuance of CBDC in conjunction with an appropriate monetary policy framework. It should be emphasized that such concerns are not merely academic but have been flagged recently by central bankers. For example, Nicolaisen (2017) specifically warns about the risks associated with a scenario in which the Norwegian economy no longer has any functional legal tender.

Loss of monetary control. Suppose paper currency becomes obsolete and the monetary base solely comprises banks' reserves held at the central bank. Will the interest rate on reserves (IOR) stay tightly linked to market interest rates, so that the central bank can continue to adjust monetary conditions as appropriate? According to the textbook view of monetary operations, IOR provides a floor for the interbank lending rate and, with a sufficiently high degree of reserves, effectively pins down the level of market rates. However, that textbook view has been contradicted by recent US experience, in which the IOR has been persistently *higher* than the overnight interbank rate as well as the short-term Treasury bill rate. Indeed, concerns about potentially weak linkages between market rates and IOR played a key role in motivating the Federal Reserve's launching of its reverse repo facility in order to engage with a much wider set of counterparties. Of course, that logic naturally leads to the rationale for introducing an interest-bearing CBDC that can be held by anyone and that ensures the central bank's ability to manage market interest rates over time.

Systemic risks. Payments networks typically exhibit substantial externalities and increasing returns to scale. Thus, in the absence of competition from CBDC, the entire payment system might well become quasi-monopolistic. Under such circumstances, any significant operational problem within the payment network could pose substantial risks to the entire financial system and to the macroeconomy.

Susceptibility to severe downturns. Although a decade has passed since the onset of the global financial crisis, there should be no illusion regarding the possibility that a similar shock could occur in coming years rather than being relegated to the distant future. Moreover, the "new normal" level of interest rates appears to be substantially lower than in the past. Thus, in the absence of an interest-bearing CBDC, the effective lower bound could pose an even tighter and more lasting constraint on conventional monetary policy, which would in turn limit the effectiveness of forward guidance (which seems most potent at horizons of a year or two) and large-scale purchases of government securities (which are intended to push down longer-term yields). In such circumstances, the central bank of a small open economy might still be able to provide monetary stimulus via foreign exchange operations aimed at depreciating its currency, but such an approach could prove infeasible or untenable for larger economies. Alternatively, the central bank might provide stimulus through credit subsidies or by financing public infrastructure spending or income transfers to households, but the viability of such coordinated monetary-fiscal policy measures could be highly dependent on the vagaries of politics. Thus, in the absence of CBDC, the central bank might find itself with no real policy alternatives and hence "out of ammunition." In such circumstances, the severity of the economic downturn and sluggish recovery could be more similar to what transpired in the 1930s than to the experience of the past decade.

In light of these considerations, a passive and inertial approach toward CBDC may *not* be the most prudent strategy. Rather, many central banks are now moving expeditiously in considering CBDC and investigating its logistical and technical details. Indeed, since our paper started with a quotation from a classical jurist, it seems fitting to conclude by quoting from two modern experts, one of whom is a distinguished legal scholar:

> Central bankers throughout the world, from Canada to Ireland, have recently indicated that they might issue digital currency in the future. Yet the U.S. has been absent from the debate. As the world's central monetary power, America should play a leading role in studying the benefits and pitfalls of a digital-currency future. . . . The march of digital commerce may eventually make the benefits seem overwhelming, and it would be wise to be ahead of the game rather than trying to catch up at the last minute. (Raskin and Yermack [2016b])

References

Agarwal, Ruchir, and Miles Kimball. 2015. "Breaking through the Zero Lower Bound." International Monetary Fund Working Paper 15-224.

Akerlof, George, William Dickens, and George Perry. 1996. "The Macroeconomics of Low Inflation." *Brookings Papers on Economic Activity* 1:1–76.

Andalfatto, David. 2015. "Fedcoin: On the Desirability of a Government Cryptocurrency." Available at http://andolfatto.blogspot.com/2015/02/fedcoin-on-desirability-of-government.html.

Arnold, Martin. 2016. "Big Banks Plan to Coin New Digital Currency." *Financial Times*, August 23. Available at https://www.ft.com/content/1a962c16-6952-11e6-ae5b-a7cc5dd5a28c.

Ball, Laurence. 2014. "The Case for a Long-Run Inflation Target of Four Percent." IMF Working Paper 14/92.

Bank for International Settlements. 2015. *Digital Currencies*. Basel: Bank for International Settlements.

Barrdear, John, and Michael Kumhof. 2016. "The Macroeconomics of Central Bank Issued Digital Currencies." Bank of England Staff Working Paper 605.

Barro, Robert. 1979. "Money and the Price Level under the Gold Standard." *Economic Journal* 89:13–32.

Beechey, Meredith, Benjamin Johannsen, and Andrew Levin. 2011. "Are Long-Run Inflation Expectations More Firmly Anchored in the Euro Area than in the United States?" *American Economic Journal: Macroeconomics* 3:104–29.

Bernanke, Ben, Thomas Laubach, Frederick Mishkin, and Adam Posen. 2001. *Inflation Targeting: Lessons from the International Experience.* Princeton, NJ: Princeton University Press.

Bernanke, Ben, and Frederic Mishkin. 1997. "Inflation Targeting—a New Framework for Monetary Policy?" *Journal of Economic Perspectives* 11:97–115.

Bewley, Truman. 2005. "Fairness, Reciprocity, and Wage Rigidity." In *Moral Sentiments and Material Interests: The Foundations of Cooperation in Economic Life*, edited by Herbert Gintis, Samuel Bowles, Robert Boyd, and Ernst Fehr, 303–38. Cambridge, MA: MIT Press.

Black, Fischer. 1987. "A Gold Standard with Double Feedback and Near Zero Reserves." In *Business Cycles and Equilibrium*, 115–20. Oxford: Basil Blackwell.

Blanchard, Olivier. 2008. "The State of Macro." NBER Working Paper 14259.

Blanchard, Olivier, Giovanni Dell'Ariccia, and Paolo Mauro. 2010. "Rethinking Macroeconomic Policy." *Journal of Money, Credit, and Banking* 42:199–215.

Boel, Paola. 2016. "Thinking about the Future of Money and Potential Implications for Central Banks." *Economic Review*, Sveriges Riksbank, 147–58.

Bordo, Michael. 1984. "The Gold Standard: The Traditional Approach." In *A Retrospective on the Classical Gold Standard, 1821–1931*, edited by Michael Bordo and Anna Schwartz, 23–120. Chicago: University of Chicago Press.

Bordo, Michael, Robert Dittmar, and Michael Gavin. 2007. "Gold, Fiat Money, and Price Stability." *Berkeley Electronic Journal of Macroeconomics* 7:1–31.

Bordo, Michael, and Barry Eichengreen. 2013. "Bretton Woods and the Great Inflation." In *The Great Inflation: The Rebirth of Modern Central Banking*, edited by Michael Bordo and Athanasios Orphanides. Chicago: University of Chicago Press.

Bordo, Michael, and Hugh Rockoff. 1996. "The Gold Standard as a Good Housekeeping Seal of Approval." *Journal of Economic History* 56:389–428.

Bordo, Michael, and Anna Schwartz. 1987. "Clark Warburton: Pioneer Monetarist." In *Money in Historical Perspective*, edited by Anna Schwartz, 234–54. Chicago: University of Chicago Press.

Bordo, Michael, and Pierre Siklos. 2017. "Central Banks: Evolution and Innovation in Historical Perspective." Unpublished manuscript.

Borio, Claudio, and Anna Zabai. 2016. "Unconventional Monetary Policies: A Reappraisal." Bank for International Settlements Working Paper 570.

Broadbent, Ben. 2016. "Central Banks and Digital Currencies." Presented at the London School of Economics, March 2. Available at www.bankofengland.co .uk/publications/Documents/speeches/2016/speech886.pdf.

Buchanan, James. 1962. "Predictability: The Criterion of Monetary Constitutions." In *In Search of a Monetary Constitution*, edited by Leland Yaeger, 155–83. Cambridge, MA: Harvard University Press.

Buiter, Willem. 2009. "Negative Nominal Interest Rates: Three Ways to Overcome the Zero Lower Bound." NBER Working Paper 15118.

Buterin, Vitalik. 2016. "A Proof of Stake Design Philosophy." *Medium*, December 30. Available at https://medium.com/@VitalikButerin/a-proof-of-stake -design-philosophy-506585978d51.

Cagan, Phillip. 1987. "A Compensated Dollar: Better or More Likely Than Gold?" In *The Search for Stable Money: Essays on Monetary Reform*, edited by James Dorn and Anna Schwartz, 261–77. Chicago: University of Chicago Press.

Clarida, Richard, Gordi Gali, and Mark Gertler. 1998. "Monetary Policy Rules in Practice: Some International Evidence." *European Economic Review* 42:1033–67.

———. 1999. "The Science of Monetary Policy: A New Keynesian Perspective." *Journal of Economic Literature* 37:1661–707.

Danezis, George, and Sarah Meiklejohn. 2016. "Centrally Banked Cryptocurrencies." Available at http://dx.doi.org/10.14722/ndss.2016.23187.

Dorn, James. 2017. *Monetary Alternatives: Rethinking Government Fiat Money*. Washington, DC: Cato Press.

Dorn, James, and Anna Schwartz. 1987. *The Search for Stable Money: Essays on Monetary Reform*. Chicago: University of Chicago Press.

Dyson, Ben, and Graham Hodgson. 2017. "Digital Cash: Why Central Banks Should Start Issuing Electronic Money." Positive Money website. Available at http://positivemoney.org/wp-content/uploads/2016/01/Digital_Cash_Web PrintReady_20160113.pdf.

Eggertsson, Gauti, and Michael Woodford. 2003. "The Zero Bound on Interest Rates and Optimal Monetary Policy." *Brookings Papers on Economic Activity* 1:139–233.

Erceg, Christopher, and Andrew Levin. 2003. "Imperfect Credibility and Inflation Persistence." *Journal of Monetary Economics* 50:915–44.

Fallick, Bruce, Michael Lettau, and William Wascher. 2016. "Downward Nominal Wage Ridigity in the United States during and after the Great Recession." Finance and Economics Discussion Series 2016-001, Board of Governors of the Federal Reserve System.

Fan Yifei. 2016. "On Digital Currencies, Central Banks Should Lead." Bloomberg, September 1. Available at https://www.bloomberg.com/view/articles/2016-09 -01/on-digital-currencies-central-banks-should-lead.

Fisher, Irving. 1913. "A Compensated Dollar." *Quarterly Journal of Economics* 27:213–35, 385–97.

Friedman, Milton. 1948. "A Monetary and Fiscal Framework for Economic Stability." *American Economic Review* 38:245 64.

———. 1960. *A Program for Monetary Stability*. New York: Fordham Press.

———. 1984. "Financial Futures Markets and Tabular Standards." *Journal of Political Economy* 92:165–67.

Friedman, Milton, and Anna Schwartz. 1986. "Has Government Any Role in Money?" In *Money in Historical Perspective*, edited by Anna Schwartz, 289–314. Chicago: University of Chicago Press.

Fung, Ben, and Hanna Halaburda. 2016. "Central Bank Digital Currencies: A Framework for Assessing Why and How." Bank of Canada Staff Discussion Paper 2016-22. Available at www.bankofcanada.ca/2016/11/staff-discussion -paper-2016-22/.

Goodfriend, Marvin. 2000. "Overcoming the Zero Bound on Interest Rate Policy." *Journal of Money, Credit, and Banking* 32:1007–35.

———. 2016. "The Case for Unencumbering Interest Rate Policy at the Zero Lower Bound." *Economic Review*, Federal Reserve Bank of Kansas City.

Greenlees, John, and Robert McClelland. 2011. "New Evidence on Outlet Substitution Effects in Consumer Price Index Data." *Review of Economics and Statistics* 93:632–46.

Greenspan, Alan. 2004. "Risk and Uncertainty in Monetary Policy." Presented at the meeting of the American Economic Association, San Diego, January 3. Available at https://www.federalreserve.gov/BoardDocs/speeches/2004 /20040103/default.htm.

Greenwood, Jeremy, Samuel Hanson, Joshua Rudolph, and Lawrence Summers. 2014. "Government Debt Management at the Zero Lower Bound." Hutchins Center on Fiscal and Monetary Policy Working Paper 5. Available at https://

www.brookings.edu/wp-content/uploads/2016/06/30_government_debt
_management_zlb.pdf.

Gürkaynak, Refet, Andrew Levin, and Eric Swanson. 2010. "Does Inflation Tar-
geting Anchor Long-Run Inflation Expectations? Evidence from Long-Term
Bond Yields in the U.S., U.K., and Sweden." *Journal of the European Economic
Association* 8:1208–42.

Hall, Robert. 1982. "Explorations in the Gold Standard and Related Policies for
Stabilizing the Dollar." In *Inflation: Causes and Effects*, edited by Robert Hall,
111–22. Chicago: University of Chicago Press.

———. 1985. "Monetary Strategy with an Elastic Price Standard." In *Price Stability
and Public Policy*, 137–59. Kansas City, MO: Federal Reserve Bank of Kansas City.

Hall, Robert, and N. Gregory Mankiw. 1994. "Nominal Income Targeting." In
Monetary Policy, edited by N. Gregory Mankiw, 79–94. Chicago: University
of Chicago Press.

Handbury, Jessie, Tsutomu Watanabe, and David Weinstein. 2013. "How Much Do
Official Price Indexes Tell Us about Inflation?" NBER Working Paper 19504.

Hayek, Frederick. 1978. *Denationalisation of Money—the Argument Refined: An
Analysis of the Theory and Practice of Concurrent Currencies.* 2d ed. London:
Institute of Economic Affairs.

Hayes, Adam. 2016. "Decentralized Banking: Monetary Technocracy in the Digital Age." In *Banking beyond Banks and Money: A Guide to Banking Services in
the 21st Century*, edited by Paolo Tasca, Tomaso Aste, Loriana Pelizzon, and
Nicolas Peronyal, 121–31. Switzerland: Springer International Press.

He, Dong, Ross Leckow, Vikram Haksar, Tommaso Mancini, Nigel Jenkinson,
Mikari Kashima, Tanai Khiaonarong, Celine Rochon, and Hervé Tourpe. 2017.
"Fintech and Financial Services: Initial Considerations." International Mone-
tary Fund Staff Discussion Note 17/05.

Jevons, William. 1875. "A Tabular Standard of Value." In *Money and the Mechanism of Exchange.* New York: Appleton. Available at www.econlib.org/library
/YPDBooks/Jevons/jvnMME25.html.

Johnson, David, Stephen Reed, and Kenneth Stewart. 2006. "Price Measurement in the United States: A Decade after the Boskin Report." *Monthly Labor
Review Online* 129 (5). Available at https://blsmon1.bls.gov/opub/mlr/2006/05
/art2abs.htm.

Ketterer, Juan Antonio, and Gabriela Andrade. 2016. "Digital Central Bank Money
and the Unbundling of the Bank Function." Inter-American Development
Bank Discussion Paper 449.

King, Mervyn. 1999. "Challenges for Monetary Policy: New and Old." Presented at the Federal Reserve Bank of Kansas City symposium, Jackson Hole, August 27. Available at https://www.kansascityfed.org/publicat/sympos/1999/s99king.pdf.

Koning, John. 2014. "Fedcoin." Available at http://jpkoning.blogspot.com/2014/10/fedcoin.html.

Kuroda, Sachiko, and Isamu Yamamoto. 2014. "Is Downward Wage Flexibility the Primary Factor of Japan's Prolonged Deflation?" *Asian Economic Policy Review* 9:143–58.

Levin, Andrew. 2014. "The Design and Communication of Systematic Monetary Policy Strategies." *Journal of Economic Dynamics and Control* 49:52–69.

Levin, Andrew, Fabio Natalucci, and Jeremy Piger. 2004. "The Macroeconomic Effects of Inflation Targeting." *Federal Reserve Bank of St. Louis Review* 86 (4): 51–80.

Levin, Andrew, Alexei Onatski, Noah Williams, and John Williams. 2006. "Monetary Policy under Uncertainty in Micro-Founded Macroeconometric Models." In *NBER Macroeconomics Annual 2005*, edited by Mark Gertler and Kenneth Rogoff. Cambridge, MA: MIT Press.

Levin, Andrew, and John Taylor. 2013. "Falling behind the Curve: A Positive Analysis of Stop-Start Monetary Policies and the Great Inflation." In *The Great Inflation: The Rebirth of Modern Central Banking*, edited by Michael Bordo and Athanasios Orphanides. Chicago: University of Chicago Press.

Levin, Andrew, Volker Wieland, and John Williams. 1999. "The Robustness of Simple Monetary Policy Rules under Model Uncertainty." In *Monetary Policy Rules*, edited by John Taylor. Chicago: University of Chicago Press.

———. 2003. "Performance of Forecast-Based Monetary Policy Rules under Model Uncertainty." *American Economic Review* 93:622–45.

Marshall, Alfred. 1887. "Remedies for Fluctuations of General Prices." *Contemporary Review* 51:355–75.

McCallum, Bennett. 1985. "Bank Deregulation, Accounting Systems of Exchange, and the Unit of Account: A Critical Review." *Carnegie-Rochester Conference Series on Public Policy* 23:13–46.

———. 1996. "Inflation Targeting in Canada, New Zealand, Sweden, the United Kingdom, and in General." NBER Working Paper 5579.

———. 2015. "The Bitcoin Revolution." *Cato Journal* 35:347–56.

Meltzer, Allan. 2002. *A History of the Federal Reserve*. Vol. 1, *1913–1951*. Chicago: University of Chicago Press.

Mersch, Yves. 2017. "Digital Base Money: An Assessment from the ECB's Perspective." Presented at Finlands Bank, Helsinki, January 16. Available at https:// www.ecb.europa.eu/press/key/date/2017/html/sp170116.en.html.

Motamedi, Sina. 2014. "Will Bitcoins Ever Become Money? A Path to Decentralized Central Banking." Tannu Tuva Initiative website, July 21. Available at http://tannutuva.org/blog/2014/7/21/will-bitcoins-ever-become-money-a -path-to-decentralized-central-banking.

Nicolaisen, Jon. 2017. "What Should the Future Form of Our Money Be?" Presented at the Norwegian Academy of Science and Letters, April 25. Available at www.norges-bank.no/en/published/speeches/2017/2017-04-25-dnva.

Patinkin. 1993. "Irving Fisher and His Compensated Dollar Plan." Federal Reserve Bank of Richmond *Economic Quarterly* 79:1–34.

Pfister, Christian, and Natacha Valla. 2017. "New Normal or New Orthodoxy: Elements of a New Central Banking Framework." Unpublished manuscript.

Powell, Jerome. 2017. "Innovation, Technology, and the Payments System." Presented at the Yale Law School, New Haven, CT, March 3. Available at https:// www.federalreserve.gov/newsevents/speech/powell20170303a.htm.

Raskin, Max, and David Yermack. 2016a. "Digital Currencies, Decentralized Ledgers, and the Future of Central Banking." NBER Working Paper 22238.

———. 2016b. "Preparing for a World without Cash." *Wall Street Journal*, August 4, https://www.wsj.com/articles/preparing-for-a-world-without-cash -1470353068.

Rogoff, Kenneth. 2016. *The Curse of Cash*. Princeton, NJ: Princeton University Press.

Schumpeter, Joseph. 1954. *History of Economic Analysis*. London: Allen & Unwin.

Scorer, Simon. 2017. "Central Bank Digital Currency: DLT or not DLT? That Is the Question." Bank Underground website, June 6. Available at https:// bankunderground.co.uk/2017/06/05/central-bank-digital-currency-dlt-or -not-dlt-that-is-the-question/.

Segendorf, Björn, and Anna-Lena Wretman. 2015. "The Swedish Payment Market in Transformation." *Sveriges Riksbank Economic Review* 3:48–68.

Selgin, George. 2008. "Milton Friedman and the Case Against Currency Monopoly." *Cato Journal* 28:287–302.

Simons, Henry. 1936. "Rules vs. Authorities in Monetary Policy." *Journal of Political Economy* 44:1–30.

Skingsley, Cecilia. 2016. "Should the Riksbank Issue e-Krona?" Presented at FinTech Stockholm 2016, November 16. Available at www.riksbank.se/en

/Press-and-published/Speeches/2016/Skingsley-Should-the-Riksbank-issue
-e-krona/.

Smith, Adam. (1776) 2003. *The Wealth of Nations*. Oxford: Penguin.

Sumner, Scott. 2011. "Re-Targeting the Fed." *National Affairs* 32 (summer): 79–96.

Svensson, Lars. 1999a. "How Should Monetary Policy Be Conducted in an Era of
Price Stability?" Presented at the Federal Reserve Bank of Kansas City symposium, Jackson Hole, WY, August 26–28. Available at https://www.kansascityfed
.org/publicat/sympos/1999/S99sven.pdf.

———. 1999b. "Price Level Targeting vs. Inflation Targeting: A Free Lunch?" *Journal of Money, Credit & Banking* 31:277–95.

Svensson, Lars, and Michael Woodford. 2003. "Implementing Optimal Policy
through Inflation-Forecast Targeting." In *The Inflation Targeting Debate*, edited by
Ben S. Bernanke and Michael Woodford. Chicago: University of Chicago Press.

Taylor, John. 1985. "What Would Nominal GDP Targeting Do to the Business
Cycle?" *Carnegie-Rochester Conference Series on Public Policy* 22:61–84.

———. 1993. "Discretion versus Policy Rules in Practice." *Carnegie-Rochester Conference Series on Public Policy* 39:195–214.

———. 1999. "An Historical Analysis of Monetary Policy Rules." In *Monetary Policy Rules*, edited by John Taylor. Chicago: University of Chicago Press.

Tobin, James. 1987. "The Case for Preserving Regulatory Distinctions." *Proceedings*, Federal Reserve Bank of Kansas City, 167–83.

Watson, Alan. 2010. *The Digest of Justinian*. Vol. 2. Philadelphia: University of
Pennsylvania Press.

Weber, Warren. 2016. "A Bitcoin Standard: Lessons from the Gold Standard." Bank
of Canada Staff Working Paper 2016-14.

Wheatley, Alan. 2017. "Cash Is Dead, Long Live Cash." *Finance & Development*
54:32–35. Available at www.imf.org/external/pubs/ft/fandd/2017/06/pdf
/wheatley.pdf.

Wicksell, Knut. 1898. *Interest and Prices: A Study of the Causes Regulating the
Value of Money*. Jena, Sweden: Gustav Fischer Press.

———. 1907. "The Influence of the Rate of Interest on Prices." *Economic Journal*
17:213–20.

Woodford, Michael. 2003. *Interest and Prices: Foundations of a Theory of Monetary
Policy*. Princeton, NJ: Princeton University Press.

Zamfir, Vlad. 2015. "Introducing Casper the Friendly Ghost." Etherium blog,
August 1. Available at https://blog.ethereum.org/2015/08/01/introducing
-casper-friendly-ghost/.

GENERAL DISCUSSION

THOMAS LAUBACH: This is fascinating stuff, and I have one suggestion and one question. So the question is, I think the general notion of providing the public with affordable access to a reliable payment system is important, and we know that even in the United States there are a bunch of unbanked people. But why do you think the central bank has to be the direct provider of access to that service?

My suggestion would be to take a look at what's been going on in India, which is a very interesting case: hundreds of millions of unbanked people, and the government is extremely active in developing technology to provide these people with a payment system that they can access but that does not necessarily involve accounts at the central bank.

ROBERT HODRICK: I'm a little worried about the negative interest rates on these digital currencies, because if multiple central banks have these nice, stable monies, it would seem relatively costless to change from dollars into euros. Accessing the foreign exchange market would be simple, and once you say you're going to start charging me 1 percent per annum, I'm going to start going into the euros. I'd like to hear what you think about that.

JOHN COCHRANE: Laurie, doesn't the blockchain get longer and longer and longer? One advantage of money is that it doesn't carry its history with it. Jesús, I know that digital currencies are currently just fiat monies, but why aren't they backed? The natural thing would be to eliminate the price volatility and say, "I promise to give you one maturing Treasury bill in return for a bitcoin." Michael and Andy, I worry a lot about eliminating all anonymity in transactions. In your system, the government has a record of every transaction you've ever made. The civil liberties and political freedom implications seem pretty dire. Also, our government passes all sorts of aspirational laws, like you shouldn't hire illegal aliens or people without the right licenses. Enforcing every law will bring the economy to a crashing halt. Finally, I have two questions. Why the Fed? Why don't we just have the Treasury issue government debt via the blockchain, and then we can trade the government debt directly, and we don't need any Fed involvement?

LAURIE HODRICK: I don't want to get too geeky answering your question, but there are technological ways to deal with how much history the ledger keeps. The amount of history needed depends on the asset, because the ledger is about keeping an asset's provenance, its true history. For assets where the long history is important, there is a need to maintain the complete record. Examples might include a house or a Hermès Birkin bag—and there are all sorts of neat applications emerging for assets where provenance is important. For other assets, only a shorter history of transactions is necessary—a monetary unit obviously much less than even a share of stock, for which the tax basis is important and a firm might want to allow shareholder voting based on tenure. So the amount of history needed in the ledger depends critically on the nature of the asset.

JESÚS FERNÁNDEZ-VILLAVERDE: There are many cryptocurrencies in the market, and every day there is a new one. I am not quite sure whether any of them have tried to do a bit of price targeting or follow some policy rule. My view at this moment is that the regulators follow some type of benign neglect and just let people try different things and see what happens. And if, in fact, cryptocurrencies are going to become a means of exchange that people want to use, my hope is that sooner or later some entrepreneur will establish a business model that is welfare improving.

Let me say something, however, about public debt. In some sense, we are ready to do that, because the best way, perhaps, to think about the US dollar is as nominative short-term government debt. And in fact, dollars were introduced during the Civil War precisely as public debt. They were payments by the federal government to finance the war. So, in some sense, it will be coming back to what we have already been doing for a long time.

ANDREW LEVIN: The question about privacy is something we've been discussing a lot with Peter Fisher. And he certainly persuaded us that actually these cryptocurrencies need to be supervised and regulated, that any financial institution which takes deposits in cryptocurrencies also needs to be a supervised institution. I hope I'm representing Peter's views accurately.

But the key issue is one of relative privacy. Because in a democratic society with a rule of law, there have to be some limits to privacy. Now, the Federal Reserve already has access to a lot of confidential, proprietary information, and it strictly protects that information. What we have in mind here is that the same kinds of protections would apply to the use of central bank digital currencies. And people would be free, if they wanted, to continue having their payments and accounts at private institutions. And as Mike said, we envision that most people would probably continue to do that.

MICHAEL BORDO: I wanted to say something. The limo driver taking me from San Francisco airport to Stanford asked me what I was doing here. I told him about my work with Andy on central bank digital currency. His reaction was, "Why would people want to have an account with the government?" I said, "It is not the government, it is the Federal Reserve." This suggests that the issue of trust in the Fed has to be dealt with.

ANDREW LEVIN: Coming to your other question, though, which I think is important, for practical purposes, the central bank would become a lot like a narrow bank. Its assets would be short-term government securities, and the bulk of its liabilities would be the digital currency. So the question you asked is, Why do you need it at all? And the answer is because the interest rate on digital currencies still has to be set. And that evolves over time, and there has to be a price-level targeting arrangement. It could be a Taylor-type rule, or a Volker Wieland rule, or a Williams rule or whatever. So that's the crucial role for a central bank committed to a stable unit of account. In principle, you could hand everything over to the Treasury and make Treasury responsible for maintaining the stability of the unit of account. But I think in our modern economies, that seems to be something that everyone agrees central banks should do.

MICHAEL MELVIN: Bob Hodrick raised a question that I was thinking about. Maybe it's not the same question, but there is a monetary theory literature on competitive monies. Theory suggests that if monies are perfect substitutes, they all have to have the same return—right?—or demand goes to zero. I haven't traded Bitcoin, but let's say all these monies have their own units of account but are really very close substitutes. How is this dealt with? It strikes me that it will be difficult to sustain many alternative competing digital monies over time.

JESÚS FERNÁNDEZ-VILLAVERDE: That gets into the details of the paper. We have two versions of the model. In one version, currencies are not perfect substitutes. Thus, you have monopolistic competition. In the second version, currencies are perfect substitutes and have the Kareken-Wallace-type result of portfolio/price indeterminacy. However, there is, as you suggested, an equilibrium condition equating the rates of return of different monies. It is precisely this equating of the rates of return of different currencies that imposes constraints on what the Fed can do. The intuition is, basically, that if the Fed is not providing the same rate of return on the other currencies, agents will move away from the Fed's money. So, yes, there is a Kareken-Wallace result at the very core of any war with multiple monies, and then the issue is how you get around that problem.

LAURIE HODRICK: And if I may add, the existing ledgers are definitely not perfect substitutes in a number of ways. As I noted in my remarks, current differences include permissions and privacy, whether they've been hacked, and how they are perceived in terms of cyber security. People definitely do not see them as perfect substitutes at this point.

ANDREW LEVIN: I'll also handle both of the questions Bob Hodrick asked. Jesús mentioned this issue with bitcoin in China. Imagine that over the next few years, some cryptocurrency becomes very popular in the United States. So popular that everyone's using it on their cell phones and people start quoting prices in that instead of US dollars. In fact, that's similar to the reasons why the Federal Reserve established its reverse repo facility. The Fed needed to deal with a wider range of counterparties, not just the depository institutions. If we had a situation where the cryptocurrency was run by . . . just think of a large country in eastern Europe that isn't always friendly. [*Laughter*] Okay? That's the sort of risk that I think we have to take seriously now. So you're right, Bob. We could be in situations where people are moving their assets quickly from one thing to another. And so it's crucial for the central bank to provide the unit of account and to maintain the public's confidence so that digital currency is widely used enough that the central bank can be effective in maintaining price stability.

JESÚS FERNÁNDEZ-VILLAVERDE: Can I add a small point that reinforces the comment you made about these two lawyers saying the United States should be a lever in this area? What has worried me in reading some of the technical details of these cryptocurrencies is that they are designed by computer scientists. God bless them, they give us great things, but their understanding of incentives and general equilibrium is not as nuanced as I would like. [*Laughter*] And what I'm worried about is we may end up accidentally using a cryptocurrency, designed by someone who hasn't taken monetary theory, that may not implement the social optimal. I think central bankers of advanced economies should play a role in designing the new means of exchange.

DAVID MULFORD: Let's assume that this system is established. If it is established, and it's established in a way that satisfies all the things that have been said here, how vulnerable is it to cyber attack by an outside force?

ANDREW LEVIN: I think that's a really important question. That's why it's probably going to take one to three years for a central bank to implement a digital currency. But in principle, because the central bank is in control of the digital currency ledger, it can look for suspicious transactions, in the same way that major credit card companies do. And in some circumstances the central bank can impose limits—say, on this account you can't withdraw more than a hundred dollars a day, or you have to call us before we approve a transaction over a thousand dollars. We know what happened with the central bank of Bangladesh. I guess you know about this, right? A hundred million dollars. These issues already exist, and it's absolutely critical, again, coming back to the quote, that the Federal Reserve and other central banks need to work on this expeditiously and carefully.

LAWRENCE SCHEMBRI: Regarding the comment about cash just disappearing, there's still going to be an inherent demand from people who want a private means of payment. So if you let cash disappear, these people are going to move into the fringes. And so there's going to be an incentive to create private currencies that are truly private. How do you manage that situation?

ANDREW LEVIN: So again, I just want to revisit what Peter Fisher taught us, which is that central banks, government agencies, and financial regulators are going to have to be on top of this. If the cryptocurrencies are being created faster, and depository institutions are taking in those cryptocurrencies faster, we could end up having financial crises and bank runs on institutions we barely know anything about. So there has to be a rule of law that's put into place here. And maybe Laurie Hodrick will be the first head of the cryptocurrency regulator!

Again, privacy has to be relative, because the government needs to prevent money laundering and other sorts of illegal activity. Even cryptocurrencies are not beyond the scope of a legitimate law enforcement transaction to find out what's going on.

MICHAEL BORDO: Look at Sweden, where cash has not been abolished but people do not use it much. There are only a few people (2 percent of the population) who still do. Our plan is not to abolish cash, but we think that as time goes by less and less people will use it.

JESÚS FERNÁNDEZ-VILLAVERDE: A simple proposal that I have presented for Europe is to issue a prepaid debit card up to some limit, let's say five hundred euros. And those prepaid credit cards can be perfectly anonymous. Five hundred euros should be enough for legitimate purposes, such as buying gifts for your partner without her knowing in advance (my problem now is that every time I try to buy a gift for my wife, she gets a notification in her iPhone from the credit card company, killing the surprise), but you are not going to finance a fraudulent operation with a few hundred euros.

JOHN DUCA: Two minor things about implementation. One, aside from the issue of the sordid substitution for currency, this strikes me as a substitute for demand deposits, even money funds, and that raises issues of how we manage the liquidity requirements on banks in a world where the federal government is now competing with them. And two, this issue of substitution involves some learning by the central bank about the optimal amount of government money and private money. This raises another issue: should we be first? Maybe it pays to see some minor advanced country try it first rather than adopt Andy's "America-first" proposal.

MICHAEL BORDO: I have a paper with Pierre Siklos, "Central Banks: Evolution and Innovation in Historical Perspective." It takes a broad historical sweep and looks at two hundred years of data for ten countries. We found that central banks learned from each other. The leader in the nineteenth century was the Bank of England. In the twentieth century, it may have been the Federal Reserve and to a certain extent the Bundesbank. In the past thirty years, it has been small open economies like Canada, Australia, New Zealand, Sweden, and Norway. The move toward central bank digital currency will come from those countries, as was the case with inflation targeting, and probably the United States will catch up.

CHAPTER FIVE

Monetary Policy Making When Views Are Disparate

John B. Taylor

I was asked to give some remarks on the themes of this conference and how they relate to monetary policy. The conference reveals a very wide range of views about monetary policy: about the proper size and pace of reduction of the Fed's balance sheet, about the effects or distortions caused by quantitative easing, about the equilibrium real interest rate, about whether low (or negative) interest rates have a positive or negative effect on the economy, about the fiscal theory of the price level, about international spillover of monetary policy actions, and of course about rules versus discretion.

In fact, the purpose of this whole conference series has been to explore a wide range of views about monetary policy. The series started during the Federal Reserve Centennial, when Mike Bordo, John Cochrane, Lee Ohanian, and I observed that conferences at that time did not portray the full range of views about monetary policy. So we decided to have a conference, which turned out to be popular, and which is now in its fourth year. (See previous conference volumes by Bordo, Dupor, and Taylor [2014], Cochrane and Taylor [2016], and Bordo and Taylor [2017].)

Of course, the range of views heard here is not exhaustive; just last week there were sessions in Washington during the IMF–World Bank meetings on the gold standard and on capital flow management. And there are new views arising all the time, including recent efforts to bring behavioral economics to macroeconomics, expanding on previous behavioral roots of macro.

So in these remarks I would like to discuss monetary policy making in practice at a time when views about monetary policy are so disparate. I will review some history and then make suggestions. To be sure, I have been quite outspoken on many of the topics about which there are disparate views: I prefer rules over discretion and a balance sheet where the supply and demand for reserves determines the interest rate; I see advantages of the "greater-than-one" principle in both Old Keynesian and New Keynesian models; I have doubts about the effectiveness of quantitative easing and excessively low interest rates; I have concerns about the international monetary system with unconventional monetary policy and argue for reform in which policy is strategic, capital is mobile, and the exchange rate is flexible. Making the case for these views using data and theory and debating them is the best way to move forward and make progress. But, despite these efforts, views are disparate, and we need to think about policy making in such an environment.

DISPARATE VIEWS CIRCA 1979

Now is not the first time there has been a disparity of views about monetary policy. Consider the situation in 1979, when Paul Volcker orchestrated the most fundamental change in monetary policy in recent memory. Views were all over the map. Milton Friedman had been writing for a decade that the long-run Philips curve did not exist, and he faced much criticism for doing so. By the late 1970s the debate had shifted from whether the long-run Phillips curve trade-off between unemployment and inflation existed to whether the unemployment costs of *reducing* inflation were too high. Jim Tobin used an Old Keynesian model to show that the costs of disinflation were so enormous we should not even try it. By then new models were replacing the Old Keynesian models:

there were the "new classical" models with rational expectations and perfectly flexible prices, and the "New Keynesian" models with rational expectations and sticky prices. I remember the February 1977 issue of the *Journal of Political Economy*, where two papers, one by Stan Fischer and the other by Ned Phelps and me, appeared with these New Keynesian assumptions.

Despite all this disagreement—which could also be found inside the Fed—Paul Volcker proceeded with the disinflation. He went with the view that reducing inflation and unemployment required a new approach to monetary policy. On October 6, 1979, he got members of the FOMC with vastly disparate views to go along with this new approach. Just one month before, in September 1979, the Federal Reserve Board had split in approving a 0.5-percentage-point discount rate hike: the vote was three to four, with the three dissenting votes being Governors Partee, Rice, and Teeters and approvals from Coldwell, Schultz, and Wallich joining Volcker (see Federal Reserve [1979] and Lindsey, Orphanides, and Rasche [2005]).

A PACKAGE APPROACH: OCTOBER 6, 1979

After that credibility-losing split vote, Volcker put together a *package* that received the support of every member of the board and every reserve bank president. History shows that his method for getting approval was similar to how George Shultz put together a strategy for instituting flexible exchange rates and got it approved when Volcker was undersecretary of the Treasury and Shultz was secretary of the Treasury (Taylor 2012).

The October 1979 package contained three key items (see Taylor 2005): First, a full-percentage-point increase in the discount rate, which appealed to those who believed the situation called for a traditional dose of monetary medicine. Second, an increase in reserves on managed liabilities, which appealed to those who wanted to take action to restrain the surge in bank lending. Third, new reserve-based operating procedures in which the interest rate would rise or fall depending on economic conditions. These new operating procedures allowed the Fed to say, with some legitimacy, that the market, not the Fed, was setting the level of the federal funds rate. The new procedure appealed to those who believed in timely and sizable interest rate responses to inflation. Importantly, it offered two-way flexibility for prompt downward movements in the federal funds rate, which appealed to those who feared a slowing economy. Though the new policy led to temporary economic weakness, which required great fortitude on the part of Paul Volcker and his colleagues, the policy paid off and led to lower inflation and unemployment and to the Great Moderation.

The international community also came along. The United States was not the only country that needed a change in monetary policy. The Fed's policy shift was followed by the United Kingdom, which adopted a monetary targeting framework. For a while others held to the view that monetary policy was ineffective in controlling inflation and that wage and price controls were needed. Over time, however, this new systemic approach to monetary policy spread around much of the world.

ROBUSTNESS TO DISPARATE ECONOMIC VIEWS

As in the 1970s, there is now a wide range of views about monetary policy, based largely on differences in economic models. Clearly central banks have different models, and different central banks have different models. One can criticize models, but there is a good message in Stanley Fischer's (2017a) reminder that Paul Samuelson said he would rather have Bob Solow than a model, but he would rather have Bob Solow with a model than without a model. So economic models are important in practice, as is the interface between models and policy. Here I think it is important to have a way of evaluating the policy impacts of the different models.

The most basic question is whether the different views found in models are important for policy. Do different models really lead to different policies? Today we have new methods that people did not have in the 1970s to answer these questions. In particular, I refer to the model comparison project—now incorporating over eighty different models—taken up by Volker Wieland and his colleagues (funded in part by a grant to the Hoover Institution). Such comparisons can be very useful to policy makers. In some surprising ways, the differences in models do not matter much for policy (Taylor and Wieland 2012): the impulse response functions are the same across a wide range of models covering three generations of dynamic stochastic general equilibrium (DSGE) models, including some that incorporate financial accelerator effects.

But optimal policy rules tend to exploit special properties of models, which means that the policy makers need to look at policy robustness across different models so that the policy does not incorrectly pay too much attention to the exotic features of any one model. Here it is essential for policy strategies or rules to be robust across different models, perhaps putting more weight on some models and less on others. I have found that an insistence on robustness across different models makes policy conclusions less disparate than views about the economy based on individual models. Again, it is much easier to evaluate robustness than it was in the 1970s.

Recent model comparison work by Binder et al. (2017) finds that newer models with financial frictions have policy implications that are all over the map. This suggests that attempts to manipulate macro-prudential policy instruments in the sense of leaning against the wind of credit growth are not ready for prime time. These are examples. Another example is John Cochrane's (2017) recent study, which considers the role of fiscal policy in price-level determination in New Keynesian and Old Keynesian models. The important point is that the Fed and other central banks could and should consider many different models and assess whether the policies are robust.

DISPARATE VIEWS ABOUT R-STAR

The disparity of views about r-star, or the equilibrium real rate of interest, has suddenly become enormous. A good way to examine the policy implications of this disparity is to place the various estimates of r-star into policy rules, an approach that would not have been possible in the 1970s, before the extensive research on policy rules. Recent speeches by Janet Yellen and Stanley Fischer provide examples.

In a recent talk here at Stanford, Janet Yellen (2017) compared current policy first with the original Taylor rule, then with a Taylor rule that is more reactive to the state of the economy, and finally with a Taylor rule with inertia. She then fed lower r-star estimates into these rules, showing that they indicate lower settings of the federal funds rate. Stanley Fischer (2017a, 2017b) gave two recent talks that take a similar approach, referring to decisions made in 2011, and in chapter 6 below he considers how rules-based approaches can be designed and evaluated with committee decision making.

However, using the same methodology, Michaelis and Wieland (2017) show that if one uses the lower r-star estimates "together with consistent estimates of potential activity, funds rate prescriptions from reference rules move back up." They add that "the decline in R-Star estimates does not justify the current policy stance. Rather, consistent application suggests that policy should be tightened." By considering the range of views about r-star in this more formal way, one finds that the range of policy implications narrows.

I think it would help further in dealing with disparate views if the process were more public, perhaps along the lines of proposed legislation where the Federal Open Market Committee would report its own strategy and compare it with well-known rules. Again quoting Michaelis and Wieland (2017), "Comparisons of Fed policy to simple reference rules show how such legislation would serve to bolster the Federal Reserve's independence. . . . Clearly, by referring to such legislation and appropriate reference rules, the Fed would be able to better stand up to such pressure and more effectively communicate its reasons to the public."

A PACKAGE APPROACH TODAY

Given that a package approach led to monetary reform thirty-eight years ago, when views were so disparate, it is natural to ask whether such a package approach would work today. Consider the issue of normalization. While there is an apparent desire to normalize policy today, some express concern that the implied higher interest rate or appreciated exchange rate would slow the economy, much like concerns in 1979. Much about the financial world has changed since then, but there are several possibilities to consider in developing a multipart package.

First, recall that the 1979 decision to target reserves reassured people like Teeters, Rice, and Partee that the policy interest rate could easily fall if need be. The emphasis now could be on a return to rules-based policy in which interest rates could fall easily should the economy falter.

Second, recall that the 1979 decision to change reserve requirements was aimed at lending and credit creation. The emphasis today could be on a plan to off-ramp regulations for financial institutions that hold sufficient capital, appealing to those who worry that normalizing interest rates with existing compliance requirements reduce credit growth. That is similar to a proposal now in the Financial CHOICE Act, which was just voted out of the House Financial Services Committee as HR 10 of the 115th Congress. It could also be implemented in part under current regulatory procedures developed at the Federal Reserve Board without a change in legislation.

Third, a rarely discussed implicit part of the actions taken in 1979 was the move by other central banks to change their approach to policy. This tended to mitigate concerns about dollar appreciation. The emphasis today might be that other central banks (the European Central Bank or the Bank of Japan) could begin to taper, which would appeal to those with exchange rate concerns. This, of course, is a most delicate issue and is best left to central banks operating in their own country's interest.

CONCLUSION

In these remarks, I have tried to suggest ways in which monetary policy makers can deal in practice with disparate views about monetary economics such as those discussed at this conference. Though objective empirical research, discussion, and debate can help narrow views and create progress, opinions today appear to be as disparate as they were at the time of the big change in monetary policy in 1979.

However, the methods of dealing with this disparity have improved. Model comparison and robustness studies are much easier to carry out. Systematic policy evaluation of alternative monetary strategies has become routine. Policy makers at the Fed can and should make better use of these advances. And though more difficult, looking for policy packages that can draw in policy makers with different views is still likely to be useful, especially if we study and learn from past experiences.

References

Binder, Michael, Philipp Lieberknecht, Jorge Quintana, and Volker Wieland. 2017. "Model Uncertainty in Macroeconomics: On the Implications of Financial

Frictions." Institute for Monetary and Financial Stability Working Paper Series 114, Goethe University, Frankfurt.

Bordo, Michael, William Dupor, and John B. Taylor. 2014. "Frameworks for Central Banking in the Next Century." Special issue, *Journal of Economic Dynamics and Control* 49.

Bordo, Michael, and John B. Taylor. 2017. *Rules for International Monetary Stability: Past, Present, and Future.* Stanford, CA: Hoover Institution Press.

Cochrane, John. 2017. "Michelson-Morley, Occam and Fisher: The Radical Implications of Stable Inflation at Near-Zero Interest Rates." *NBER Macroeconomics Annual.*

Cochrane, John, and John B. Taylor. 2016. *Central Bank Governance and Oversight Reform.* Stanford, CA: Hoover Institution Press.

Federal Reserve. 1979. Press release, November 23, https://www.federalreserve .gov/monetarypolicy/files/fomcropa19791006.pdf.

Fischer, Stanley. 2017a. "I'd Rather Have Bob Solow Than an Econometric Model, But . . ." Paper presented at the Warwick Economics Summit, Coventry, United Kingdom, February 11.

———. 2017b. "Monetary Policy: By Rule, by Committee, or by Both?" Paper presented at the U.S. Monetary Policy Forum, Initiative on Global Markets at the University of Chicago Booth School of Business, New York, March 3.

Lindsey, David E., Athanasios Orphanides, and Robert H. Rasche. 2005. "The Reform of October 1979: How It Happened and Why." *Federal Reserve Bank of St. Louis Review* 87 (2): 187–236.

Michaelis, Henrike, and Volker Wieland. 2017. "R-Star and the Yellen rules." Vox-EU website, February 3, http://voxeu.org/article/r-star-and-yellen-rules.

Taylor, John B. 2005. "The International Implications of October 1979: Toward a Long Boom on a Global Scale." *Federal Reserve Bank of St. Louis Review* 87 (2): 269–75.

———. 2012. "When Volcker Ruled." *Wall Street Journal*, September 8.

Taylor, John B., and Volcker Wieland. 2012. "Surprising Comparative Properties of Monetary Models: Results from a New Model Data Base." *Review of Economics and Statistics* 94 (3): 800–16.

Yellen, Janet L. 2017. "The Economic Outlook and the Conduct of Monetary Policy." Paper presented at the Stanford Institute for Economic Policy Research, Stanford University, Stanford, California, January 19.

GENERAL DISCUSSION

DAVID PAPELL: You discussed thinking about robustness across models when you look at policy rules. But if you look, for example, at your *Review of Economics and Statistics* paper with Volker Wieland, the three models all had the result that, in the basic Taylor rule, the optimal policy rule is inflation gap tilting with a higher coefficient on the inflation gap than on the output gap. In contrast, Robert Tetlow's *International Journal of Central Banking* paper had the result that, in the 2007 variant of the FRB/US model, the optimal policy rule is output gap tilting with a higher coefficient on the output gap than on the inflation gap. The optimal policy rule in the current version of the FRB/US model is even more output gap tilting than the rule in the 2007 version. How do you think about robustness when the leading models give completely opposite answers?

JOHN TAYLOR: First of all, I think what's happened to the models over time is quite relevant. Tetlow also has pictures in his paper that show a radical movement in the policy rules from the same model as it is evolving over time. The model comparison allows you to deal with different vintages of models. So you can see what is different about the FRB/US model, how the older MPS model was different, and then examine that. You also have other models to compare. You offer a really good example, because you don't want to be so dependent on the most recent model; one event such as the Great Recession or an unusual policy may have influenced it so much.

BILL NELSON: So the initial Humphrey Hawkins required the Fed to communicate its policy intentions and what it was going to do in terms of money growth. And over the years, that sort of solidified into the money growth cones. Ultimately, those cones didn't change for years on end, and they used boilerplate language that didn't convey any information whatsoever, I think because they'd become largely irrelevant. So if the committee were required to communicate in terms of a rule or rules, how would you suggest that kind of obsolescence be avoided?

JOHN TAYLOR: First of all, that is a very important lesson. The Congress did require that the Fed report these money growth ranges. Originally, the Fed objected strenuously. Eventually, when they saw it was going to happen, they worked with the Congress to get something more reasonable that they could work with. And so that became part of the law—I believe it was 1977. And so they worked that way. And the discussion that Volcker went through in 1979 to some extent was bringing money into the conversation. And it may have helped. He did emphasize money growth. Eventually, he went off it, of course, in 1982. But I think the discussion of money growth was beneficial. That requirement was removed from the Federal Reserve Act in 2000. I didn't complain about it at the time. But the rationale was just what you say. It really wasn't very helpful anymore. Technology was changing, how you measure the M's was also changing, so they just took it out of the law, and that made Greenspan's life easier. But I think its removal is the reason why something else is needed. We now think of policy more in terms of interest rate rules of different kinds, and there's a reason for that: money has not been as stable. By the way, I think we ought to try to bring money back in to some extent. But short of that, the legislative proposal would have the Fed simply be required to state its strategy. It would be their job to define it completely, and then check it against some other well-known policy rules. It's not that different from what Janet Yellen has said recently in speeches. Of course, the world is always changing, and so the strategy may have to be changed in the future. But there's been lots of experience with this type of strategy—probably more experience than with money growth targeting at the time—so I think it's promising.

ROBERT HELLER: As you said, 1979 was a year of divergence, and soon thereafter came the Great Convergence. Then you had, after a minor revolt on the board in 1986, a period under Volcker, as well as Greenspan, with great unanimity. There wasn't anyone who was really disagreeing with the policy. So what do you think changed to break up this unanimity? Was it research?

JOHN TAYLOR: It was research and experience that drove the first change toward unanimity. I think the experience was tough those first few years of disinflation, to be sure. But eventually, you had a much better economy. The Great Moderation began. I think that convinced a lot of people that policy that was the way to go. And then research was certainly a part of it. Rich Clarida did work on showing that the response of the Fed did change about that time, and it's related to the improved performance. So it's a combination of research and experience. There was a whole set of new models that followed the original New Keynesian models. They took a while to seep into the central banks, including the FRB/US model. John Williams, who was a student here at Stanford, went to the Fed and was part of the reason that new modeling came in. The Bank of Canada brought the new models in too. It was with a lag, to be sure. But the policy change occurred before that. But maybe that affected the views.

JAMES BULLARD: As you're saying, the CHOICE Act now says that the Fed should report using policy rules. How should we handle the zero bound? Should the rule also specify how the committee thinks it will react in a zero bound situation?

JOHN TAYLOR: It's a good question. I should say it's up to you. [*Laughter*] But since you're asking, I would first propose a kind of mega-rule. That's like the Reifschneider-Williams approach. And if we hit the zero bound, the central bank would stay at zero for longer. I think that's where I would start.

I agree that it's hard to make this work in practice, but the FOMC has to be thinking about a strategy. "Adopting" may be too strong a word, but there has to be a fair amount of agreement. If it is not very specific about magnitudes, then the direction of movement in interest rates and the response to certain variables should be given. The Fed already has had a discussion of r-star. They've already had a discussion of the target inflation rate. So they are close. I think some discussion of a strategy for other kinds of actions would be useful, such as interest on excess reserves, the size of the balance sheet. That might require a compromise of some kind, as in my example of Volker's experience in 1979.

CHARLES EVANS: John, that was a great talk on the history going back to 1979. I really enjoyed that. Your comments on robustness are really important and something that we should all think about in terms of what rules survive different models. As I have not thought about this enough, let me ask an impossible question that I myself couldn't answer: How do you have confidence that you've considered an appropriate span of models that takes into account mechanisms that might be common to most models that economists write down. And as I go out and talk to people about low interest rates, negative interest rates—which are extraordinarily unpopular—I also wonder how we can cover these more unusual issues. How would you think about incorporating models that do so? I don't have an answer myself.

JOHN TAYLOR: I appreciate that you can't answer your own question. I can't either, but here is a try. Volker Wieland has eighty models in his database. Some of them are not all that different, but a lot of them are different. Some bring in the financial accelerator, financial frictions. The models are beginning to examine the impact of negative or very low interest rates on the spreads. The banking sector is not described as well as it might be. So I'd look for different approaches like that. But ultimately, you're right. You can't do every model, and no robustness study is foolproof. But you can try, and I think central banks can do better with this.

LAWRENCE SCHEMBRI: John, you mentioned the international aspect, namely taking into account the behavior of other central banks. Things are very different now than they were in 1979, in the sense that we all basically have 2 percent inflation targets. We're all moving in the same direction to some extent. Do you think the same extent of coordination is needed now as was perhaps needed in 1979, when we didn't have the same viewpoint as to the goal of monetary policy?

JOHN TAYLOR: There's a lot to be learned from the previous efforts to coordinate, like the Plaza Accord, which I don't think worked very well. That agreement basically moved Japan off what would have been a good policy. But what comes out of the experience is that if each central bank focused on what is best for its own country, and each central bank believes that other central banks will do the same, then it's very close to a global optimum. And you don't need much more. You don't need to argue, "Hey, you should do this, that, or anything." The optimality result just automatically falls out. There's research on that, and I think there should be more research.

CHAPTER SIX

MONETARY RULES AND COMMITTEES

Stanley Fischer

In this chapter, I offer some observations on monetary policy rules and their place in decision making by the Federal Open Market Committee (FOMC).[1] I have two messages. First, policy makers should consult the prescriptions of policy rules, but—almost needless to say—they should avoid applying them mechanically. Second, policy-making committees have strengths that policy rules lack. In particular, committees are an efficient means of aggregating a wide variety of information and perspectives.

MONETARY POLICY RULES IN RESEARCH AND POLICY

Since May 2014, I have considered monetary policy rules from the vantage point of a member of the FOMC. But my interest in them began many years ago and was reflected in some of my earliest publications.[2] At that time, the literature on monetary policy rules, especially in the United States, remained predominantly concerned with the money stock or total bank reserves rather than the short-

---

1. Views expressed in this presentation are my own and not necessarily the views of the Federal Reserve Board or the Federal Open Market Committee. I am grateful to Ed Nelson of the Federal Reserve Board for his assistance.
2. See, for example, Cooper and Fischer (1972).

term interest rate.[3] Seen with the benefit of hindsight, that emphasis probably derived from three sources: first, the quantity theory
of money emphasized the link between the quantity of money and
inflation; second, the research was carried out when monetarism
was gaining credibility in the profession; and third, there was a
concern that interest rate rules might lead to price-level indeterminacy—an issue disposed of by Bennett McCallum and others.[4]

Subsequently, John Taylor's research, especially his celebrated
1993 paper, was a catalyst in shifting the focus toward rules for the
short-term interest rate.[5] Taylor's work thus helped change the terms
of the discussion in favor of rules for the instrument that central
banks prefer to use. His 1993 study also highlighted the practical
relevance of monetary policy rules, as he showed that a particular
simple rule—the rule that now bears his name—provided a good
approximation to the behavior of the federal funds rate during the

---

3. There was, however, a long tradition of monetary analysis in the United Kingdom
and continental Europe centered on the authorities' use of the interest rate as an instrument.
See especially Keynes (1930) and Wicksell (1936). In the post–World War II decades, this
tradition continued in the UK research literature on monetary policy: examples include
Currie and Levine (1987) and Flemming (1993). In addition, an interest rate was the policy
instrument in some key contributions to open-economy monetary theory, such as Meade
(1951) and Mundell (1960). These traditions likely reflected the long-standing use of bank
rate as a policy instrument in the United Kingdom and the fact that, for most of the period
from the Treasury/Federal Reserve Accord of 1951 until the 1990s, central banks in countries other than the United States tended to be more explicit than the Federal Reserve chose
to be about their use of short-term interest rates as their primary policy instrument. Even
in the US context, however, there was a certain amount of research on interest rate policies. For example, it was common practice among builders of large econometric models to
consider different Federal Reserve interest rate strategies (see Ando 1981). In addition, the
empirical and simulation properties of the Federal Reserve's interest rate reaction function
were the concern of such studies as Dewald and Johnson (1963), DeRosa and Stern (1977),
Dornbusch and Fischer (1979), and Henderson and McKibbin (1993), while Sargent and
Wallace (1975) and McCallum (1981) examined the analytical properties of interest rate
rules. A later magisterial study of the analytics of interest rate rules was Woodford (2003).
4. See McCallum (1981). I should add that when we presented work based on Cooper
and Fischer (1972), we were urged by several economists to focus on the interest rate as
the monetary policy instrument. Among these economists were Albert Ando and Franco
Modigliani, who were then working with others on building the MPS (MIT–Pennsylvania–
Social Science Research Council) model.
5. See Taylor (1993).

early Greenspan years. The research literature on monetary policy rules has experienced a major revival since Taylor's seminal paper and has concentrated on rules for the short-term interest rate.

Consideration of interest rate rules has also, as I will discuss, come to have a prominent role in FOMC discussions, with the Taylor rule being one benchmark that we regularly consult. But— building on recent remarks I made elsewhere—I will also indicate why policy makers might have good reasons for deviating from these rule benchmarks and why, in pursuing the objectives of monetary policy, they could appropriately behave in ways that are not well characterized by simple monetary policy rules.[6] In particular, I will point to reasons why the FOMC's discussions might lead to decisions that depart—temporarily or permanently—from the prescriptions of baseline monetary policy rules.

RULES AS A BENCHMARK FOR POLICY DISCUSSIONS

Some perspective on the status of policy rules in FOMC discussions is provided by considering what has changed over the past twenty years. Donald Kohn, at a landmark conference organized by John Taylor in January 1998, described the role played by monetary policy rules in the FOMC briefing process.[7] His account noted that Federal Reserve staff members presented FOMC participants with prescriptions from several policy rules, including the Taylor (1993) rule. This description remains true today. Publicly available Blue Books and Teal Books of successive years demonstrate that the

---

6. For my earlier speeches in this area, see Fischer (2017a, 2017b).

7. See Kohn (1999). At the time, Donald Kohn was director of the Division of Monetary Affairs at the Federal Reserve Board. The conference proceedings were published as Taylor (1999a).

coverage of policy rules in the briefing material provided by the board staff expanded considerably in the years after Kohn spoke.[8]

Kohn noted that policy rule prescriptions served two functions: as a "benchmark for the stance of policy" and "to structure thinking about the implications of incoming information for the direction of policy action."[9] These two functions continue to be important: Policy rule prescriptions provide a useful starting point for FOMC deliberations and a convenient way of organizing alternative arguments about the appropriate policy decision. Policy rule prescriptions, particularly prescriptions obtained from a dynamic model simulation, also help policy makers take to heart a key message of the literature on policy rules—namely, that monetary policy decisions should concern the appropriate *path* for the policy instrument and not merely the current setting of that instrument.

Kohn also observed, however, that "in truth, only a few members look at this or similar information regularly, and the number does not seem to be growing." That state of affairs has probably changed in the two decades since Kohn wrote. It is clear from transcripts in the public record that rule prescriptions have frequently been cited at FOMC meetings.[10] The prominence that interest rate rules have achieved in Federal Reserve policy makers' analysis of monetary policy was underscored by Chair Yellen in her speech at Stanford University earlier this year.[11]

---

8. The Federal Reserve Board's website (https://www.federalreserve.gov/monetarypolicy/fomc_historical_year.htm) provides downloadable copies of the briefing books (the Green Book and Blue Book, which were replaced in 2010 by the Teal Book) distributed to FOMC members and other participants ahead of each FOMC meeting. At present, the most recent year for which these materials are available on the site is 2011. The "Monetary Policy Strategies" portion of the Blue Book (and later, the Teal Book) contains prescriptions from interest rate rules.

9. Kohn (1999, 195). The first of these functions of policy rule prescriptions was one I also had highlighted. When considering McCallum's (1988) proposed rule for monetary base growth, I described it as "a useful benchmark against which to judge policy" (Fischer 1994, 289).

10. Searchable transcripts of FOMC meetings up to 2011 are available on the board's website at https://www.federalreserve.gov/monetarypolicy/fomc_historical.htm.

11. See Yellen (2017).

Further, as is clear from Taylor's econometric derivation of his 1993 rule, actual monetary policy decisions may—and probably should—exhibit systematic patterns that can be described as a rule. In fact, as I have already noted, one attraction of the 1993 Taylor rule was that it described US monetary policy patterns well over a certain period, one that was associated with a reasonable degree of economic stability.

Nevertheless, central bankers who are aware of the merits of the arguments for policy rules have on occasion deviated substantially from the prescriptions of standard policy rules. Further, while the implications of different monetary rules are described in the Teal Book and typically referred to in presentations by FOMC participants, the overall discussion in FOMC meetings is not generally cast in terms of how it relates to one version or another of the Taylor or any other rule. The other set of rules mentioned frequently in FOMC discussions is Wicksellian, for there is often a discussion of r^*, which in some formulations of the Taylor rule is also the constant term.

The period since 2008 bears testimony to central bankers' willingness to depart from the prescriptions of a prespecified rule. In the wake of the financial crisis, policy makers found it necessary to follow a more accommodative monetary policy appropriate for the new economic conditions.[12] In addition, structural changes in the US economy have apparently lowered the value of the interest rate—that is, r^*—consistent with neutral policy.[13]

Such structural changes were not anticipated in advance.[14] Of course, once a structural change has occurred and been ascertained

---

12. See especially Engen, Laubach, and Reifschneider (2015). Because the federal funds rate was at its effective lower bound from late 2008 to late 2015, policy choices about that rate largely involved decisions concerning the forward guidance provided by the FOMC. These decisions in turn rested on judgments regarding the period over which the rate should remain at its lower bound, as well as about the pace and magnitude of the subsequent policy firming.

13. See, for example, Board of Governors (2017).

14. Indeed, Milton Friedman's advocacy of a policy rule consisting of constant monetary growth rested in part on the existence of uncertainty, as he suggested that economists lacked

by policy makers, they know what rules would likely have performed well in the face of that change. For this reason, policy makers might change their judgment about which monetary policy rules constitute reasonable benchmarks—or, over time, they might develop a procedure for revising the monetary rule. But a frequently revised rule does not really qualify as a rule in the sense that we currently use the term.

Consequently, when considering the relationship between monetary policy decisions and monetary policy rules, we can expect two regularities to hold. First, actual monetary policy will sometimes appropriately depart from the prescriptions of benchmark rules even when those benchmarks describe past decisions well. Second, in their use of rules, policy makers will from time to time change their assessment of what rule they regard as the appropriate benchmark. Both regularities have been amply observed in recent years, but they were also present twenty years ago, as reflected in Kohn's remark that policy makers "do not see their past actions as a very firm guide to current or future policy."[15] Or, as a teacher of mine at the London School of Economics, Richard Sayers, put it much earlier, "There is no code of eternal rules. . . . We have central banks for the very reason that there are no such rules."[16]

As I will now elaborate, I believe the fact that monetary policy is made by committees in most economies is important in understanding both of these regularities.

---

the knowledge about economic relationships required to improve on that simple rule. See Friedman (1972) for a concise version of his case for the rule and Dornbusch and Fischer (1978, 278–80, 516) for a textbook account of Friedman's rule that emphasized the uncertainty aspect of his argument for the rule. Of course, the fact that a policy rule is simple far from guarantees that the rule will generate satisfactory economic outcomes in the face of uncertainty and economic change. For example, Friedman's rule would likely perform poorly in an environment in which the trend rate of growth of monetary velocity underwent a major shift, while the Taylor rule could perform unsatisfactorily if the assumption about potential-output behavior embedded in the rule proved to be badly mistaken. The latter possibility was stressed in Orphanides (2003).

15. Kohn (1999, 195).
16. Sayers (1958, 7).

THE ROLE OF COMMITTEES IN
POLICY FORMATION

Monetary policy decisions in the United States and elsewhere typically arise from the discussion and vote of a committee.[17] In principle, a monetary policy committee could decide to follow a rule. But a decision of this kind is unlikely to occur in practice. Committee discussions bring into policy-making features that a rule lacks. A committee-based decision process is, I suggest, likely to produce policy decisions that depart from the prescriptions of benchmark rules.

A policy rule prescription is more consistent with a single perspective on the economy than with the pooling of multiple perspectives associated with a committee policy-making process. Roger Lowenstein's book *America's Bank* details how the founding of the Federal Reserve involved reconciling a large number of interests in the United States.[18] In a similar vein, the modern FOMC framework involves participation by twelve reserve bank presidents, each of whom represents a different district of the country. The FOMC framework also balances centralized and decentralized decision making by having most of the permanent voting members—specifically, the Board of Governors—based in Washington, DC.

All of the FOMC participants have common goals—maximum employment and price stability—which are given by the Federal Reserve's statutory mandate. They have also agreed, for pursuing that mandate, on the Statement on Longer-Run Goals and Monetary Policy Strategy.[19] But while they have this common ground, each FOMC participant brings to the table his or her own perspective or view of the world. Part of their role in meetings is to

---

17. I discussed some of the literature on monetary policy committees in Fischer (2017b).
18. See Lowenstein (2015).
19. See Federal Open Market Committee (2017).

articulate that perspective and perhaps persuade their colleagues to revise their own perspectives—or vice versa.

A member of a committee may well have valuable economic information not known by their colleagues until he or she relays it. This point has been brought home to me by reserve bank presidents' accounts of recent economic developments in their districts. These narratives shed light on the real-world developments that lie behind the recorded economic data. They also help shape my interpretation of what part of incoming data may be an important signal and what part may reflect transitory factors or mismeasurement.

The information underlying a policy decision is, therefore, crucially shaped by a committee system. Committees can aggregate a large volume of diverse information about current and expected future economic conditions. The information includes anecdotes and impressions gleaned from business and other contacts, which can provide insights that are not recorded in current data releases.

In practice, it is likely that the information obtained and processed by the committee will leave the FOMC less inclined to follow a benchmark rule. For example, the committee's discussions might point up factors that have not yet affected real economic activity and inflation. Such factors would not lead to an immediate change in the prescription for the federal funds rate obtained from a rule like the Taylor rule, as this prescription is a function of current values of the output gap and inflation. The committee might nevertheless wish to adjust the federal funds rate immediately because the newly unearthed factors are likely to affect output and inflation in coming months.

In addition, and as I have suggested, policy makers might also encounter unexpected or unusual events, or both, or they might perceive changes in the structure of the economy. A committee process is conducive to assessing the appropriate policy response to these developments. A case in point is the decline, as I mentioned, in estimates of the neutral interest rate. The concept of the neutral interest rate is a way of summarizing the various forces, many of them unobservable, that shift the relationship between monetary policy and economic activity. Bringing to the table diverse perspectives is a pragmatic way of confronting such deep sources of uncertainty and deciding how to deal with them. A committee discussion can flesh out the factors behind changes in the neutral rate, and a committee would likely be able to identify such changes more promptly than would a statistical exercise, because of the wider set of information from around the country that the committee is able to process.

The decision-making environment that I have described involves more flexibility for FOMC members than they would have if they simply followed a policy rule. But transparency and accountability must figure heavily in this more flexible environment. The FOMC's policy communications include its post-meeting statement, the minutes of its meetings, the chair's quarterly press conference, the chair's semiannual monetary policy testimony to the Congress, and other public remarks by individual FOMC members. In this framework, policy makers articulate the reasoning behind each decision and, in particular, explain how the policy decision contributes to the achievement of the committee's statutory mandate.

There remains a deeper question about committee decision making: Why have almost all countries decided that monetary policy decisions should be made by a committee rather than by a rule? One answer is that laws in most countries are passed by institutions in which committee deliberation is the norm. Of course, we then have to ask why that has become a norm in almost all democracies. The answer is that opinions—even on monetary policy—differ among experts, while the economy is in a constant process of change.

Because opinions differ among experts, democracies tend to prefer committees in which decisions are made by discussion among the experts—and, in many cases, other representatives of the public—who discuss, try to persuade each other, and must at the end of their deliberations reach a decision. But those decisions have to be explained to the public and to other parts of the government—and hence the appropriate emphasis on transparency and accountability. That is the democratic way of making decisions when opinions differ, as they often do in the monetary field.

I have been a governor of two central banks and, even as the sole decision maker on monetary policy in the Bank of Israel, sometimes found that my initial view on the next decision changed as a result of discussions with the informal advisory committee with which I consulted at that time. Those discussions, which recognize human frailty in analyzing a situation and the need to act despite considerable uncertainty, are the reason why committee decision making is, *on average*, preferable to the use of a rule.[20]

Emphasis on a single rule as *the* basis for monetary policy implies that the truth has been found, despite the record over time of major shifts in monetary policy—from the gold standard, to the Bretton Woods fixed but changeable exchange rate rule, to Keynesian approaches, to monetary targeting, to the modern frameworks of inflation targeting and the dual mandate of the Fed, and more. We should not make our monetary policy decisions based on that assumption. Rather, we need our policy makers to be continually on the lookout for structural changes in the economy and for disturbances from hitherto unexpected sources.

CONCLUDING REMARKS

The prescriptions of monetary policy rules play a prominent role in the FOMC's monetary policy deliberations. And this is as it should be, in view of the usefulness of rules as a starting point for policy

---

20. The existing literature on monetary policy committees has found that committee decisions tend to be better than decisions made by a sole policy maker. See, for example, Blinder and Morgan (2005); Lombardelli, Proudman, and Talbot (2005); and Warsh (2016).

discussion and the fact that comparison with a benchmark rule provides a useful means of articulating one's own preferred policy action. But, for the reasons I have outlined, adherence to a simple policy rule is not the most appropriate means of achieving macroeconomic goals—and there are very good reasons why monetary policy decisions are typically made in committees, whose structure allows participants to assess the varying conditions of different regions and economic sectors, as well as to reflect different beliefs about the working of the economy.

References

Ando, Albert. 1981. "On a Theoretical and Empirical Basis of Macroeconometric Models." In *Large-Scale Macro-Econometric Models: Theory and Practice*, edited by J. Kmenta and J. B. Ramsey, 329–68. New York: North-Holland.

Blinder, Alan S., and John Morgan. 2005. "Are Two Heads Better Than One? Monetary Policy by Committee." *Journal of Money, Credit, and Banking* 37 (October): 789–811.

Board of Governors of the Federal Reserve System. 2017. "Minutes of the Federal Open Market Committee, December 13–14, 2016." Press release, January 4.

Cooper, J. Phillip, and Stanley Fischer. 1972. "Stochastic Simulation of Monetary Rules in Two Macroeconomic Models." *Journal of the American Statistical Association* 67 (December): 750–60.

Currie, David, and Paul Levine. 1987. "Does International Macroeconomic Policy Coordination Pay and Is It Sustainable? A Two-Country Analysis." *Oxford Economic Papers* 39 (March): 38–74.

DeRosa, Paul, and Gary H. Stern. 1977. "Monetary Control and the Federal Funds Rate." *Journal of Monetary Economics* 3 (April): 217–30.

Dewald, William G., and Harry G. Johnson. 1963. "An Objective Analysis of the Objectives of American Monetary Policy, 1952–61." In *Banking and Monetary Studies*, edited by Deane Carson, 171–89. Homewood, IL: R. D. Irwin.

Dornbusch, Rudiger, and Stanley Fischer. 1978. *Macroeconomics*. New York: McGraw-Hill.

———. 1979. *The Determinants and Effects of Changes in Interest Rates: A Study Prepared for the Trustees of the Banking Research Fund*. Chicago: Association of Reserve City Bankers.

Engen, Eric M., Thomas Laubach, and David Reifschneider. 2015. "The Macroeconomic Effects of the Federal Reserve's Unconventional Monetary Policies" (PDF). Finance and Economics Discussion Series 2015-005. Washington, DC: Board of Governors of the Federal Reserve System.

Federal Open Market Committee. 2017. "Statement on Longer-Run Goals and Monetary Policy Strategy" (PDF), amended effective January 31 (original version adopted effective January 24, 2012).

Fischer, Stanley. 1994. "Modern Central Banking." In *The Future of Central Banking: The Tercentenary Symposium of the Bank of England*, edited by Forrest Capie, Charles Goodhart, Stanley Fischer, and Norbert Schnadt, 262–308. New York: Cambridge University Press.

———. 2017a. "'I'd Rather Have Bob Solow Than an Econometric Model, But. . . .'" Speech delivered at the Warwick Economics Summit, Coventry, United Kingdom, February 11.

———. 2017b. "Monetary Policy: By Rule, by Committee, or by Both?" Speech delivered at the 2017 US Monetary Policy Forum, sponsored by the Initiative on Global Markets at the University of Chicago Booth School of Business, New York, March 3.

Flemming, John. 1993. "Money, Interest and Consumption in the *General Theory.*" In *Monetary Theory and Thought: Essays in Honour of Don Patinkin*, edited by Haim Barkai, Stanley Fischer, and Nissan Liviatan, 74–83. London: Macmillan.

Friedman, Milton. 1972. "The Case for a Monetary Rule." *Newsweek*, February 7.

Henderson, Dale W., and Warwick J. McKibbin. 1993. "A Comparison of Some Basic Monetary Policy Regimes for Open Economies: Implications of Different Degrees of Instrument Adjustment and Wage Persistence." *Carnegie-Rochester Conference Series on Public Policy* 39 (December): 221–317.

Keynes, John Maynard. 1930. *A Treatise on Money*. 2 vols. New York: Harcourt, Brace.

Kohn, Donald L. 1999. "Comment." In *Monetary Policy Rules*, edited by John B. Taylor, 192–99. Chicago: University of Chicago Press.

Levin, Andrew T., and John C. Williams. 2003. "Robust Monetary Policy with Competing Reference Models." *Journal of Monetary Economics* 50 (July): 945–75.

Lombardelli, Clare, James Proudman, and James Talbot. 2005. "Committees versus Individuals: An Experimental Analysis of Monetary Policy Decision Making." *International Journal of Central Banking* 1 (May): 181–205.

Lowenstein, Roger. 2015. *America's Bank: The Epic Struggle to Create the Federal Reserve*. New York: Penguin Press.

McCallum, Bennett T. 1981. "Price Level Determinacy with an Interest Rate Policy Rule and Rational Expectations." *Journal of Monetary Economics* 8 (November): 319–29.

———. 1988. "Robustness Properties of a Rule for Monetary Policy." *Carnegie-Rochester Conference Series on Public Policy* 29 (Autumn): 173–203.

Meade, James E. 1951. *The Theory of International Economic Policy.* Vol. 1, *The Balance of Payments.* New York: Oxford University Press.

Mundell, Robert A. 1960. "The Monetary Dynamics of International Adjustment under Fixed and Flexible Exchange Rates." *Quarterly Journal of Economics* 74 (May): 227–57.

Orphanides, Athanasios. 2003. "The Quest for Prosperity without Inflation." *Journal of Monetary Economics* 50 (April): 633–63.

Reifschneider, David. 2016. "Gauging the Ability of the FOMC to Respond to Future Recessions" (PDF). Finance and Economics Discussion Series 2016-068. Washington, DC: Board of Governors of the Federal Reserve System.

Sargent, Thomas J., and Neil Wallace. 1975. "'Rational' Expectations, the Optimal Monetary Instrument, and the Optimal Money Supply Rule." *Journal of Political Economy* 83 (April): 241–54.

Sayers, R. S. 1958. *Central Banking after Bagehot.* Rev. ed. Oxford: Clarendon Press.

Taylor, John B. 1993. "Discretion versus Policy Rules in Practice." *Carnegie-Rochester Conference Series on Public Policy* 39 (December): 195–214.

———, ed. 1999a. *Monetary Policy Rules.* Chicago: University of Chicago Press.

———. 1999b. "The Robustness and Efficiency of Monetary Policy Rules as Guidelines for Interest Rate Setting by the European Central Bank." *Journal of Monetary Economics* 43 (June): 655–79.

Warsh, Kevin M. 2016. "Institutional Design: Deliberations, Decisions, and Committee Dynamics." In *Central Bank Governance and Oversight Reform*, edited by John H. Cochrane and John B. Taylor, 173–93. Stanford, CA: Hoover Institution Press.

Wicksell, Knut. 1936. *Interest and Prices: A Study of the Causes Regulating the Value of Money.* Translated by R. F. Kahn. London: Macmillan.

Woodford, Michael. 2003. *Interest and Prices: Foundations of a Theory of Monetary Policy.* Princeton, NJ: Princeton University Press.

Yellen, Janet L. 2017. "The Economic Outlook and the Conduct of Monetary Policy." Speech delivered at the Stanford Institute for Economic Policy Research, Stanford, CA, January 19.

GENERAL DISCUSSION

JOHN TAYLOR: Stan, in this talk, you've again hit on one of the most important issues I can think of, which is how you can have strategies or rules where committees are making decisions. I have lots of questions, but I just want to raise a quick one. Greenspan, when he was chair, said the Fed deserved an assist in creating the Taylor rule. And so, there is a sense in which there are periods when there's more or less a strategy. And so, it's not impossible to think about committees coming to agreement on a strategy. There are laws. Laws are passed. I'm not saying it should be all one way. But a law is a way to come to an agreement, and some people disagree. But there's compromises. So it's not impossible, and we have some history. I agree one hundred percent that you've focused on a very important issue here. But it seems to me it's not impossible to put committee-making decisions and rules-based policy together.

STANLEY FISCHER: Well, I think that's right. It's not impossible and can be done for a period of years. Agreements always break down, and then you have to figure out what set of rules you're going to have for changing the rules. In Canada, they have inflation targeting, but every five years the central bank and the finance minister have to reach a fresh agreement on it. That's a way of dealing with the uncertainties that's not impossible to envisage.

I'm always struck by one thing, John, and you'll excuse me explaining this to the audience. Whenever John and I have a conversation on monetary rules, I come out thinking, Why do people argue about this issue? But then, people do argue about this issue. We've got to ask ourselves, What is the problem? I think the problem is we're describing a rule for monetary policy that is like the rule of the Medes and the Persians—it's never going to change. But we know that it is going to change. And that, I think, is why we have not been willing to agree to a rule. So I can envisage, say, in the case of inflation targeting, a procedure in which you can change the target, or you can change the other variables that are involved on some regular basis, through some regularly undertaken calculation, and you say, "That's my rule." My rule is an equation at a moment in time, combined with footnotes that tell you how to deal with special circumstances and combined with another few paragraphs that tell you how to revise it over the course of time. If that's a rule, it sounds like a law. It's something that I can envisage.

ROBERT HELLER: Stan, you talked eloquently about the advantages of the diversity of views that you get in the FOMC and the various opinions, and how that really helps. Why do you think there is such enormous pressure on people to have unanimity in the FOMC? Why not have, like the Supreme Court does, split votes of seven to five, or six to whatever. That would reflect the diversity of views you so value.

STANLEY FISCHER: I think the issue relates to the size of the committee and the need to drive it to a decision on a particular date. Mervin King used to say that he wanted to be in the minority from time to time, just to show that he could be in the minority and the world didn't end nor did the Bank of England break down on that particular day. Well, that's not been the tradition in the Fed. The tradition in the Fed goes the other way. And if you have a fair number of dissents, you already start being in trouble, as happened to Paul Volcker, who people held in high regard, yet in the end he had difficulty getting some of his decisions through. The system could tend to break down. What happens if there isn't somebody, some group, trying to drive decisions in a particular direction over the course of time? If you were very close to having two political parties among the nineteen members of the board, I think you'd have very bad monetary policy. And it's that need for some coherence in what comes out of the meeting that pushes the Fed in the direction of preferring minimal dissent.

In preparing for this lecture, I read some of the papers and books edited or written by John Taylor. The literature on the optimal committee size says five. I was chair of a committee of six, which had originally been seven, just to tell you about Israel. I thought, "Well, it'll be fine. So we'll have four outsiders and three insiders." So we put that into law and I sent that to the Treasury, and the head of the Treasury called me and said, "Listen, Stan. You're not in New Zealand. You're in Israel. If you don't start with some advantage, you're going to be outvoted very, very often." So we got down to six, with a double vote for the chairman if there was a tie. So we had a small committee with that characteristic.

And then something interesting happened, which relates to the Fed in some ways. I never used the double vote. But somewhere near the end of my term, as the meeting progressed, I thought I was going to have to use the double vote for the first time. And then we had the vote, and my view won, four to two. So at the end of the meeting, I spoke to the guy who I knew for sure preferred the opposite decision. And I said to him, "Why didn't you vote as I expected you to vote?"

He said, "I thought this issue was too small for you to have to break the rule of not using the double vote."

So that's when you see a committee trying to work as a committee and not as six different people. Now there are questions about that. The principles set out for the Bank of England are that everybody votes as a person and not as members of the committee. I'm not sure which is better. Because you've got to keep meeting. You've got to keep making decisions. And you've got to be able to speak freely if you're going to make good decisions. I don't know which way was the right way. On that particular day, I appreciated that guy's choice, but it wasn't critical in any way. It was just something about forming a group of people to make a decision.

GEORGE SHULTZ: You have a broad mandate. And you have certain specified tools. But sometimes you must see that the tools you have aren't enough to satisfy the mandate. Maybe you think tax policy should be different or spending policy should be different. To what degree do you feel a compulsion to speak up on behalf of your mandate to get other people to do what they should do?

STANLEY FISCHER: Well, the answer is, at first thought, very often I'm tempted. And then I say to the people around me, "I'm going to go and say something this time."

And they'll say, "You can't do that!"

And then I say, "Why not?"

And then they explain to me why I can't do that. The last thing we need is a war with the Congress, for example. So in the end, I rarely express my views. That was not the case in Israel, but it's a different culture. On the first day I was there, I said to a fairly large staff, "What I don't want to hear from you is what you think my views are. And if I find examples of that, I'll be very irritated." Well, I didn't suffer from that problem at all. They don't care. They just say what's on their mind, and that's a very attractive way—to my mind—that their society works. But it may only work in a small country. I'm not sure it works in a very large country.

MICHAEL BOSKIN: Stanley, my question is a corollary of George's. To what extent does, and to what extent should, the FOMC take into account the effect of its behavior on enabling fiscal policy that might be deleterious in the long term? For example, enabling greater government long-term debt issuance, especially when the deleterious effects may be well outside what you're looking at in the short-term determination of monetary policy?

STANLEY FISCHER: I've thought about that often in having arguments with the European non–central bank officials about what they want the ECB to do. And I decided I'm not going to play that game. I'm not going to be somebody who undertakes a policy to influence something that is not in my area, which is the clearly defined responsibility of someone else—the finance minister or the government, as the case may be—because I will inevitably have to start lying at some stage if I go down that route.

They ask, "Why do you say this, Mr. Fischer?" And then you start giving some story that is not exactly the true story. So I told European policy makers, "You're asking me to do your job. You're the finance minister. You want this small budget. You wanted to have a small deficit. Well, go out and argue for it. I'm not going to go out and argue for it on your behalf through my actions." It's a very tough point to get to. But I think that having to go out and play the other game is not one you'll be capable of doing for any length of time.

I'm sure that, Mike and George, sometimes there will be things about which you say to yourself, "Dammit, I just have to say something." But the bar is very high. And should be very high. It's not our job.

ANDREW LEVIN: I really like the approach that Peter Fisher proposed last spring, and I'm wondering if you would react to it. Peter has recommended several times (including at this conference a couple of years ago) that the central bank, at its organizational meeting every January, should adopt a specific quantitative strategy. It would indicate clearly to the public that it's going to follow that benchmark strategy through the year, explain to the Parliament or the Congress why it has adopted it, and how it's relevant for the future and the past. The strategy could be formulated in terms of a Taylor rule or a variant of the Taylor rule or a set of contingency plans. This approach would solve the cacophony problem to a large extent. It would be flexible, because it could change it in future years. Or, if it works well, the central bank could stick with it. It seems so sensible to me, and of course I think of Peter Fisher being very sensible. Why isn't that approach the right way forward?

STANLEY FISCHER: Because I don't understand the logic of it. What is it? You can fix it for a year, and you can change it, and in the middle something happens that indicates you left something out of your rule. That's what happens. You get into a crisis, you have to do something, and you do it. You do things that are within your power. We don't have the capacity that the British have, which is that the the governor of the Bank of England can make a deal with the finance minister or the chancellor of the exchequer that will stick. I think a deal between the Fed chair and the secretary of the Treasury on something that is important will not stick. We don't have such flexibility with regard to the law. And that is a problem.

But Andy, what is the benefit of that approach? We're telling people in the market, "Look guys. We're just a terrible source of noise." When we take actions normally, we take actions that may not be intended to help the economy. If you want to know what we're going to do, decide what people like us do on the basis of our record, and put your money where your mouth is. And I frequently think, and this is impolitic of me to think that way, what is the job of people who make their living off the financial markets? It's to make a living off the financial markets and to thereby, if you believe in some invisible hand, cause the markets to move in the direction that supports or, if we are erring, makes more difficult the job of the central bank. So they've got to do something, and I can't figure out, aside from making their lives easier, what we're doing. That's a question, Andy.

ANDREW LEVIN: Fed officials have repeatedly emphasized the importance of being data dependent, not calendar dependent. That's what a benchmark is. The basic purpose of a quantitative strategy and contingency planning is to explain how things would change if something happens during the year.

MICHAEL BORDO: Stan, my question is, why was Alan Greenspan so successful in following what may be, ex post at least, rule-like policy? Was it good luck or good policy? This is an old question, and the reason people often give for the departure from that strategy in the last decade is "Well, we had a big financial crisis." My question is, Was the crisis a climacteric? Was there a permanent change in the world? Or are we going back to something like the normality we observed before the crisis? My reading of American economic history is that we will go back to something like normalcy. And if that is the case, why can't we have a rules-based system?

STANLEY FISCHER: But what is the benefit of the rules-based system if you appoint decent people to the job, and they say, this is what we plan on doing, but they don't follow a rule that is publicly announced? What is the benefit of that?

I'm going to stick to this. I know that there will be occasions when it's wrong. Why did I have to say that?

MICHAEL BORDO: Didn't you say before that rules need to be contingent?

STANLEY FISCHER: Yes, but the question is, Am I committed to this thing or not? Are there occasions on which I will be doing things I otherwise wouldn't do if I didn't have the rule?

ROBERT HELLER: You do it from one FOMC meeting to the next, or for six weeks at a time. You can say, "For the next six weeks, the fed funds rate. . . ."

STANLEY FISCHER: That's true. The Bank of India has, I think, only four scheduled meetings a year, but they're allowed to change the rate between meetings, and apparently, they meet every week to change. I'm not sure that's what we do.

MICHAEL BORDO: Rules are contingent. It's what you said before.

CHAPTER SEVEN

THE EURO CRISIS

Markus Brunnermeier

This chapter is based on my book *The Euro and the Battle of Ideas*, written with Harold James, a historian at Princeton University, and Jean Pierre Landau at Sciences Po. I discuss how differences in economic thinking and philosophies made a quick resolution of the euro crisis difficult. This story ends on a positive note since these differences are not cast in stone.

First let me highlight the watershed moments in the euro crisis. Strains in the European banking system emerged in 2007–8, when the US subprime crisis spilled over to Europe. By late 2009 large budgetary gaps began to appear in some euro area members, especially in Greece. The crisis that began in 2010 involved a massive power shift in the governance of the euro area. In the spring of 2010 power shifted from the European Commission to the European Council, away from Brussels and toward the capitals of the member states of the European Union. Then, in October 2010, Angela Merkel and Nicolas Sarkozy took a famous walk on the beach in Deauville, France, and decided on a restructuring of Greek sovereign debt. This involved the private sector taking a haircut (Private Sector Involvement, PSI). From then on, everyone knew that any political move or even statement would impact the interest rates in countries on Europe's periphery. This limited the political space for initiatives in the crisis countries, and from then on France and especially Germany were in the driver's seat. Then in the summer of 2012, just prior to the Olympic Games in London, Mario

Draghi gave his famous "Whatever It Takes" speech. The outcome of the speech drastically reduced sovereign debt spreads, yet not a euro was spent by the European Central Bank (ECB). Another watershed moment occurred in the spring of 2013 with the Cyprus bail-in, involving a shift from a bailout to a bail-in philosophy. And finally, there was Brexit in June 2016.

There are four dimensions of philosophic disagreement between France and Germany, the two most powerful players in the euro area. When these two countries agree, things move forward in the euro area. If they do not agree, little happens. Moreover, many other countries in the euro area fall into this Rhine divide: the Nordic countries think more like Germany, while many countries on Europe's periphery think more like France. Indeed, the Rhine essentially divides the views of France and Germany. This is an old division going back to the work of Max Weber.

The first dimension relates to a theme of this conference: rules versus discretion. The Germans are primarily rule driven. They want to have ex ante setup of rules that must be followed, whereas the French are much more interventionistic and favor using discretion.

However, the difference between the two nations is not so simple: the French approach is much more subtle than just using discretion. When you have discretion, the time inconsistency problem arises. The policy maker promises today to do something tomorrow, but when tomorrow comes he may use his discretion to change the plan. Of course, the public anticipates this, so promises are not credible. For this reason, the French approach is much more nuanced: In certain dimensions, they go for a strict commitment without wiggle room—a straitjacket—in order to overcome the commitment problem. In other dimensions, however, they like to maintain full flexibility. In this multidimensional space, the policy maker forcefully locks in his response in certain dimensions, but in others there is great flexibility. By contrast, the Germans like a system with rules, escape clauses, and autonomous safety values so that they do not have to intervene ex post at all. This is a very different approach.

There are some important examples of French straitjacket commitments. First, the French never want to restructure debt. No default. Recall that it was the Germans who pushed through PSI— Greek debt restructuring—at Deauville in October 2010. How can one fulfill a straitjacket commitment never to default? This leads us directly to the current heated debate on how to regulate banks' sovereign bond holdings. If domestic bonds are stuffed with their own countries' sovereign bonds, then a sovereign default will destroy the banking system. Faced with the possibility that a restructuring will bring down the banking system, it is unlikely that a government will choose that option. In a sense, domestic banks are taken hostage to credibly signal/commit that a government is unlikely to default on its bonds. This is a powerful commitment device.

The Germans, by contrast, favor a different approach to banking regulation. They favor risk weights on sovereign bonds such that banks hold an extra equity cushion for the event of a sovereign bond restructuring. In this arrangement, debt restructuring would not destroy the banking system. Indeed, a battle is going on at the moment on this issue. Should we force banks to hold an extra equity cushion? The French say, "Definitely not. This ruins our commitment not to default."

Without an extra bank equity cushion, the diabolic (doom) loop between sovereign risk and banking risk emerges. When sovereign risk increases, the banks suffer because bonds decline in value. This lowers banks' equity, possibly to such an extent that they have to be bailed out. As the bailout probability goes up, sovereign debt further declines in value, which in turn hurts the banks, and so on. In addition, there is a second diabolic loop. As banks suffer losses, they also lend less to the economy. Economic growth slows down, which then lowers government tax revenue. With lower tax revenue, the fiscal situation worsens, and government bonds decline further. This produces further losses for the banks, and so on.

If there is a lot of risk weight on sovereign bonds and the banks have to hold considerable equity as shock absorbers, you do not have this problem. This dimension is playing out prominently.

Another example of a straitjacket commitment is the French insistence during the Maastricht Treaty negotiations not to have any rules for exit from the monetary union. Once you commit to be part of the monetary union, there is no way to get out of it without causing havoc. More generally, the French prefer pegged exchange rates. The commitment to a pegged exchange rate is of course strongest in a monetary union (without exit). By contrast, the Germans have always favored flexible exchange rates. So if you think about the old debate between pegged and floating exchange rates, the Germans were always in favor of flexible exchange rates, along with the Canadians, while the French (straitjacket) commit to low exchange-rate volatility.

In the Mundell-Fleming trilemma, you can pick two of three desired features. France favors managed fixed exchange rates and is willing to give up free capital flows. Germany favors free capital flows and is willing to give up fixed exchange rates. Both want autonomous monetary policy. In the French approach, you commit in certain dimensions not to exit from a currency union or strict peg but then have to actively manage the other dimensions with a lot of discretion. In the German approach, you do not have to actively manage the economy, so lots of flexibility is built into a self-governing, autonomous system.

The first dimension pits discretion against rules. The second dimension pits solidarity against liability. Solidarity was a central value during the French Revolution. The French favor a fiscal union with joint liability, whereby everyone is liable for everybody else. In contrast, in German Ordoliberalism, liability is paramount. If you are in charge, you are liable. You never separate control from liability. These two elements have to be united. There will be no bailouts. Germany favors a bail-in approach and despises joint liability. The French pushed for joint liability in Eurobonds, while the Germans refused any joint liability bond structure. Angela Merkel insisted that "never in my lifetime will there be a Eurobond." Note that the French approach is not totally inconsistent: if you have a straitjacket commitment where you never default on your bonds, then you can have joint liability because participants will not default even in difficult circumstances. However, in extreme circumstances, when you really have to default, the country will be in deep trouble.

A third dimension where the two countries differ considerably involves liquidity and solvency. When faced with financial difficulties, the French say, "There is a liquidity problem. We have to intervene," while the Germans say, "There is a fundamental solvency problem. You are just throwing good money after bad." There are two types of liquidity problems. One is a multiple equilibrium liquidity problem—a situation where the economy goes from a good equilibrium to a bad equilibrium. All it takes to avoid a bad equilibrium is a "big bazooka." Just show the big bazooka, and the monetary problems will be solved. The term "big bazooka" was actually coined by then UK prime minister David Cameron, and others also argued for it. One could argue that Mario Draghi's London speech in the summer of 2012 announcing the Outright Monetary Transactions (OMT) program was such a bazooka. The OMT was ultimately specified only in the late summer and never activated. Not a single euro was ever spent on the OMT. Nevertheless, the interest rate spreads declined significantly during the summer. French observers claimed that this proved Europe was suffering from a problem of liquidity and not solvency. The Germans, however, argued that OMT was just a guarantee extended by the ECB, and that is why the spreads came down.

A second liquidity problem arises due to amplification and spiral effects. This occurs when strategic complementarities are less pronounced, and the demand curve is not inverted or *s*-shaped, but is like an inverted integral (script *S*-shaped). In such circumstances, if one puts in an extra euro (of bailout money), one gets a benefit that far exceeds this single euro. In other words, the expected net present value of a bailout is positive—a good deal. And what is the net present value of a bailout? It is the present value of bailing out versus the present value of not bailing out. The present value of not bailing out depends on your estimates of the size of contagion, or systemic risk. If refusing a bailout leads to huge spillovers across the whole euro area, the cost of not bailing out is huge. There is considerable disagreement over this issue. From a French perspective, the contagion effects are very large, while the Germans think they are manageable.

This difference played out dramatically in the Cyprus crisis in the spring of 2013. Part of Cyprus's business model as a country was to establish a banking sector that attracted black market money from Russian oligarchs so as to develop into an international financial center. Cyprian banks held a lot of Greek sovereign debt. The restructuring of Greek debt ruined their assets. Given their liabilities—deposits owed to Cyprian citizens and Russian oligarchs—the banks were insolvent. Even after wiping out all equity holders, the assets were insufficient to cover the deposits. The Germans argued that if not bailing out Russian oligarchs is systemic, then everything is systemic. Thus the no-bailout rule enshrined in the Maastricht Treaty would become totally irrelevant, leading to bailouts everywhere. From a French perspective, bailouts would have been appropriate to avoid the contagion risk. In the Cyprus crisis, the Germans prevailed. Equity holders, creditors, and even large deposit holders were bailed in and suffered losses. Contagion was limited, since capital controls were put in place in advance. Overall, the Cyprus bail-in led to a significant shift in the rethinking in Europe. A general bail-in rule book was established. Here again, issues of solvency and liquidity arise.

The fourth dimension is the old debate between Keynesian stimulus on the one hand and austerity and reforms on the other. Everyone agrees that in a recession aggregate demand is depressed, and you do not want to create additional uncertainty by introducing reforms that further depress demand. French observers' push for Keynesian stimulus relies primarily on this argument, while Germans put forward a political economy argument. One has to use a crisis to push through reforms. Only during a crisis can a government convince the public that reforms are unavoidable for the long-term sustainability of the country. The essential difference regards timing and whether one emphasizes economic arguments or political economy arguments.

One might conclude that the situation in Europe was hopeless because the two main countries driving the process of economic and political integration have such different economic approaches. How can there be any consensus in the European Union in the long run?

I argue that there is hope. The hope can be seen if you observe that the two countries have switched sides in terms of which approach they follow. In other words, these differences are not written in stone but are actually quite flexible. At first sight, it appears that France is absolute—a centrally organized country. You can always intervene ex post. Discretion is very powerful, while in Germany you can't do this, because you have a federal structure, and thousands of little dukes will intervene. So you need ex ante rules to govern the system.

Interestingly, a historical perspective makes clear that laissez-faire reluctance to intervene is a French idea. The great free-market thinkers before the twentieth century were French. And in the eighteenth and nineteenth centuries Germany was characterized by cameralism, a strong-state tradition, and intervention. Frederick the Great intervened a lot in Prussia, as did imperial Germany in the nineteenth century. It was only after World War II that these positions reversed themselves. In Germany, of course, it was the Nazis who were in favor of centralized power and extensive state intervention in the economy.

After the war, the Ordoliberals—an economic school with roots in Freiburg—argued against the arbitrariness in continuous government intervention. They posited that there is a need to restrain government power by ex ante rules to limit intervention. They also strongly promoted competition to avoid any concentration of power, be it political or economic. The Allies emphasized competition because it distributed power away from Berlin. Germany then had its economic miracle after World War II. Things went well, and everyone fell in love with the new arrangement.

France went in the opposite direction. There was considerable austerity in the 1930s. The government's budget was severely cut, and at that time, the biggest part of the budget was military spending. Then in 1940, after Germany quickly defeated France, it was argued that austerity measures were partly to blame for the France's vulnerability to the German attack. Thus the dirigiste, interventionist approach became much more powerful, and France switched to the other side. The overall—and hopeful—message is that the difference in economic approaches is not permanent.

In sum, the battle lines during the Maastricht Treaty negotiations before 1992 were along four dimensions, but financial stability and banking sector aspects were to a large extent ignored. When the Maastricht Treaty was negotiated in the late 1980s and early 1990s, the world had not yet lived through the Asian crisis with its huge waves of contagion. Financial stability was not at the forefront of people's minds; instead, fiscal aspects dominated. The diabolic (doom) loop—which one side sees as a commitment mechanism and the other as an amplification mechanism and destabilizer—came later. One reason the diabolic loop was so prevalent during the euro crisis was the absence of any safe asset across the euro area.

Let me outline a safe asset proposal that I, together with the Euro-nomics group, put forward in 2011. Our European safe bonds (ESBies) proposal ensures that the safe asset is provided symmetrically by all member countries in the euro area. During the euro crisis, the worsening situation led to a flight to safety from peripheral countries to core countries, because safe assets are provided by only a subset of euro area countries. Instead of having a Eurobond with joint and several liability, one can create a European safe asset via securitization. We initially called this safe asset the European safe bond. Officials now refer to it as a sovereign bond-backed security (SBBS). The idea is to first pool national sovereign bonds—say, up to 60 percent of a country's GDP. Then one tranches the pool into a senior bond—the safe asset—and a junior bond. Importantly, this is not a Eurobond since there is no joint liability. It is just simple pooling and tranching. Banks would hold only the senior bonds, not the junior bonds. When a crisis occurs, the senior bonds do not lose their value because they are protected by the junior bonds. The diabolic (doom) loop will not emerge. We are doing away with the commitment device but stabilizing the banks. A second advantage is that if there is a flight to safety, it will not go across borders, from the periphery to the core; it will go from the junior bond to the senior bond, and both bonds are European. These are bonds without a passport.

In conclusion, one reason the euro crisis was so difficult to manage was that different countries have divergent ideas on how to manage an economy. And ideas matter, not only interests. Importantly, one sees interests through the lens of ideas. There are many examples where the interests of Germany and France are aligned, but the lenses through which the two countries look at these interests are different and hence they push for different policies. In 2010, a huge power shift occurred away from Brussels and toward the European capitals, with the involvement of the IMF. Power moved away from a supranational arrangement in Brussels toward an intergovernmental arrangement. With the famous Deauville decision in October 2010, the influence of Paris and especially Berlin was further strengthened. This is why I focus on the differences in economic approach between France and Germany—that is, along the Rhine divide. Importantly, these approaches with their many dimensions can change. Hence, there is hope for convergence down the road. The European safe bond (ESBies or SBBS) proposal bridges both approaches. It redirects cross-border flight to flows from a European junior bond to a European senior bond. As both bonds are European, flight-to-safety capital flows are less destabilizing. This program can shift Europe into a different equilibrium. In addition, with the appropriate banking regulation, ESBies/SBBS take the sovereign risk out of the banks' balance sheets and thereby switch off the diabolic (doom) loop between banking and sovereign risk.

References

Brunnermeier, M. 2015. "Financial Dominance." Baffi Lecture, presented at Bank of Italy, Rome, December 1.

Brunnermeier, M., L. Garicano, P. Lane, M. Pagano, R. Reis, T. Santos, D. Thesmar, S. Van Nieuwerburgh, and D. Vayanos. 2011. "European Safe Bonds." Euronomics Group, www.VoxEU.org.

———. 2016. "The Sovereign-Bank Diabolic Loop and ESBies." *American Economic Review Papers and Proceedings* 106 (5): 508–12.

Brunnermeier, M., H. James, and J. P. Landau. 2016. *The Euro and the Battle of Ideas.* Princeton, NJ: Princeton University Press.

GENERAL DISCUSSION

VOLKER WIELAND: Markus, you mentioned the change in Germany following World War II. An important element was outside intervention, and it was a terrible experience. I'm a professor in Frankfurt. We're located nowadays in what used to be the headquarters of I. G. Farben, a big chemical conglomerate. This facility was used as the US Army headquarters in Europe and the seat of the military government after World War II. From this building in Frankfurt, the military government handed down guidelines to the heads of the German states regarding many rules and institutions of the state. For example, the so-called Frankfurt Documents influenced what became the so-called Basic Law (Grundgesetz), our version of the Constitution. Same with our new currency, the deutsche mark. So it's this combination that drove the change, the horrible experience of disaster and external intervention.

And if we move to the discussion today, the German position you describe also has a lot to do with experience. Unlike France, we have a federalist structure. There is in the population a big group that would say yes to a federal union. But the experience on the fiscal side of federalism hasn't been all that good, because unlike the United States, we haven't had working budget discipline. The focus on no bailout at the European level is influenced by the fact that we have had repeated bail-ins within Germany. Within Germany, we have the German states, that is, the German *Laender,* and among them are permanent recipients of transfers—Bremen, Berlin, Saarland. So that's where the proposals are coming from. And without going further, I think it's not going to be sufficient to just invent another financial instrument, where you have to ask yourself, Why is the market already offering that? But I think what you need is to unify control and liability on the same level. to make this work and not have Marine Le Pen win in France. If you're in control of your budget, of your policies, you also have to be responsible, liable, for your policies. And without going to a central government, which the French want the least, as you can see from the number of votes Marine Le Pen gets, this requires reviving the no-bailout clause of the Maastricht Treaty.

MARKUS BRUNNERMEIER: I agree with several aspects. Yes, having a federal structure raises additional challenges. Our book is very detailed in outlining the importance of the United States in Germany's rethinking of its economic philosophy. On the other hand, the decision of Ludwig Erhard, Germany's first economic minister after World War II, to lift all price controls was against US wishes. This step was essential for Germany's economic miracle after the war. In addition, the Ordoliberalists were also important at the University of Frankfurt.

   Should one conclude that a drastic change in economic philosophy requires an extreme and violent event, like a war? We do not think so. The euro crisis was a severe event for many of the citizens in Europe, and it led to a debate, which is the first step toward a common economic philosophy. One might argue that in certain dimensions there are first signs of convergence. A key example is the shift toward a bail-in philosophy. Of course, some of these aspects are very technical, so a rethink can take some time to trickle down to the average citizen.

   The disagreement about this liability principle can be cast in the modern literature of principal-agent type models. Moral hazard limits full risk sharing, but some risk sharing, especially of tail risks, is optimal. Of course, one has to agree about whether an event is a tail event or a normal risk event. People have to come to an agreement on what events are extreme enough to warrant risk sharing across nations, since the moral hazard implications can be contained.

Additionally, the moral hazard that arises from excess fiscal debt levels and common bonds with joint liability is something Germany is familiar with historically. In the late nineteenth century, after the first unification of Germany in 1871, the federal structure was very loose—recall that Bavaria and Prussia had their own separate armies. At that time, Bismarck complained that some smaller "German member states" behaved irresponsibly in fiscal matters and simply relied on bailouts from the larger member states of Germany. It took imperial Germany several decades to unify.

Finally, I share the skepticism about Eurobonds. ESBies are not Eurobonds, but they solve specific problems without requiring active intervention. In answer to the question of whether ESBies will solve all the problems, I don't think so. ESBies are an attractive way to solve two problems without requiring joint liability. The two problems are the diabolic (doom) loop and flight-to-safety capital flow. First, with appropriate bank regulation ESBies will eliminate the diabolic loop between banking risk and solvency risk. This would also make possible restructuring of sovereign debt in extreme circumstances, but of course it also removes a "straitjacket commitment device." Second, ESBies rechannel flight-to-safety capital flows away from cross-border flows to flows across asset classes, from a junior bond to a senior bond.

DAVID MULFORD: In your presentation, the word "Brexit" appeared. You made the comment that it doesn't necessarily take a war to make change. So I wonder if you could look forward over the next couple of years of Brexit negotiations and speculate or explain how you think this might affect euro development, core ideas, and the ideas that you made in your presentation. Because I think we're entering a very significant and uncertain period here.

MARKUS BRUNNERMEIER: I agree with you that Brexit will be a challenging process, in particular because expectations, particularly the expectations projected to the population, are not consistent. In the United Kingdom, most people believe that the transition will be smooth and the country can still enjoy the benefits of a common market. Great disappointment is likely. And the danger is significant that politicians will play the national card later on.

There are several recent developments besides Brexit that encourage continental Europeans to collaborate more closely. Donald Trump's initial indication that he would closely cooperate with Russia worried many Europeans about the security of eastern Europe. Also, Trump's initial comment that other nations should consider an exit triggered more unity on the continent than the reverse. Overall, I think it would be nice to keep the United Kingdom as closely linked as possible with continental Europe. This is important for at least two reasons: trade and geopolitical security. The United Kingdom is still an important European military power.

CHAPTER EIGHT

MONETARY POLICY REFORM

Kevin Warsh

We find ourselves in the foothills by the bay on another perfect day at the epicenter of the innovation economy.

The long drought is over. The flowers are in full bloom. And the construction boom is on full display—even we at Hoover cannot resist erecting a new edifice.

Students are gravitating to novel fields of study. Their ideas are funded as they walk to the edge of campus. Exceptional skills are rewarded like never before.

Deep interconnectivity, low-cost computing power, novel analytic tools, and tremendous advances in artificial intelligence are driving massive changes in industry structure.

According to popular lore, Silicon Valley finds itself in the middle of long epoch of prosperity. And we are assured this is a sustainable, durable equilibrium.

What could possibly go wrong?[1]

• • •

That is the central question central bankers should be asking.

The Fed was founded in response to a crisis. Financial and economic shocks tested the central bank with some frequency in the

---

1. Tail risks run in both directions. A subject for another day is, what could possibly go right? The more material constraint on further economic expansion is on the productive side of the economy. If a pro-growth reform agenda were adopted across a range of macroeconomic policies, higher labor and capital supply into the real economy would cause economic growth to track substantially above Fed forecasts.

century that followed. And shocks test the resilience of the economy. Economic and financial shocks threaten to knock the Fed farthest from its statutory price stability and employment objectives.

Leading Fed officials are confidently predicting a benign external environment for the next several years: steady growth, stable inflation, and financial assets trading at fair values. Policy makers have all but proclaimed their monetary mission accomplished, their employment and inflation targets largely achieved. The dot forecasts from members of the FOMC are nearly on top of one another.

The last time I recall such uniformity of opinion—among central bankers, academics, and market pros—was just over ten years ago.

We gather at this year's Hoover Institution Monetary Policy Conference at an important time for the US economy and the broad conduct of US macroeconomic policies.

Many of the issues addressed over the last day mirror the agenda of the Federal Reserve in recent years. A few observations: We should not encourage policy makers to fiddle with the non-accelerating inflation rate of unemployment (NAIRU) to rationalize the near-term conduct of monetary policy. We should not accept the Fed's newfound conviction that a very low neutral equilibrium real short-term interest rate (r^*) is a fixed feature of future monetary policy.[2] We should resist the pseudoscientific precision being assigned to the Fed's preferred measure of inflation, and we should not consider it a good arbiter of the output gap or a good proxy for financial stability.

Judgments on these issues are of tactical importance and keen academic interest. But they should be considered in the context of the Fed's most difficult and consequential mission: to mitigate

---

2. Total factor productivity fell markedly in the past decade, reasons for which are uncertain and were assuredly not foreseen. I see little reason for the Fed to assume that low productivity is a permanent feature of the forecast.

the likely damage to the economy that may arise from the next shock. The Fed's price stability and employment mandate demand nothing less.

The central bank and the academic community should engage in a fundamental rethinking of the Fed's strategy, tools, governance, and communications. A reform agenda could improve the modal outlook for the US economy by clarifying the Fed's responsibilities, improving its decision making, and bolstering its credibility. No less, a reformed central bank would prove useful to mitigate the risks of the next crisis and essential to a forceful and efficacious response to the inevitable challenges on the horizon.

There is no holiday from history. Policy makers should not squander the grace period on a victory lap.

• • •

My crystal ball is scarcely perfect. But neither is the Fed's.

The most important trait in a forecaster is humility. The most important forecasting measure is the confidence interval, not the point estimate. The most common forecasting error is groupthink. The best forecasting fix is to assemble a humble, independent, diverse, intellectually rigorous, and cohesive group.

The Fed has a lot riding on its outlook, and its institutional inclinations give me pause. Policy makers should evaluate the tail risks of their forecasts with more care than the central tendency. And scrupulously judge their ability to respond in less likely but more disruptive scenarios.

Maybe the scars of the last crisis burden me with unnecessary worry. Maybe the levers of macroeconomic policy are sufficiently improved that business, economic, credit, and financial cycles are an artifact of history. Maybe the economy gets another decade of moderate growth and inflation.

We should not mistake the present situation for permanence.

We should not confuse the postcrisis period of benign, however modest, aggregate macroeconomic conditions with a sustainable, durable equilibrium.

We should not be comforted by the low implied measures of volatility across financial markets. We should query whether a sudden shift in expectations would make asset prices an amplifier of distress rather than a shock absorber.

We should not encourage the financial markets to be the handmaiden of the central bank. We should allow asset prices to be an independent source of economic insight and discipline.

We must not allow a failure of imagination, a failure of preparation, or a lack of courage to keep monetary policy makers from pursuing a robust reform agenda equal to the risks ahead.

And we should not conflate a forward-looking policy of reform with a policy of *revanchism*, pining for the good old days when monetary policy was ostensibly perfected. The conduct of monetary policy has never been easy or simple. And the lessons learned in the last decade about money, credit, banking, finance, markets, and global interconnectedness should be incorporated into a twenty-first-century monetary framework.

The challenges of the next several years are different from those that confronted the Fed in the late 1970s when Paul Volcker stood tall, or those that confronted the Fed in the darkest days of the financial crisis when Ben Bernanke stood strong. But the challenges are no less consequential.

What type of reforms could make a real difference? A few observations.

STRATEGY

The familiar refrain from the last crisis was that "a plan beats no plan." True, but a strategy beats a plan every time. A durable strategy can be understood and relied upon. It should be operative through the business and financial cycle. It would scarcely require Fed speakers to rush to update their guidance to market participants between blackout periods.

A reformed Fed strategy should make the medium-term time horizon its North Star. The Fed would not be beguiled by the caprice of day traders and the variance of lagging data. The Fed's reaction function should be less sensitive to normal financial market ups and downs.

A reformed strategy should account for the possibility of demand- and supply-side changes to the economy. And it should show greater respect for the micro-foundations of macroeconomics.

To inform future inflation and output, it should take special note of contemporaneous, real-time data and pay careful attention to forward-looking trends.

International spillovers in monetary policy include intellectual spillovers. The G20 relies upon the leadership of the United States to deliver strong economic growth as the anchor of the global economy. Foreign central banks and finance ministers also rely upon a steady and well-understood Fed strategy. Absent reform of the Fed's framework, foreign central bank policy choices risk limbo. And the lack of reform by the Fed makes it more likely that the next foreign financial shock finds its way to our shores.

TOOLS

The Fed's comfort with its conduct of monetary policy seems based, in part, on the Dodd-Frank-inspired changes in the regulatory area. The argument goes that monetary policy's mission can be focused on the modal outlook because micro- and macroprudential policies will manage tail risks.

Would it were so.

Microprudential regulatory changes in the postcrisis era are likely inadequate to deal with the next financial shock. And the macroprudential tool kit is underdeveloped with regard to systemic risks. Until those areas of regulation and supervision are made more robust, monetary policy bears the substantial burden.

I am confused by the Fed's "normalization" strategy in monetary policy. Its preferred sequencing of rate increases and balance sheet reductions differs markedly from what was agreed when we conceived quantitative easing in the "war room" amid the crisis. There might be good reason. But the transmission mechanisms of rate changes and balance sheet adjustments are markedly different than projected. So too are the distributional effects. This merits a more robust public explanation.

According to the Fed's recent commentary, the balance sheet taper could well come by year end. The Fed would be prudent to engage in substantive discussions with the Treasury Department, so that the flow of issuance is well coordinated and the duration of outstanding securities understood. The absence of clarity around important questions at this late date does no favors to the Fed, the rest of government, or the broader economy.

GOVERNANCE

The Fed's existing model of governance is ripe for reform. The Fed should straighten itself from its defensive crouch. And it should resist the reflexive response that any proposed changes in governance are a threat to the institution's independence.

My time at the Fed and subsequent experience reviewing the Bank of England's institutional structure confirm the wisdom of Peter Conti-Brown's recent exhortation: "Having the right institutional design . . . isn't a side show to the real questions of monetary policy and financial regulation. Governance may in fact be the whole show."[3]

Changes are in order regarding how the Fed organizes itself, conducts its business, deliberates policy choices, and makes its monetary policy decisions. In short, deliberations should be more robust and decisions less constrained. The existing governance structure reinforces a groupthink of the guild. It places the Fed at considerable institutional risk when the next crisis strikes. And it makes the next crisis more likely to be more harmful to the economy.

COMMUNICATIONS

The Fed has come a long way from Montagu Norman's famed motto "Never explain, never excuse." Nothing compares with the zeal of the converted: the Fed of modern times is always communicating.

Communication has become so important to Fed policy makers that they now find themselves communicating about communicating, lest they be misunderstood.

Leading Fed policy makers believe that the so-called taper tantrum of 2013 was a communications failure that caused financial instability, and so they must toil to ensure that the error is not repeated. The spike in volatility of the long bond, however unanticipated, was a useful reminder to investors that complacency is a killer. If that's the magnitude of the tail risk event that consumes the central bank, we indeed have much about which to worry. Some emerging market economies were pushed to put their houses in order. And bond investors were made a bit less complacent.

In the monthly window between FOMC meetings, policy makers provide the minutes of the preceding meeting and make dozens of statements, speeches, interviews, forecasts, and other predic-

---

3. Conti-Brown (2016, 261).

tions. They pay great attention to the latest payroll data and inflation prints and their immediate effect on the next decision. There
is, however, little to be learned from the latest Fed forecast, little
insight to be gleaned from the last piece of government data.

I worry that Fed policy makers find themselves settling scores
with one another while Fed watchers score-count hawks and doves.
All the while, the big questions for the economy go unanswered.
And the big risks over the horizon go unaddressed.

Walter Bagehot captured the essence of this dynamic when he
said, "Two hosts of eager disputants on this subject ask of every
[discussant] the one question—are you with or us against us? And
they care for little else."

There is much else about which we should care.

CONCLUSION

Those in the bright white lab coats in the life sciences lab on the
other side of Stanford campus should be the starry-eyed true believ-
ers. The t-shirt-wearing coders in the Palo Alto garages should be
the eternal optimists. And those in the venture community can play
the role of evangelists. I wish them nothing but fame and fortune.

But central bankers should be different. Their fifteen minutes
of fame should end with the crisis. And they should use the inter-
regnum to take stock, deepen their knowledge base, bolster their
capabilities, and work to reform the institution before the next
siren sounds.

When the next shock strikes, the Fed is unlikely to have conventional or unconventional armaments in sufficient supply. So the
Fed's credibility will be at premium. Its credibility would be significantly enhanced by first reforming its own policies and practices.

References

Boyle, Andrew. 1967. *Montagu Norman: A Biography*. New York: Weybright and Talley.

Conti-Brown, Peter. 2016. *The Power and Independence of the Federal Reserve*. Princeton, NJ: Princeton University Press.

Warsh, Kevin. 2014. "Transparency and the Bank of England's Monetary Policy Committee." Hoover Institution website, December 17, www.hoover.org /research/transparency-and-bank-englands-monetary-policy-committee.

———. 2017. "America Needs a Steady, Strategic Fed." *Wall Street Journal*, January 30, www.hoover.org/research/america-needs-steady-strategic-fed.

GENERAL DISCUSSION

ANN SAPHIR: I just wanted to ask a quick political economy question to Kevin. What kind of indications are you seeing that the administration wants the kind of approach to the Fed and the kind of changes that you've been advocating?

KEVIN WARSH: The good thing about being back at Stanford is that we are able to explain what we think is the right outcome. We do not have to be burdened by the opinion polls or the latest comings and goings in Washington. I would say this: Both in the context of Dodd-Frank on the regulatory side and in the conduct of monetary policy, there's much Congress might choose to do to change the law. But there's also a lot of self-help that can be applied by the Fed. Almost all the authority granted to the Federal Reserve under Dodd-Frank was authority that—broadly speaking—the Federal Reserve already possessed. There are some exceptions, of course. Almost all the changes I've discussed today—the need for a robust strategy, the importance of fixing Fed governance, the need to be clearer to the public about the differing transmission channels of the Fed's tools and their distributional consequences, and changing Fed communications— these are reforms that can be taken up by the institution without delay. In some sense, if the institution doesn't look first to itself for reform, then its leaders might not like what happens at the other end of the political lens (i.e., Congress), particularly after the next slowdown, the next recession, the next shock. So my remarks are really a call for self-help. You and others can judge whether it's feasible in the broader Washington context. But part of the benefit of being three thousand miles from Washington is that we can focus on what we think is the best public policy choice. And leave it to others who are now burdened with official responsibilities to decide whether they wish to take up a reform agenda.

JAMES BULLARD: I have a question for Kevin. You seem to characterize one of the major problems for the Fed as groupthink. First of all, I'm not sure that is the core problem, but maybe you can defend that a little bit. What would you do to break down groupthink? What do you think the Fed should do in that dimension?

KEVIN WARSH: It's a great question. I've written a paper about it, but I'll try to summarize a couple of the ideas here, Jim. As Stan Fischer suggests, when Congress establishes a committee as large as the FOMC, there is a tendency to try to find an anchor, try to find some commonality. That's a natural part of human behavior.

And FRB/US—the dynamic, stochastic, general equilibrium model that has served at the core of the Fed's thinking for decades—ends up being the leading device through which a lot of discussions are conducted in formulating policy. This was assuredly true in my day, though I departed the Fed six years ago. The flaws in the dominant model should not be hidden but exposed.

Allow me to mention a couple of nontrivial things missing from the model. First, financial markets: there are virtually no asset prices in the model. Why would that be? In a prior period, it might well have been believed that assets are always perfectly efficient, so the Fed need not clutter up its elegant model with such things. But much has been learned about efficient markets in recent decades, most recently since the global financial crisis. The economic literature, including Markus Brunnermeier's work about booms and busts and other shocks, reveals a more nuanced view: market prices are often efficient but not always so. The Fed's dominant model scarcely includes asset prices, yet much of the purported benefit of monetary policy through quantitative easing happens through asset prices.

Second, the Fed's predominant model hardly includes the dynamic effects of the economies of the rest of the world on the US economy. Adding a couple of lines to the model to account for net exports is insufficient to capture the interconnectedness of the United States to the rest of the G20. A few decades ago, a closed-economy model might serve as a fair approximation of output and employment in the United States, but no longer.

My friend and former colleague Ben Bernanke might reply to my critique with a famed aphorism: It takes a model to beat a model. Well, if we had that other model, I'd be serving it up here. We don't. But we shouldn't hide from the frailties of the dominant model and the dominant economic framework. We shouldn't hew without reservation to a model that we know is fundamentally flawed and missing key elements. So a broader discussion about what ails the conduct of policy would be very useful to mitigate groupthink.

Groupthink does not come from bad intentions. It comes from a desire for comity in the committee, a will to get along. This is about good intentions of patriots who are trying to do the right thing for the economy. But if the intellectual backgrounds of the participants are so similar, if the long tenured history in the system is beyond reproach, some fresh air could be useful— fresh air from the real side of the economy, fresh air from financial markets, fresh air from overseas.

In an understandable attempt at civility, the Fed finds itself at press conferences and in testimonies seeking to use dominant models and their outputs, however unreliable, to show the commonality among committee participants. The Fed's dot-plot forecasts of growth and inflation are an example. These dot plots have proven quite inaccurate for most of the postcrisis period, and the cluster of dots suggests a groupthink about future prospects for both output and inflation.

Imagine, for example, that at the next FOMC press conference, Fed leadership did not dwell on the change in the forecasts by a tenth of a point to inflation, a tenth of a point to GDP. Instead, imagine if the Fed leadership discussed the central issues driving the Fed's decision making, such as the productivity puzzle. If the Fed doesn't wrestle—privately and publicly—with productivity, for example, it is unlikely that the Fed will be able to correctly assess r-star, the unobservable neutral equilibrium real rate. If the Fed doesn't assess r-star rightly and rigorously, it won't be able to conduct monetary policy optimally.

It is not a sign of weakness for the Fed to be uncertain about the future. It's a sign of strength. Reforms in governance, including those undertaken by the Bank of England, for example, could ensure more robust deliberations and greater comfort of participants in sharing their heterodox views.

The Fed expends a couple billion dollars of taxpayer money. The dollars should be deployed on the most difficult and fundamental questions confronting the US economy. The incredible brainpower of the hundreds of economists—and the leaders of the Fed system that gather around the FOMC—should be focused on these bigger, harder questions, like productivity, financial shocks, the role of markets and asset prices, and international flows. There is plenty of opportunity therein to break with groupthink in pursuit of better economic outcomes.

CHAPTER NINE

POLICY PANEL

James Bullard, John H. Cochrane, Charles L. Evans,
and Eric Rosengren

JOHN COCHRANE: I'd like to welcome everyone to the policy panel. This panel is an emerging tradition of this conference. We sum up and think about how the big issues we have discussed affect policy. I'd like to welcome our guests: Jim Bullard from St. Louis, Charlie Evans from Chicago, and Eric Rosengren from Boston. I'm going to tee up some questions. They won't be big surprises: I'm going to ask our panelists their views on the themes of this conference, and how they see the discussion going in the policy community, and the FOMC. I'll then ask if there are an important questions that I've left out, and their answers. Then we'll move on to questions from the floor. We not only have current reserve bank presidents and FOMC members here, but we have some people who have been on the FOMC or run a bank previously. I'll give them the first shot at comments and or questions. Then we'll go to general Q&A.

Let's start where we started the conference: the balance sheet. What's the new normal for reserves? Should the Fed keep a big supply of interest-paying excess reserves? Should it further open access to reserves to nonbanks? (The reverse repo program essentially allows financial institutions that are not banks to hold interest-paying reserves at the Fed.) Should the Fed run monetary policy as it used to do, with a very small amount of non-interest-paying reserves? Should we continue as now with a trillion dollars in reserves and paying interest on excess reserves? Or how about my wide-open balance sheet: to set interest rates at 3 percent, say to banks and financial institutions, "Come and get it. Give us your Treasuries and we will give you 3 percent (say) on reserves"? Should the size of the balance sheet be a separate tool? Should we do more quantitative easing (QE) in the next recession? That's the liability side of the Fed's balance sheet. The asset side poses interesting and novel questions: Does quantitative easing (QE) work? If you think it does, does it do so on the asset side, by buying up bonds, mortgage-backed securities, and other assets, and so driving prices up, or on the liability side by "printing money"—by forcing the system to hold more reserves? What kind of assets should the Fed buy? Do you welcome restrictions, or precommitments (two words for the same thing)? Or should the Fed buy widely, among long-term Treasuries, mortgage-backed securities (MBS), corporate bonds, stocks, commercial paper, or whatever else the Fed seems to think needs buying?

CHARLES EVANS: There's so much there—I'll just take the one that I have the strongest opinion on. Our balance sheet is very large. Everybody recognizes that. And nobody expects that we're going to keep the balance sheet at $4.5 trillion, which is its current level. The committee has indicated this through various communications. Of course, the balance sheet is not going to be as small as it was back in 2007, at a minimum because the economy has grown and there's more currency out there. But we have not yet decided how big the balance sheet will be in the long run. Our communications have been pretty clear in describing the committee's deliberations over the various issues. We're actively discussing the benefits of a larger balance sheet that could be consistent with a floor system for some financial stability reasons versus perhaps going back to the previous model, in which reserves were scarce and we had an active interbank market. Given my twenty-five years in the Fed, there are times when I have some sympathy for the old model. Certainly a large balance sheet does open you up to political interests weighing in on its use. And Congress could pass a law directing you to do something particular with it. That is democracy: Congress can pass laws. I don't know where we'll end up, but the committee is thinking about the issue.

JAMES BULLARD: I agree with Charlie that the $4.5 trillion level that we're at now for the size of the balance sheet is larger than we'd like. So I've been an advocate of beginning to shrink the balance sheet by ending the reinvestment policy. I think we could go as low as $2 trillion, because the currency is about $1.5 trillion, and a couple of hundred billion for reserves would probably get you down to a floor system, although I wouldn't be firm on that. That gives you an idea on how far away we are from where we'd need to be, even if you wanted to run a floor system. I think we have a long way to go and we might as well get started.

One of the questions is, Would there be QE in the next recession? I think that's a distinct possibility. Therefore, the prudent thing would be to create policy space on the balance-sheet side like we are doing on the policy-rate side. If a future committee wanted to contemplate that kind of policy if we hit the zero bound in the future, they'd be able to do so. I also think we have a rather odd "twist operation" going on. We're raising the policy rate and therefore trying to normalize conditions, but we haven't changed the balance sheet. According to our rhetoric and our statement, that balance sheet is putting downward pressure on long- and medium-term yields. It's a bit odd to be saying we're going to raise the short-term rate, which would normally be thought to raise everything along the yield curve, all else equal. Nevertheless, we're putting downward pressure on other parts of the yield curve. I think that's an inconsistency that needs to be ironed out. That's another reason why I've advocated that we get going on balance-sheet normalization.

On whether QE works or not, I would challenge people here because a lot of times you get people saying that QE didn't have any effect. I think I heard John Cochrane sort of say that yesterday. Let me push back on that a bit. I think you have a distinct set of empirical facts associated with QE, and any theory has to explain these facts. We have experiments in Europe, in the United States, and in Japan, and it seems pretty clear what happened. Equity prices react a lot. You have big movements in exchange rates: we saw that in 2014 with the euro, and we saw that in Japan. You also saw important effects on term premiums and long-term interest rates. And then, puzzlingly, for me anyway, not much effect on inflation or on inflation expectations. So whatever theory you choose, I think it has to confront those facts. They aren't easy to confront in a model. So some people say it didn't do anything. It did something, but it's maybe not something as conventional as we thought it was.

ERIC ROSENGREN: I'll just follow up on a couple of things Jim talked about. One was his question about the likelihood that we could see a swollen balance sheet again. Clearly, the system design has to incorporate what you think about what's occurring right now—whether you think it's a one-time event or it's likely to occur more frequently. I think it is important to note the Summary of Economic Projections (SEP) by FOMC participants, which suggests that policy makers think we'll have a long-term federal funds rate around 3 percent. Combine that with how the Federal Reserve normally responds to a recession, where it's not at all uncommon to lower the federal funds rate by five hundred basis points. So if you have three hundred basis points in the longer run for the federal funds rate, but you need to go down by five hundred basis points, it means that you're going to hit the zero lower bound pretty frequently in easing situations.

Why is it that we're likely to be at the zero lower bound more frequently? I think there are several reasons. One of the benefits right now is we do have a low, roughly 2 percent inflation rate. And I think inflation expectations are getting to be well anchored. During previous periods, we had a much higher inflation rate. I don't think that's a desirable thing. But the result is that there's less of a buffer between where the nominal interest rate is and zero. Furthermore, it's not just the United States that's encountering this. Japan is experiencing it, and so is Europe. In terms of other trends, population growth is much slower than it was a few decades back. That's true in the United States. It's true in Europe. It's true in Japan. It's not only slower births but less immigration, and that seems likely to continue.

Concerning productivity trends, I agree with Kevin: we don't completely understand why productivity growth is as slow as it is, but it seems to be relatively slow. So you combine a low population growth, low productivity, and a 2 percent inflation rate, and it's not surprising that much of the committee comes up with a number around 3 percent.

So as I said, that means we are going to be here—approaching zero—pretty frequently. And if we're going to be here pretty frequently, we need to come up with a system design that is well equipped to address what we are going to do when we come up against the zero lower bound. So I personally think it is inevitable that we're going to be talking about the balance sheet expanding in future recessions—actually in most recessions, unless they're very, very mild.

JOHN COCHRANE: Let me push you guys a bit. I presume you view QE as working not so much by the issuance of reserves but by asset purchases. You heard Charlie Plosser in our first panel, warning about the political pressure to buy certain assets rather than other assets, and political pressure to prop up certain prices rather than other prices. You're taking credit risk and term risk onto the balance sheet. Does that worry you at all? Or do you favor just a pure Treasury strategy? Or do you think it's actually the reserves that matter, not the purchases anyway?

ERIC ROSENGREN: So the political economy question certainly worries me. I think it is a significant issue. But we have to deal with the reality—if you're going to have a fed funds rate that's 3 percent and recessions occur, what are you going to do when you hit the zero lower bound? So you need an alternative. In Europe, they've tried negative interest rates. There's probably a limit to how negative rates can be—at least until we get some of the new currencies that were talked about in the previous chapters, but I don't think that's likely to happen in the near term. So we need an alternative that reflects what we're going to do when we do hit the zero lower bound. As I said earlier, in discussing what the Federal Reserve should do, we should recognize that it is possible we will be confronted with a situation where inflation's below 2 percent, the unemployment rate's very high, and the short-term interest rate is at zero.

Importantly, I do think there is a fair amount of empirical evidence that the large-scale asset purchases did make a difference. The long-term Treasury rates did move down. And I think you can look at even more recent experience, as in the United States we've gotten closer to normalization and stopped the purchase program, but the Europeans and the Japanese have not. Their ten-year government bonds are at rates much lower than our ten-year Treasury, and I don't think it's necessarily because they're viewed as much better credit risks than the United States. I think part of it is that they have a very different monetary policy than we have right now.

When I give talks, particularly to financial audiences, they spend much more time asking me about the balance sheet than they do about the federal funds rate path—which tells me that at least financial market participants think it matters. I think there is a fair amount of empirical evidence that the balance sheet has had an effect. I do think it lowers long-term interest rates, and I think it had an impact on the economy, and I think it is one reason why the United States is at full employment or possibly a bit below, and why inflation is pretty close to 2 percent. And those countries that waited much longer before they engaged in quantitative easing are not nearly as far along as we are.

JOHN COCHRANE: Is this something that needs a strategy, a plan, a rule, for what assets you buy and when you buy the assets? Or is it "Well, we'll go into the firehouse and pull out whatever we think when the time comes"?

JAMES BULLARD: I think the near-term challenge for the Fed is to realize that we're probably going to have to at least have QE available in the future. I think we should be creating policy space for that. My near-term goal for Fed strategy is to incorporate QE into the Fed's arsenal without bringing up the political economy problems that people have outlined here, which are very serious.

CHARLES EVANS: First, with regard to what we might buy, we are constrained in the assets we are allowed to purchase. We cannot buy equities; we can't take on risk like that. The Federal Reserve Act doesn't allow us to. The Federal Reserve's assets have to be safe. So we buy only Treasuries and mortgage-backed securities (MBS). There is no great credit risk with these purchases. If our MBS defaulted, we would get paid back by the guarantees the government-sponsored enterprises provide.

Second, what about when to buy? I'm not looking forward to any future episodes at the zero lower bound. However, I think it's extremely important that we make sure we can hit our policy objectives. So we need the ability to act the way we're supposed to if we find ourselves threatened with the ZLB. I'm with Ben Bernanke on this. He has said—and he's a scholar of the 1930s Great Depression—that if you look at the shocks that hit the system during the Great Depression and the shocks that hit the US economy after Lehman, the latter were bigger. The unemployment rate during the last crisis was horrible at 10 percent—but it wasn't 25 percent like during the Great Depression. I think this was because of all of the efforts the Fed undertook in conjunction with the administration: the liquidity programs, the stress testing, and making sure the banks had capital. And it also was because of the Fed's ability to provide stimulus through alternative tools, such as QE, once we hit the ZLB. We need to make sure we always have the capability to respond to adverse shocks. Of course, it would also be good to make sure we have the most vibrant economy we can, so that we've got inflation at target and we're at full employment, so that we would be less likely to face such a situation again anytime soon.

JOHN COCHRANE: I think that brings us to the next question, really, because you mentioned inflation. R-star. If indeed the long-run real rate is falling, how should the Fed adapt? I think Eric described the standard view: we keep the 2 percent inflation target. That means if real rates and r-star decline to 1 percent, we're going to end up at a 3 percent federal funds rate and probably run into the zero bound every recession. But I might channel Charlie saying that we need more headroom over the zero bound. We need to get the nominal rate back up to 4 percent or so, and that means we're going to have to raise the inflation targets, say to 3 percent. Or maybe, as discussed in the earlier panel, we need to rethink the whole business. Perhaps the Fed should think about changes in interest rates, raising them and lowering them in response to events only, and not the levels of interest rates at all. Or perhaps you have more extreme ideas, such as going to zero inflation, a price-level target, or a nominal GDP target. If this low real interest rate world keeps going, how do we adapt?

JAMES BULLARD: On r-star, the main failing of modern macro-economics is the treatment of the trend. Even estimated models often say, "We're just going to take averages over long periods of time. We're going to relate those to the balanced growth path that underlies the model, and we're going to analyze fluctuations around that balanced growth path." From looking at history in the United States and across the globe, we know that these trends do change over time. In the model, any change in the trend would change the behavior of everyone in the model and would have to be taken into account. I've actually worked with models like that. They're not easy to work with. But from a policy-maker perspective, we understand that these trends might be changing.

One way to handle changes is to look at regime-switching models.[1] I like those because they keep some level of stationarity in the system, as opposed to a random walk. Let's say there's a high-growth regime and a low-growth regime. You might be switching very occasionally, for example, with ten years as the expected duration of a particular regime. But given the regime, everything behaves as if that would be the balanced growth path forever. To make monetary policy in that environment, you have to know which regime you're in.

I think this is a good conceptual way to think about r-star. Eric just outlined some things that you might think are lower today and higher in the past. Productivity growth is low today, while it was higher in the 1995–2005 period. Labor force growth was higher precrisis and lower postcrisis. Both would feed into this balanced growth path and, therefore, into the real interest rate associated with that path.

In addition, you've got a longer-run trend for increasing demand for safe assets that has been going on since the 1980s.

---

1. See J. Bullard, "The St. Louis Fed's New Characterization of the Outlook for the U.S. Economy," Federal Reserve Bank of St. Louis announcement, June 17, 2016, https://www.stlouisfed.org/from-the-president/commentary/2016/new-characterization-outlook-economy.

You had a period where there was a relatively normal demand for safe assets. Today, there's high demand for safe assets. That's pushing the safe real yield down as well.

I like this kind of framework. I think it keeps policy makers on their toes about what's actually going on in the economy, without disrupting the entire framework and saying that you can't do anything because you don't know what the state of the world is. I would be sympathetic to the idea that you could go with the growth-rate type policy rules, which would do a better job of tracking where you are in this regime-switching world, as opposed to simply assuming that you're always dealing with a constant balanced growth path.

ERIC ROSENGREN: We had a very good session earlier in the conference about estimating r-star. It's not observable. Of course, there's a big standard error around any kind of equation that economists run, but I'd say that r-star in particular has a fairly large standard error. So I agree with the empirical work that suggests it's quite uncertain. What we're seeing in productivity trends is a lot of uncertainty as to whether they'll continue or not. I don't think there's much uncertainty about what the population trends are going to be. The Fed doesn't get to pick productivity or population growth. And for those who want to make sure we don't do asset purchases in the future, I would suggest that they have to come up with an alternative for what we're going to do when we hit the zero lower bound.

Whether you think it's exactly 3 percent or not, it's clearly not 5 percent. I think it's pretty clear that it's not 5 percent— which means that in most recessions it's going to be a problem. I don't think the r-star estimation is really what's going to be driving whether we hit the zero lower bound. Because even though there's a pretty big standard error, as I add it up between what the inflation rate is, population growth, and productivity, it seems very likely we're going to hit the zero lower bound in most recessions.

So I think it is important to try to estimate it. It's a good policy tool. However, I don't think it's something that hinges on whether we're going to be using balance sheets in the future.

CHARLES EVANS: This is a wide-ranging question, so let me pick up on the different-ways-to-do-policy aspect. I tend to favor— especially given where we've traveled from over the last ten years—focusing on outcome-based policy. This encompasses making sure we have a long-run strategy that is informed by modern economic theory; this includes concepts such as the natural rate of interest and the thinking on it going back to Milton Friedman. Outcome-based policy also incorporates an inflation target, which is our price-stability objective. To execute our strategy, we focus on making sure we provide monetary and financial conditions to support full employment and price stability. We state what we mean by full employment—that's why we adjust our description of it in our long-run goals and strategy statement every year; that's a very natural thing to do. We also state our inflation objective and affirm that it is symmetric. Two percent is not a ceiling. We have to be willing to go above 2 percent periodically and also be below that. Following these elements of outcome-based policy is very important.

Now, this isn't necessarily just pure discretion. But it's also not following any one rule all the time. We need to use a range of models, and we have to recognize—as Kevin said—when those models have obvious shortcomings. Macroeconomics as a literature has had difficulty fitting models to the data for the postwar US experience to a first approximation. Some of the difficulties I see today are in modeling the financial and international sectors. So, when you're facing unusual circumstances—something like a tail risk—you need to be mindful of the fact that our standard models don't cover the situation well. We have to incorporate other analyses, and adding them in can be a very "artful" exercise. This can be quite uncomfortable if you're accustomed to, and would like to have, a nice single, unified model. But such a model doesn't exist. That's a statement about the profession, not just central banks.

Stan gave a very good talk this morning in which he mentioned that Don Kohn had said that the committee's been informed about Taylor rules and different alternatives going back as far as 1995. These analyses have been very useful. But I think you have to be mindful of tail risks. This means you need to make a judgment about when you should focus on something other than the center of the distribution. A policy rule is going to be focused on the center of the distribution. It tries to be robust against deviations, but if you're going to be serious about tail risks, you also need to be ready to say, "Now's a time when I need to do something a bit different." I think that's what the Bernanke Fed did in response to the financial crisis, with 10 percent unemployment and inflation not expected to get up to our objective anytime soon. I would note that the rest of the world was slower to get to that point than the United States, and they also lagged in the recovery.

JOHN COCHRANE: I want to press you on this. If the zero bound is a problem, why not raise the inflation target to 3 percent, so you've got more headroom?

JAMES BULLARD: Let me set you right on this. If you have higher inflation, you're distorting the economy all the time because of the higher inflation. So do you want to distort the economy every day so that on occasion you're able to conduct a little better stabilization policy? The literature has a clear answer to this, which is that the distortion caused by everyday inflation is much bigger—an order of magnitude bigger—than the benefits of the stabilization policy. That's the received wisdom from the literature. You could write down different models, but that's the way the debate should be stated. I don't think the additional benefits from better stabilization policy would outweigh the day-to-day distortion that would come from the higher inflation target, so I don't think that's a good trade-off. I also think there are things you can do at the zero bound, including quantitative easing. I have been an advocate. It's not perfect, but there are some things you can do. So it's not like you're out of ammunition when you're at the zero lower bound.

JOHN COCHRANE: Well, I'll take the answer I like and move on. I also notice you guys are taking productivity—and, thank goodness, population growth—as exogenous to the Fed. Whereas of course, there's an alternative story that it's secular stagnation, and the Fed should be doing more about productivity growth and labor force participation.

What are the lessons of the recent quiet period? Marty Eichenbaum had a very interesting graph. The Fed, along with me and it seems everybody else, got forecast after forecast wrong, expecting a robust recovery that never came. Marty used that fact to say that people are irrational expecters. But, of course, those were Fed forecasts. Maybe the Fed is an irrational expecter too? The Phillips curve fell apart. The deflation spiral never came. Growth is too low, but does that have anything to do with monetary policy? Or maybe we and Japan are just living the optimal quantity of money, and growth is too low for real reasons unrelated to monetary policy. In the end, the Fed achieved its objectives: low inflation, maximum employment—at least as much as monetary policy can give you—and tiny interest rates. Maybe the Fed should just have a big party? What lessons do you see from this recent, surprisingly quiet period?

ERIC ROSENGREN: I agree with what Charlie highlighted earlier, that monetary policy should be focused on outcomes. Inflation and unemployment are things we should definitely be focused on.

You've just stated a whole bunch of things that can change over time, where there's a fair amount of uncertainty about what values they are going to be at for any particular point in time. It really kind of reiterates Stan's comments earlier, about having a fixed policy rule. But if you think a lot of these relationships are uncertain and possibly changing, the last thing you'll want to do is tie yourself to a rule that might be wrong.

So we do have an ability to monitor what's happening with inflation and unemployment. I think actually that should be the focus of congressional oversight: when we're missing on both variables, that is a discussion we should be having. But I'm not sure having Congress or the GAO determine what goes into getting that outcome is particularly productive.

JAMES BULLARD: So the question is about the "quiet" zero lower bound. I would take the main lesson from this era to be that, to paraphrase Friedman, near-zero interest rates do not everywhere and always imply higher inflation. That's a puzzle I don't think the profession has come to grips with even now. It came out of left field. I don't think anyone expected that. If I had told most of the people in this room eight years ago where interest rates would be and what the size of the balance sheet and the monetary base would be eight years in the future, you would all have said, "I bet inflation is high, or at least higher than targeted." And you would have been wrong.

That has been a shocking development from the point of view of received economic theory. At the St. Louis Fed, we're kind of overachievers on providing new ideas, so we provided two possibilities on what's going on or what might be going on. One is to bring out the Benhabib/Schmitt-Grohé/Uribe type analysis and think about the possibility that there's another steady state.[2]

---

2. See J. Bullard, "Seven Faces of the 'Peril,'" *Federal Reserve Bank of St. Louis Review* 92 (September/October 2010): 339–52; J. Benhabib, S. Schmitt-Grohé, and M. Uribe, "The Perils of Taylor Rules," *Journal of Economic Theory* 96 (January 2001): 40–69.

That steady state is very robust across models, because it only relies on the idea that there's a Fisher relation, a Taylor rule, and a zero bound, most of which would be in any of our models. Maybe we're somehow getting stuck at that steady state, or you could interpret Japan as Benhabib et al. did, as getting stuck at that steady state. I still think that's a reasonable idea. I'm not sure you really want to bring it in as the focal point of monetary policy, but that's a reasonable idea of what has happened. And the other idea is neo-Fisherian. If you just keep the interest rate low for a long time—or a permanent peg, as John Cochrane has discussed—eventually the private-sector expectations of inflation will become consistent with the very low nominal interest rate, and inflation will simply come down.[3] That seems to be a good model for Japan as well: for twenty years the policy rate has been below fifty basis points, and not too much is on the horizon as far as changes. After a while, the private sector throws in the towel and says, "Well, I'm just going to expect the amount of inflation that's consistent with that level of nominal interest rates, given that the real interest rate has to be determined by supply and demand conditions in that economy." I'm not saying neo-Fisherian effects would immediately dominate. But if you're going to keep the policy rate in the same place for a long period of time, I can imagine that private-sector inflation expectations will adapt, as opposed to real output or other variables.

CHARLES EVANS: One thing Jim just demonstrated quite well is that he's been willing to bring different views forward to the FOMC: he has spoken about different growth regimes, neo-Fisherian thinking, Schmitt-Grohé and Uribe multiple equilibriums, and so on. I'll be honest: I don't always like it. You know? [*Laughter*] For example, the neo-Fisherian models get inflation up by increasing interest rates. That is kind of counterintuitive, and

---

3. See J. Bullard, "Permazero," speech delivered at the Cato Institute's 33rd Annual Monetary Conference, "Rethinking Monetary Policy," Washington, DC, November 12, 2015.

I'm not sure it's right. But I benefit from talking to my staff and having them educate me about these topics. We benefit by understanding where those results come from. Either you buy into it or you think, as we do with some results, "Oh, that involves a slavish devotion to the Taylor rule all the way down—into the deflationary spiral, through the gates of Hell, into Hades, all the way down and not stopping. Because if you stop, say, because you've got some threshold, then that's going to kill the transversality condition in the infinite limit, and then. . . ." Okay, we don't have to think about that anymore. But the point is that this type of exercise is a way of getting around the groupthink Kevin mentioned.

We also listen to alternative views from outside the committee. I have spent a lot of time talking about forward guidance and explicit thresholds as a means of communication to people who were skeptical about their usefulness. These people are like those in Marty's chart who always thought the funds rate would go back up because it always has. And every time I saw such a funds rate forecast, I thought, "We're not getting as much accommodation in place as we would like." So hearing these different views helped me realize we needed some forceful way to demonstrate our conditional commitment to keep interest rates low as long as we had to. And we had good committee discussions about this topic.

Yet another example is Eric's talk about financial stability issues and areas where we could run afoul, with financial exuberance leading to a large increase in unemployment. Those are risky propositions.

Anyway, I think all of these are good examples of the committee benefiting from a variety of viewpoints. And they dovetail with Stan's comments about different perspectives on the committee.

JOHN COCHRANE: I'm getting a sense that one response to Kevin's worries is that regional Federal Reserve Banks are an excellent antidote to groupthink and allow you to come up with alternative ideas to bring to Washington.

JAMES BULLARD: Let me just follow up on that. One of my favorite examples is Charlie Evans, so this is a mutual admiration society. Charlie came up with the idea of thresholds for policy. When he first gave the "thresholds speech," I didn't know what he was talking about—I had never heard of it or even thought that way. He stayed at it for about a year or maybe more. And lo and behold, that entered into actual FOMC policy. Now, if the chair had gone out and said something about thresholds, all hell would have broken loose. I think there are some advantages to having the big committee in a world that has been turned upside down; you do need new ideas to flow into the policy process, but you can't just spring them on global financial markets. You don't know what would happen. There are advantages to this system we have of allowing different viewpoints to be stated and trying out different ideas before they actually get into the full weight of policy making.

JOHN COCHRANE: Let me move on to some issues Kevin Warsh brought up in his talk. In public, the Fed talks a lot about point forecasts. What should we do, assuming the economy continues to grow and inflation stays low? What's the path of normalization? It's a very quiet scenario that we were talking about. It is full of questions like, Do we raise twenty-five basis points first, then slowly squeeze down the balance sheet later? Let us hope those are the problems we deal with in the future. There is a danger that this starts to feel like we're congratulating ourselves on the Great Moderation in about 2006. So let's talk about what could go wrong, about variance, about confidence bands, about bad scenarios. The Fed puts banks through stress tests. Surely there are stress tests for monetary policy too? Now, you may not want to talk about this in public, but what scenarios keep you guys up at night? What scenarios keep the Fed up at night? What are the Fed's internal stress tests about? How can we avoid being caught flat-footed once again when the next truly unpredictable but in retrospect it-looked-predictable crisis comes? Do you worry about China blowing up? The euro blowing up? The United States blowing up? Some sort of sovereign default? Banks, student loans, state pensions? What are you thinking about for where the next crisis might be and what the Fed might do about it. In some sense as long as inflation stays under 2 percent, that's not really a big worry, and crisis management is much, much more what the Fed's about. What keeps you up at night?

ERIC ROSENGREN: I'll answer the first part about stress tests. With the Teal Book, we have different scenarios that we look at. We look at scenarios where there are unanticipated shocks—for example, something happening in China or Europe that we didn't anticipate—and also the uncertainty about economic relationships. For example, maybe we have a very different set of economic relationships than our standard models are telling us.

And so, the staff normally puts together four or five of those kinds of scenarios. That is part of the discussion at each of the meetings. My own staff also goes through various scenarios that they think might be relevant. Those scenarios change over time depending upon geopolitical situations, depending on which economic relationships are breaking down.

So I would say we do think about various scenarios. We tend to be focused on the modal forecast because it's much easier to explain the modal forecast than it is to explain standard errors, fan charts, and all the uncertainty that revolves around these relationships. But these are things that we do around every meeting. So if you go back five years, where you can see the Teal Books, part of that discussion includes these various scenarios.

And at each meeting, the scenarios change as different economic data come in.

So in sum, I completely agree with you that we should be spending a lot of time thinking about what goes wrong. Those things change over time, and that is something we take into account when we have our deliberations.

JAMES BULLARD: I agree with Eric. We do scenarios, and I think it's a good thing. We definitely look at what if productivity comes in lower than we think? Or what if various shocks hit from around the world—China hard landing, things like that? But let me just elaborate a bit.

I don't think what we do is sufficient, so in that sense I would agree with Kevin Warsh's comments. Here's how I think about robustness. If you have a model where everything is going to return to the balanced growth path no matter what you do, and it's just a matter of how big the deviations will be, that's going to give you one view of the world and one view of the type of risk you have to manage. But if you have a model that says most of the time you're on the balanced growth path, but sometimes all hell breaks loose and you go to a completely different state of the world, that gives you a very different picture of what you're trying to do. Because in that world, all you're trying to do is stay away from the edge of the cliff. You don't really care about the fluctuations around the balanced growth path. You just want to say, "Well, what types of policies are going to keep me from falling off the cliff?" We don't have that kind of stuff. We don't talk in those terms, except anecdotally, and it's not part of our models, and we don't work with models that have problems like that. There are models in the literature. Probably the best-known sequence of papers—there must be several hundred papers— analyzes Diamond-Dybvig-style bank runs. In those models, you're thinking about what gets rid of the bad equilibrium. What keeps me from falling off the cliff? That dominates the thinking in that literature. We don't have that for ordinary monetary policy. We treat the world as if it's quite a stable place—even though you could be subject to pretty big shocks, you would still eventually come back to the balanced growth path you started with.

So I think we could do a better job on that.

CHARLES EVANS: I'm not all that optimistic about the proposals on digital payments and currency, where all of the sudden it becomes easy to implement negative interest rates. I don't think those actions would be popular politically. I'm not sure how such a policy would be perceived. But the jury is still out on such proposals.

The kinds of things I worry about—and I've talked a lot about this—are the risks that would take us back to the zero lower bound, or the effective lower bound, if you want to describe it that way. I think these risks are really important because of the following asymmetry. On the one hand, if inflation picks up, we know how to deal with it. We know how to raise rates. It's not good, and we'd rather not be there. Volcker had to go through an awful lot to bring down inflation, and it was extremely costly. You wouldn't want to dissipate that credibility. But we do know how to raise rates. On the other hand, providing more accommodation when there are factors standing in the way (such as the ZLB) and the economy is suffering is a very big challenge. So that's why I think these issues are very important.

Now, just to provide a little balance, I have for the longest time not given a lot of airtime to this question: What if the low-inflation risk turns into the high-inflation risk? I haven't because, frankly, it has become hard to imagine this scenario. John, I've never understood all the ins and outs of the fiscal theory of the price level. There's a certain elegance to the inflationary implications of the consolidated intertemporal budget constraint that you have pointed out many times. But all the ins and outs of active fiscal policy playing out against passive monetary policy are a big part of the story. I always go back to Leeper's very important paper in 1991 to think about this, and I've got a colleague, Leonardo Melosi, who has distilled this into a very nice descriptive piece.[4] Start with a certain period of time—like maybe eight quarters—when fiscal policy becomes irresponsible. That kicks it all off. Deficits become so large that the real value of the debt has to go down. How's that going to work? Well, it's going to work through an increase in prices. And you can get some large inflation rates out of that. Now, active monetary policy would react to this inflation. Such a situation would be very challenging, because it would get monetary policy and fiscal policy actively working against each other. The resulting equilibrium is not well laid out. This would put you into the realm that Jim, I think, is talking about—sort of outside the normal approach.

JOHN COCHRANE: Well, a global sovereign debt crisis would be challenging. [*Laughter*]

JAMES BULLARD: I just had one other thought that I wanted to hit on here. The idea of having eighty (or eighty-four) models and that you should check what's going on with many different frameworks—this is what Volker Wieland and John Taylor were talking about—and see which things appear to be consistent across models and which things are not consistent. That might be a good way to get better robustness in decision making. I actually think that's quite a good idea, as opposed to what we do now, which is to run different scenarios within FRB/US. Now you're getting to a world with better IT, better computing. You

---

4. See Eric M. Leeper, "Equilibria under 'Active' and 'Passive' Monetary and Fiscal Policies," *Journal of Monetary Economics* 27, no. 1 (1991): 129–47; and Francesco Bianchi and Leonardo Melosi, "The Dire Effects of the Lack of Monetary and Fiscal Coordination," NBER Working Paper no. 23605, July 2017.

could probably do the eighty-four models with not exactly a push of a button, but you could probably automate a lot of that and look at different scenarios and different models.

JOHN COCHRANE: Quantity versus quality on models . . . I like it.

I'm just going to ask one last question, and then we'll open it up. There is an elephant in the room. I won't ask you to comment on the CHOICE Act or other specifics, but clearly this is a moment when our country is rethinking the Fed's general structure, the nature of congressional oversight, and your relations with the Treasury. I welcome any comments that you're willing to make on good or bad aspects of this. How should reporting be improved? Should it be more relative to rules or not? Do you favor the separation of monetary policy and supervision and regulation? Should the Fed welcome limitations on what it does, because limitations on actions are also limitations on responsibility? Should the Fed and Treasury come to a new agreement or accord, and stop this business where the Treasury sells long-term debt and then the Fed buys it all back up again? Really, who is in charge of the maturity structure of the debt anyway? Should the Fed and Treasury routinely swap securities so that the Fed doesn't end up holding maturity and credit risk for long periods of time, as Charlie Plosser suggested? Are there any structural and supervision issues of that sort you're willing to comment on?

ERIC ROSENGREN: You had a long list there, so I'll take a couple of them. We've talked a little bit about monetary rules. I want to emphasize that we do look at rules. We spend a lot of time looking at rules. And we don't just look at one or two rules—we look at a lot of rules. I think it is very important to think about rules, to think about why you're diverging, and to come up with coherent explanations for why you're coming up with a different answer than a particular rule.

That, however, is very different from legislating a rule that you have to follow, which gets audited by the GAO and results in congressional hearings. I'm not in favor of legislation that would provide a rule, or have us regularly provide a rule and then have to meet it, for many of the reasons that Stan highlighted. That aspect of the legislation I don't find particularly productive.

You mentioned supervision. I think it's impossible to divorce monetary policy from supervisory policy. One of the reasons the financial crisis and its aftereffects became so serious and damaging for so many people was because of the problems at financial institutions. In fact, it's not at all unusual around the world that in instances where recessions coincide with severe problems in the financial sector, they're much more severe, take much longer to recover from, and have broad implications for society in general.

So I do think it's important that we understand those trade-offs. The topics came up a couple of the questions earlier. I don't think we can divorce supervisory responsibilities from monetary policy responsibilities. I think we have to think about those two things and how they interact. This is a very important aspect of what the Federal Reserve does, and I wouldn't want to see that change.

JAMES BULLARD: I'm going to mention some areas of Fed reform I've advocated in the past that I think we could do unilaterally without congressional action and that I think would help alleviate some of the pressure on the Fed.

One thing we could do is have a press conference at every meeting, make each meeting ex ante identical, allowing the committee to move at any juncture. Other central banks do this. We're one of the few that don't. I think this is important because the markets and the wider monetary policy community want to hear from the chair, because the chair and the chair only speaks for the committee. Whatever you decided a month ago or six weeks ago, there has been intervening data—this and that have happened—and they want reassurance that you're still on track, or if you're adjusting slightly, they want to know you're adjusting slightly. My vision is that communication should be more or less continuous because developments in the economy are a more or less continuous process. If you had a model based on continuous time and Brownian motion, the policy maker would react in continuous time. You want this idea of continuous communication in epsilon amounts: almost nothing is said on any particular day, but because you're communicating all the time, markets are never surprised by monetary policy. I think press conferences would take us a step in that direction. As it is now, between press conferences we're at the mercy of the speaking schedule. Sometimes that doesn't work out all that well, especially over the holiday period in the United States. So I think we could do more.

We could also have a monetary policy report at quarterly intervals, which would lay down a baseline for markets and for the policy makers on the committee itself. Here's what we're thinking at some very basic level on what's going to happen in the economy. You could compare what private-sector forecasters are saying. And then everyone on the committee could give their own views relative to that baseline. So I think a monetary policy report could go a long way to improve Fed communications. In addition, that report could include all kinds of reporting relative to monetary policy rules, because, let's face it, John Taylor revolutionized how we do macro and monetary economics. We already give long speeches in terms of monetary policy rules. Janet Yellen did it here at Stanford just recently, but this has been going on for years. We already talk in terms of monetary policy rules. We could put that into the report, in the appropriate way, and this would provide a benchmark for everybody: here's what this rule says, and here are some reasons why we're not doing exactly what is prescribed by that rule, or the committee's judgment was that it wasn't the right thing to do at this point. I think you could get this idea of rules reporting going if you had a monetary policy report.

None of these things require legislation. I think the Fed could take steps in this direction, and then we might not stress our lawmakers quite as much, because they have a lot of other things they need to be doing.

CHARLES EVANS: It's extremely important for us to be accountable to Congress and the American public and to explain what we're doing. I often think that as central bankers we use language that strikes me as a bit arrogant. For example, some say, "We need independent monetary policy." Independence in a democracy? What are you talking about? That's why accountability is so important. So the chair goes up to Congress and testifies twice a year and schedules talks to the congressional Joint Economic Committee (JEC). (Indeed, the taper tantrum started when Bernanke made some comments during a JEC meeting.) And system officials go up to the Hill at other times when called upon. I think that's appropriate.

Because of this accountability, it's natural for us to talk about communication. You could wonder, "Why do you always have to talk about communication? That must be a sign something's not right." But it's more a sign that it is appropriate for us to continually assess our transparency.

On the quarterly Summary of Economic Projections, let me just offer what may be a minority opinion on a subtopic, which is the dot chart. Now, the dot chart is something that you either like a lot or do not like—and you may also say you don't understand it. I think Kevin said he thought the dots were on top of each other. They might be on top of each other for forecasts made late in the current year, when there's no action we could do that's different from what we all know we will do. But at one year or two years ahead, the dots put our disagreements on full display—for example, when somebody has eight increases over the next year or two, and someone else has none. People ought to want to know why that is. I think answering that question is one reason why FOMC participants go out and explain their views. And I think those communications are very useful.

Charlie Plosser, I apologize if I didn't ask you about this ahead of time, but I hope you will be fine with what I am about to say. Charlie and I didn't always agree on the policy path for the next couple of years. But I'm pretty sure we might have submitted about the same inflation forecast two or three years ahead, along with a similar outlook for the unemployment rate, and that we both thought output growth would be at trend. What was different? It was the underlying assumptions about the economy and the policy needed to achieve our forecast. And the dots showed that difference in policy. In other words, some FOMC participants said, "I'm going to get there, but I'm going to get there with higher rates because I'm fighting inflationary pressures." While others would say, "I'm going to get there, but I need low rates to do so because we have to get inflation up." I think this distinction is very informative, and that's part of what we need to have the public understand.

GENERAL DISCUSSION

JOHN COCHRANE: I promised I'd reserve the first three questions for
our ex-FOMC members, and then everyone else gets a chance.
So do you guys have something you want to ask?

CHARLES PLOSSER: I have a few observations. First, I want to follow
up briefly on Charlie's last point, since there's a degree to which
I take some responsibility for the dot plot and having it there in
the first place. I spent a lot of time in speeches trying to explain
to people what it meant and what it didn't mean. I'd often use the
example that Charlie just gave, which was that participants may
have the same or similar economic projections but very different
ways of getting there—that is, their underlying policy assumptions may be quite different. Partly what's incomplete about the
presentation of the SEPs is that readers of the summary can't
match up those individual forecasts with the corresponding dot.
Many of us have argued for a long time that publishing the full
matrix, which matches up the forecasts and policy assumptions,
would be helpful in understanding some of these issues.

My second observation elaborates on Jim's comment about a
monetary policy report and how we treat rules. At this conference three years ago, I gave a talk where I said that what the Fed
could and should be doing to help promote and communicate
a more systematic policy strategy is actually to make the rules
and projected outcomes that the staff produce part of a public
monetary policy report. This has several benefits. For example,
while it doesn't require adopting a specific rule, it does offer an
opportunity for the committee to compare its decision to the
guidelines provided by a range of plausible and robust rules
suggested in the academic literature. In doing so, it provides an
opportunity to elaborate on the logic and thinking behind the
decisions and explain why it chose to deviate or not from the

guidelines. This would improve the committee's communication and be helpful in articulating or revealing a monetary policy strategy. I'm glad Jim's talking about that. I hope the committee is considering such an approach. Had it been adopted sooner, you could have headed off some of this stuff that the Congress is trying to impose and micromanage through legislation. And by the way, Mike Dotsey and I provided a sort of model report about how you might go on about doing that—and I think Philadelphia is still doing it.

The other observation I have concerns the treatment of tail risks. This has come up a lot during the recent recession and crisis. Central bankers are naturally a worrisome lot: they wring their hands, and they're always afraid about what can happen. I suspect that's appropriate to some degree. It's kind of the nature of the beast. But I worry about overstressing unusual events and thinking of them as regular events. For example, when I was first learning macroeconomics and thinking about building models for the macroeconomy, a very common reaction you'd get in academic circles was, "Well, that's great. That looks good. You got everything working fine. We understand it. But your model doesn't explain the Great Depression. And if your model doesn't explain the Great Depression, I'm not interested in it." Well, we still don't understand the Great Depression. It's what—eighty years later? And people are still writing papers and debating causes and the choice of policies. There are revisionist views about what happened, why it happened, what policies worked, what policies didn't work. Lee Ohanian's been writing about different ways of thinking about the effects of fiscal policy. So there's a lot we still don't understand. I think there's a lot we don't understand about this crisis too. And I suspect, sixty years from now, economists are still going to be speculating about what happened and why, and which of the panoply of policies were effective and which were not.

So I want to ask, Do we get too focused on tail events and risk avoiding policies that may be effective because we think some rare or low-probability event might occur? Such risk management approaches have costs as well as benefits. Moreover, we may not even know what the right policy would be in the rare event. The world of what-ifs is quite large, limited only by our imagination, and placing meaningful probabilities on such tail events is difficult at best. Yes, forecasting is hard but necessary, and it is difficult enough to consider deviations from modal outcomes and normal uncertainties, but are we, and the economy, well served by holding policy decisions hostage for fear of truly rare events? While risk management strategies sound appealing, they are exceedingly difficult to execute effectively. When undertaking them, how does one evaluate the trade-offs and the uncertainties of rare events occurring and the consequences of their occurrence? Do you design policies or mechanisms that solve the big problems and then not worry about the normal problems? Or vice versa? How do you approach assessing the trade-offs? I think this line of thought poses interesting and challenging issues about the design of policies and bears more work and thought.

ROBERT HELLER: I heard a lot of willingness to engage in future market operations here, QE-type operations. As I look around the world, the biggest risks I see out there are the black swans: the insurance companies and especially the pension funds. A lot of them are underfunded by enormous amounts, so how are you going to deal with that if you then want to do QE?

And in the same vein, if you have higher inflation—and some people have advocated that on this panel—a lot of these pension funds will take losses, because as public pension funds they are fully indexed. So higher inflation is no way out of the dilemma you're facing, and you've got a big black swan that you can actually see. What are you going to do about that?

ERIC ROSENGREN: Let me combine the two, actually, because you're talking about a specific tail risk. And I think understanding what could cause problems for leveraged financial institutions is critically important. Insurance companies, banks, and other types of financial intermediaries could be significantly impacted. Charlie made the argument that maybe we spend too much time on tail risk. I'd actually make the opposite argument, that it's really costly to have an unemployment rate at 10 percent. If the unemployment rate rises from 4.4 to 4.6 percent, that's not a significant problem, but if it is rising and the unemployment rate is already 10 percent that is a huge problem. We're still suffering a decade after the last event; a lot of this discussion is tied to what happened in that event. The problem with tail risk is that it has long tails, and it takes a long time to recover. So I think we should always ask ourselves, what kinds of problems could generate these very severe outcomes?

I agree with your point that you don't want to construct a design for the kind of monetary policy you want, just for bad outcomes. But recessions are not, in some respects, that big a tail risk. They happen periodically. It's not like we have one every fifty years; unfortunately, it has been one every ten years or so. So if you design a system such that every time you hit a recession you're going to have a problem, that's probably not an ideal system. You should be thinking about the tail risk and trying to avoid it. Monetary policy may not be the right tool to avoid it. In fact, in the case of insurance companies and pension funds, probably regulatory approaches are far more appropriate than monetary policy approaches.

CHARLES EVANS: Well, long-duration liability managers have obviously been challenged in the environment of low interest rates— life insurance companies, pensions, and the like. It's very easy to go to some event, sit down at dinner, and find that your hosts have steered you toward sitting next to someone like that—and then they kind of say, "What?" [*Laughter*] Interest rates are low, and they often think you are really hurting them. Similarly for savers, who've done everything right throughout their lives and now are suddenly facing low interest rates on their assets.

Monetary policy has tried to reduce longer-term interest rates through portfolio balance effects in order to induce more risk-taking and get us back to better growth. But it's not just monetary policy. For example, after the taper tantrum, term premiums went up a hundred basis points and then retraced that rise. The decline wasn't because we expanded our asset purchases; it was because worldwide interest rates were falling. There have been many factors at work, such as the ones George Shultz talked about in terms of AI and 3-D printing and their differential impacts on labor markets for different segments of the population. And trend output growth rates are lower, and these reduce r-star.

Monetary policy does live in this low-interest-rate space, and this means there likely are going to be more periods in which we have to deal with the zero lower bound. That's why I say the zero lower bound is the risk that worries me most—I'm not sure we can handle it as effectively as we would like.

DENNIS LOCKHART: I'll ask a fairly concrete question about, say, 2018 Fed policy, and that is the relationship between tapering the balance sheet and rate increases. What's your current thinking as to how much accommodation will be removed through various scenarios of tapering the balance sheet versus increments of twenty-five basis point increases in the policy rate?

CHARLES EVANS: I carefully consulted the minutes of our March meeting during the break just to make sure I understood what we had all said. It's pretty much what people have been saying in speeches. The committee is looking forward to the upward-sloping funds rate path being confidently in place. Today, the fundamentals for the economy are good, so we're moving toward this place. When well under way with the rate increases, then

we'll start adjusting the size of our balance sheet by not rein-
vesting the maturing securities. The minutes indicate that many
participants thought this could begin before the end of 2017.
They also indicate that we discussed whether we would let the
full amount mature and not be reinvested or, in some cases, only
reinvest part of the maturing securities. I think if you look at the
monthly patterns, some months have larger maturities, and that
could get in the way of some of the Treasury funding. So adjusting reinvestments to smooth out those patterns is one possibility.
But, you know, I'm not sure it's essential. Those are some of the
issues we talked about.

JAMES BULLARD: We adopted this regime switching view. We think
we're in a very low real interest rate regime right now for a variety of reasons. We don't really see the factors that are affecting
that regime switching very soon. So over the forecast horizon,
we have a very low policy-rate path. Our dots are definitely not
sitting on top of everybody else's dots. If we went up twenty-five
basis points, or even fifty basis points, I don't think that would
be the end of the world. But what I do object to is the idea that
you have to go on this very long march up to two hundred basis
points or more over the next two years to keep unemployment
low and inflation near target. I don't think you have to do that
given the current circumstances.

If that's the view you take—and it should be—then the logical
approach is to allow the rest of the yield curve to adjust normally
and naturally. So you'd want to take the pressure coming from
the big balance sheet off the longer-term rates. You could allow
for the runoff of the balance sheet. You could manage that, or
you could let it all run off. The chair will have to make a decision
about that.

ERIC ROSENGREN: The committee hasn't made decisions on this, so
I can only speak for myself. But my preference would be that
we start reducing the balance sheet relatively soon, and we do

it in a very gradual, highly tapered way, so it can serve "in the background." If it's highly tapered and pretty gradual, you can continue to focus on the federal funds rate as the primary target for meeting your inflation and unemployment objectives. And so, those are the two principles that I would focus on: highly tapered so it's not disruptive, and it's not the primary tool that you're relying on. And I wouldn't wait all that long.

I have a slightly different view than Jim. We're at 4.4 percent unemployment. My estimate for full employment is 4.7 percent, so we're already low. A lot of the private-sector forecasts have GDP growth that's in excess of 2 percent. My own estimate of potential is 1.75. That would imply continued pressure on labor markets. So I am a little worried that we need to take away the accommodation. We've been doing it very gradually by historical standards, and I think that's appropriate. I want to continue doing it gradually, and the best way to do it gradually is to continue so we end up hitting our dual mandate in terms of both inflation and employment.

MARTIN EICHENBAUM: There's an important interaction between regulatory policy and many of the questions we've been discussing, such as the level of r-star or the size of the Fed's balance sheet.

Let me give two examples.

First, banks pay enormous attention to key regulations involving liquidity coverage and common equity ratios. Safe assets like excess reserves play a special role in the way these ratios are calculated. For example, excess reserves don't take a haircut when you calculate the numerator in the liquidity coverage ratio. In addition, that type of asset gets little or no weight when calculating the value of risk-weighted assets for the denominator of the common equity tier 1 ratio. So these assets have an important value beyond their direct pecuniary yields.

The growth of regulations involving liquidity coverage and common equity ratios has led to a dramatic rise in the demand for safe assets. You can see this effect directly in the composition of banks' portfolios. Banks have gone from holding around 4 percent of their assets in Treasury bills to something around 8 percent. The rise in banks' demand for safe assets is a very real, concrete phenomenon. This rise has arguably contributed a lot to the fall in interest rates related to r-star.

To the extent that the rise in regulations has contributed to the fall in r-star, there are interesting trade-offs to consider when balancing monetary and macro prudential policies. For example, do we want to increase r-star a bit by relaxing some of the bank regulatory ratios? Another example involves efforts to reduce the size of the Fed's balance sheet. Suppose the Fed sells some of its risky assets to the private sector. Those sales will inevitably remove excess reserves from the system. But remember that those reserves play a special role in the regulatory ratios. Banks will have to somehow adjust the size and composition of their assets to comply with regulations. Presumably that adjustment will involve an increase in safe assets that substitute for excess reserves. That type of adjustment will push yields on safe assets down, not up. That's very different from the conventional view of how a smaller Fed balance sheet will affect rates. While the regulatory effects may not dominate the net effect on yields, it will almost certainly have effects that we need to take into account as we move forward.

JAMES BULLARD: Part of the regime idea is exactly that the demand for safe assets has increased, not just in recent years but over the last three decades. The one-year ex post real rate on a US Treasury was in the 5 percent or more range in the mid-1980s. It's now −1 percent. So you're down six hundred basis points. It's a long-term trend, and it doesn't look like it's turning around anytime soon.

If you talk to people in financial markets, they say exactly what Marty Eichenbaum just said: "We're being required to hold these safe assets for various regulatory reasons. The demand in some sense has skyrocketed, not just in the United States but worldwide, so what do you expect? The prices are going to be very high and the yields are going to be very low." These are exactly the rates that are most relevant from a monetary policy perspective, and they provide a baseline for a Taylor-type policy rule. This is part of what we've taken on board in our regime view, in addition to lower productivity and lower labor force growth. That's why we think we're in this low-rate environment, at least over the forecast horizon. So I do think there is some interaction. I'm not sure I'd go so far as to say, "Well, you should back off of those kinds of requirements" on the grounds that you want to have a higher r-star for monetary policy. I think monetary policy should probably adapt to the regulatory policy environment, and that's what we're trying to do.

ERIC ROSENGREN: I completely agree with your fundamental point that when we think about monetary policy, we have to be thinking about how supervisory policy interacts with it. Liquidity requirements, though, are actually a critical component of how we think about what happened in the last crisis. The dependence on wholesale funding was one reason investment banks were subject to runs and why we had the kind of problems we saw in 2008. So I'm not sure the answer to safe assets is to allow the banks to once again get into a situation where they're potentially illiquid.

I strongly believe that we need to focus on making sure that financial institutions are able to weather liquidity shocks. And I wouldn't do it by pulling back on liquidity requirements. I do think that the Treasury has a way of providing more safe assets. Debt management, if it's worried about this, could involve issuing much more at the short end of the market to relieve some of these concerns. That seems much less costly, particularly for stress scenarios, than trying to change the liquidity requirements. But I think your more general point—that whenever you think of system design for monetary policy, you have to take into account how regulatory requirements interact with monetary policy supply design—is critically important.

JOHN COCHRANE: What Marty brings up is that there are two sides of this balance sheet: there are the assets and the liabilities. We got ourselves into talking about the assets—how you're buying very long-term debt as the effective long end of the yield curve—and Marty brings us back to liabilities. Wait a minute! These vast quantities of reserves are actually important now, not just because of reserve requirements but because of other things. Perhaps the other way out of the conundrum is that the Fed gets rid of the longer-term assets and the MBSs but keeps a large balance sheet funded by short-term Treasuries, and that way you can keep the big reserves as well.

CHARLES EVANS: I'm trying to figure this out. . . . [*Laughter*] We'd be taking those Treasuries off the market, and they are safe assets. But you're right that we'd also be supplying safe reserves. That was my back-and-forth thinking on the subject.

JAMES BULLARD: I don't think reserves are a perfect substitute for short-term Treasuries, so I think the Treasuries are more valuable in the marketplace.

JOHN COCHRANE: Treasuries are more valuable than reserves. Yes. That's an interesting observation. We're used to thinking of money as suffering rate of return dominance because it's more liquid than debt, but now it's the other way around.

Contributors and Discussants

Editors:

MICHAEL D. BORDO is a Board of Governors' Professor of Economics and director of the Center for Monetary and Financial History at Rutgers University, New Brunswick, New Jersey. He a distinguished visiting fellow at the Hoover Institution currently doing research on a Hoover Institution book project *The Historical Performance of the Federal Reserve: The Importance of Rules.* He is currently president of the Economic History Association and is preparing a speech and paper titled "Financial Stability and Monetary Policy Regimes: A Historical Approach." He is also working on projects on the evolution of central banks; the profiles of SOMC members; and the timing of exits from episodes of loose monetary policy: a comparison of the 1932 open market operations with QE1. He is a research associate of the National Bureau of Economic Research, Cambridge, Massachusetts, and a member of the Shadow Open Market Committee. He received a PhD in 1972 from the University of Chicago. He has published many articles in leading journals and sixteen books on monetary economics and monetary history. He is editor of a series of books for Cambridge University Press: Studies in Macroeconomic History.

JOHN H. COCHRANE is a senior fellow at the Hoover Institution, a research associate of the National Bureau of Economic Research, and an adjunct scholar of the Cato Institute. Cochrane earned his PhD in economics at the University of California at Berkeley. His recent publications include the book *Asset Pricing* and articles on dynamics in stock and bond markets, the volatility of exchange rates, the term structure of interest rates, the returns to venture capital, liquidity premiums in stock prices, the relation between stock prices and business cycles, and option pricing when investors can't perfectly hedge. His monetary economics publications include articles on the relationship between deficits and inflation, the effects of monetary policy, and the fiscal theory of the price level. His PhD Asset Pricing class is available online via Coursera. Cochrane contributes editorial opinion essays to the *Wall Street Journal,* Bloomberg .com, and other publications. He also maintains the *Grumpy Economist* blog.

AMIT SERU is a senior fellow at the Hoover Institution, the Steven and Roberta Denning Professor of Finance at the Stanford Graduate School of Business, a senior fellow at the Stanford Institute for Economic Policy Research, and a research associate at the National Bureau of Economic Research. Seru's primary research interest is in issues related to financial intermediation and regulation. His papers in this area have been published in several journals, including the *American Economic Review,* the *Quarterly Journal of Economics,* and the *Journal of Political Economy.* He is a coeditor of the *Journal of Finance* and an associate editor of the *Journal of Political Economy.* Seru earned a BE in electronics and communication and an MBA from the University of Delhi and a PhD in finance from the University of Michigan. He was formerly a faculty member at the University of Chicago's Booth School of Business.

Contributors:

MARKUS K. BRUNNERMEIER is the Edwards S. Sanford Professor at Princeton University. He is a faculty member of the Department of Economics and director of Princeton's Bendheim Center for Finance. His research focuses on international financial markets and the macroeconomy with special emphasis on bubbles, liquidity, and financial and monetary price stability. He is also a research associate at NBER, CEPR, and CESifo. He is a member of several advisory groups, including the IMF, the Federal Reserve of New York, the Bundesbank, the US Congressional Budget Office, and, formerly, the European Systemic Risk Board. Brunnermeier was awarded his PhD by the London School of Economics. He is a Sloan Research Fellow, fellow of the Econometric Society, Guggenheim Fellow, and the recipient of the Bernácer Prize for outstanding contributions in the fields of macroeconomics and finance.

JAMES BULLARD, as president and CEO of the Federal Reserve Bank of St. Louis, participates in the Federal Open Market Committee and directs the activities of the bank's head office in St. Louis and its branches in Little Rock, Arkansas, Louisville, Kentucky, and Memphis, Tennessee. He has published widely and currently serves as coeditor of the *Journal of Economic Dynamics and Control*. Bullard sits on the advisory council of the economics department at Washington University and also serves on the board of the St. Louis Regional Chamber and on the senior committee of the Central Bank Research Association. He is the chair of the United Way USA Board of Trustees. Bullard earned his doctorate in economics from Indiana University in Bloomington.

MARTIN EICHENBAUM is the Charles Moskos Professor of Economics in the Weinberg College of Arts and Sciences at Northwestern University and the codirector of the Center of International Macroeconomics. His research focuses on understanding aggregate economic fluctuations. He is currently studying the causes and consequences of exchange-rate fluctuations, as well as the effect of monetary policy on postwar US business cycles. He is a fellow of the Econometric Society and the American Academy of Arts and Sciences, as well as a research associate of the National Bureau of Economic Research. He was the coeditor of the *American Economic Review* and is currently the coeditor of the *NBER Macroeconomics Annual*. He has served as a consultant for the IMF, the World Bank, and the Federal Reserve Bank of Chicago. He is currently a consultant at the Federal Reserve Banks of Atlanta and San Francisco. He is an advisory council member of the Global Markets Institute at Goldman Sachs and on the board of directors of the Bank of Montreal. He holds a PhD in economics from the University of Minnesota and a bachelor of commerce in economics from McGill University.

CHARLES L. EVANS is president and CEO of the Federal Reserve Bank of Chicago. He serves on the Federal Open Market Committee, the Federal Reserve System's monetary policy-making body. As head of the Chicago Fed Evans oversees the work of twelve regional Reserve Banks across the country and roughly 1,400 employees in Chicago and Detroit who conduct economic research, supervise financial institutions, and provide payment services to commercial banks and the US government. Before becoming president in September 2007 Evans served as director of research and senior vice president. His research has focused on measuring the effects of monetary policy on US economic activity, inflation, and financial market prices and has been published in the *Journal of Political Economy, American Economic Review, Journal of Monetary Economics, Quarterly Journal of Economics,* and the *Handbook of Macroeconomics.* He received his doctorate in economics from Carnegie-Mellon University in Pittsburgh.

JESÚS FERNÁNDEZ-VILLAVERDE is professor of economics at the University of Pennsylvania, visiting professor at University of Oxford, visiting scholar at the Federal Reserve Banks of Chicago and Philadelphia and the Bank of Spain, advisor to the Hoover Institution at Stanford University's Regulation and Rule of Law Initiative, and a member of the National Bureau of Economic Research and the Center for Economic Policy Research. In the past, he has held academic appointments at Princeton University, Yale University, Duke University, and New York University, among others. He has been visiting scholar at the Federal Reserve Banks of St. Louis, Minneapolis, Cleveland, and Atlanta, was research professor at FEDEA (Spain), and was the director of the Penn Institute for Economic Research. He is editor of the *International Economic Review*. In the past, he served on the editorial boards of several other learned journals.

STANLEY FISCHER was sworn in as vice chairman of the Board of Governors in June 2014 and was a member of the Board of Governors of the Federal Reserve System until October 2017. Before his appointment to the board Fischer was governor of the Bank of Israel from 2005 to 2013 and vice chairman of Citigroup from February 2002 to April 2005. Additional appointments include serving as the first deputy managing director of the International Monetary Fund; chief economist of the World Bank and a fellow at the Guggenheim Foundation, the American Academy of Arts and Sciences, and the Econometric Society, as well as a research associate at the National Bureau of Economic Research and an honorary fellow at the London School of Economics. He has published many articles on a variety of economic issues and is the author and editor of several scholarly books. He received his PhD in economics from the Massachusetts Institute of Technology in 1969.

LAURIE SIMON HODRICK is the A. Barton Hepburn Professor of Economics in the Faculty of Business at Columbia Business School, a visiting fellow at the Hoover Institution, and a visiting professor of law and a Rock Center for Corporate Governance Fellow at Stanford Law School. With many research and teaching plaudits to her name, she is especially known for her groundbreaking research on corporate financial decisions, with a particular interest in corporate cash holdings and capital allocation, including share repurchases and dividends, takeovers, and equity offerings. Her past appointments include serving as a national fellow at the Hoover Institution, the founding director and chair of the advisory board of the Program for Financial Studies at Columbia Business School, managing director at Deutsche Bank where she was Global Head of Alternative Investment Strategies, and as an independent director/trustee for Merrill Lynch Investment Managers. She is currently an independent director for Corporate Capital Trust and Prudential Retail Funds. Hodrick received her PhD in economics from Stanford University.

ARVIND KRISHNAMURTHY is the John S. Osterweis Professor of Finance at the Stanford Graduate School of Business and a research associate at the National Bureau of Economic Research. Krishnamurthy's research interests include financial intermediation, debt markets, housing markets, financial crises, monetary policy, and financial regulation. Krishnamurthy's research on financial crises and monetary policy has received national media coverage and been cited by central banks around the world. He received his PhD from MIT and his undergraduate degree from the University of Pennsylvania.

ANDREW T. LEVIN is a professor of economics at Dartmouth College. He worked as an economist at the Federal Reserve Board for two decades, including two years as a special adviser to the chairman and vice chair on monetary policy strategy and communications. He subsequently served as an adviser at the International Monetary Fund. Professor Levin is currently an external adviser to the Bank of Korea and a regular visiting scholar at the Bank of Canada and the IMF. He has also served as a consultant to the European Central Bank and a visiting scholar at the Bank of Japan and the Dutch National Bank; he has provided technical assistance to the national banks of Albania, Argentina, Ghana, Macedonia, and Ukraine. He received his PhD in economics from Stanford University in 1989.

LEE E. OHANIAN is a professor of economics and director of the Ettinger Family Program in Macroeconomic Research at the University of California at Los Angeles, where he has taught since 1999. He is a senior fellow at the Hoover Institution and also associate director of the Center for the Advanced Study in Economic Efficiency at Arizona State University. Ohanian is an adviser to the Federal Reserve Bank of Minneapolis and has previously advised other Federal Reserve banks, foreign central banks, and the National Science Foundation. His research, which focuses on economic crises, has been published widely in a number of peer-reviewed journals. He is codirector of the research initiative Macroeconomics across Time and Space at the National Bureau of Economic Research. He received a PhD in economics from the University of Rochester.

CHARLES I. PLOSSER served as president and CEO of the Federal Reserve Bank of Philadelphia from 2006 to his retirement in 2015. He has been a longtime advocate of the Federal Reserve's adopting an explicit inflation target, which the Federal Open Market Committee did in January 2012. Before joining the Philadelphia Fed in 2006, Plosser served as dean from 1993 to 2003 at the University of Rochester's Simon School of Business. He is a research associate of the National Bureau of Economic Research as well as a visiting scholar at the Hoover Institution. Plosser served as coeditor of the *Journal of Monetary Economics* for two decades and cochaired the Shadow Open Market Committee with Anna Schwartz. His research and teaching interests include monetary and fiscal policy, long-term economic growth, and banking and financial markets. Plosser earned PhD and MBA degrees from the University of Chicago.

ERIC ROSENGREN became the Boston Fed's CEO in July 2007, after holding senior positions in both the bank's economic research and supervision functions. Rosengren joined the Federal Reserve Bank of Boston as an economist in the Research Department in 1985. During his time in the Supervision Department, Rosengren was active in domestic and international regulatory policy and wrote extensively on macroeconomics, international banking, bank supervision, and risk management, including articles in leading economics and finance journals. Much of Rosengren's research, analysis, and public speaking have focused on how problems in the financial sector affect the real economy. He is a director of the United Way of Massachusetts Bay & Merrimack Valley, the chair of Colby College's Board of Trustees, and a member of the University of Wisconsin's Economics Advisory Board. Rosengren earned his PhD in economics at the University of Wisconsin, Madison.

DANIEL SANCHES is an economic advisor and research economist at the Federal Reserve Bank of Philadelphia. Sanches earned a PhD in economics from Washington University in St. Louis in 2010. His research has focused on the implications of privately created monies for macroeconomic stability. He has published scholarly articles in leading economics journals, including the *Journal of Economic Theory*, the *International Economic Review*, and the *Review of Economic Dynamics*.

JOHN B. TAYLOR is the Mary and Robert Raymond Professor of Economics at Stanford University, the George P. Shultz Senior Fellow in Economics at the Hoover Institution, and the director of Stanford's Introductory Economics Center. He served as senior economist on the President's Council of Economic Advisers in 1976–77 and later as a member of the Council from 1989 to 1991. From 2001 to 2005 he served as undersecretary of the Treasury for international affairs. He received the 2016 Adam Smith Award from the Association of Private Enterprise Education, the Truman Medal for Economic Policy for extraordinary contribution to the formation and conduct of economic policy, the Bradley Prize for his economic research and policy achievements, the Adam Smith Award from the National Association for Business Economics, the Alexander Hamilton Award and the Treasury Distinguished Service Award for his policy contributions at the US Treasury, and the Medal of the Republic of Uruguay for his work in resolving the 2002 financial crisis. Taylor received a PhD in economics from Stanford.

KEVIN WARSH is the Shepard Family Distinguished Visiting Fellow in Economics at Stanford University's Hoover Institution and lecturer at Stanford's Graduate School of Business. He advises several private and public companies, including serving on the board of directors of United Parcel Service. He is a member of the Group of Thirty. He was a member of the Board of Governors of the Federal Reserve System from 2006 to

2011. He served as the Fed's representative to the Group of Twenty; the board's emissary to the emerging and advanced economies in Asia; and administrative governor, managing and overseeing the board's operations, personnel, and financial performance. Previously Warsh served as special assistant to the president for economic policy and as executive secretary of the White House National Economic Council. Prior to his government service he was a member of the Mergers & Acquisitions Department at Morgan Stanley & Co. in New York, serving as vice president and executive director. Warsh received his AB from Stanford University and JD from Harvard Law School.

VOLKER WIELAND holds the Endowed Chair of Monetary Economics at the Institute for Monetary and Financial Stability at Goethe University of Frankfurt and has served as its managing director since June 2012. He received his PhD in economics from Stanford University in 1995. His appointments include professor of monetary theory and policy at Goethe University and member of the German Council of Economic Advisers. He has served as a consultant to the European Central Bank, the European Commission, the Federal Reserve Board, and the Reserve Bank of Finland. In 2008 Wieland was awarded the Wim Duisenberg Research Fellowship by the European Central Bank. Academic activities included a stint as coordinating editor of the *Journal of Economic Dynamics and Control* from 2002 to 2006 and as associate editor of the *European Economic Review* (2001–4). He has recently been coordinating the creation of a public archive of macroeconomic models, Macroeconomic Model Data Base, for comparative purposes.

General Discussion Participants:

MICHAEL J. BOSKIN is a senior fellow at the Hoover Institution, the Tully M. Friedman Professor of Economics at Stanford University, a research associate at the National Bureau of Economic Research, and former chair of the President's Council of Economic Advisers.

RICHARD CLARIDA is the Lowell Harriss Professor of Economics at Columbia University, Global Adviser with PIMCO, and the former assistant secretary of the US Treasury for economic policy.

MICHAEL DOTSEY is executive vice president and director of research at the Federal Reserve Bank of Philadelphia.

JOHN V. DUCA is vice president and associate director of research at the Federal Reserve Bank of Dallas, where he leads and conducts research in macroeconomics and finance.

DARRELL DUFFIE is the Dean Witter Distinguished Professor of Finance at Stanford University's Graduate School of Business and professor, by courtesy, in the Department of Economics at Stanford University.

PETER R. FISHER is a senior fellow at the Center for Business, Government & Society at the Tuck School of Business at Dartmouth, where he is also a clinical professor.

ROBERT HELLER is a former member of the Board of Governors of the Federal Reserve System and former president and CEO of Visa USA.

ROBERT HODRICK is the Nomura Professor of International Finance at Columbia University's Graduate School of Business and a research associate of the National Bureau of Economic Research.

KENNETH L. JUDD is the Paul H. Bauer Senior Fellow at the Hoover Institution.

THOMAS LAUBACH is the director of the Federal Reserve Board's Division of Monetary Affairs.

STEVE LIESMAN has been a senior economics reporter at CNBC since 2002. He was a *Wall Street Journal* reporter from 1994 to 2002, serving as an economics reporter, energy reporter, and Moscow bureau chief. He received his BA from SUNY Buffalo and master's in journalism from Columbia University.

DENNIS LOCKHART served as the fourteenth president and CEO of the Federal Reserve Bank of Atlanta from March 2007 to February 2017.

MICHAEL MELVIN is the executive director of the Masters of Finance Program at UC San Diego's Rady School of Management and former managing director and senior research advisor in multi-asset strategies at BlackRock.

DAVID MULFORD is a distinguished visiting fellow at the Hoover Institution, former US ambassador to India, former undersecretary of the US Treasury for International Affairs, and former vice chairman international at Credit Suisse.

EDWARD NELSON is a senior adviser at the Federal Reserve Board of Governors' division of monetary affairs. He has written many journal articles and also the forthcoming book *Milton Friedman and U.S. Economic Debate, 1932–1972*.

WILLIAM (BILL) NELSON is executive managing director, chief economist, and head of research, The Clearing House association, and Chief Economist of The Clearing House Payments Company. Bill contributes to and oversees research and analysis to support the advocacy of the Association on behalf of the owner banks.

DAVID PAPELL is the Joel W. Sailors Endowed Professor and chair of the Department of Economics at the University of Houston. His fields of expertise are macroeconomics, international economics, and applied time series econometrics.

ANN SAPHIR reports on the Federal Reserve, monetary policy, and the US economy for Reuters.

LAWRENCE SCHEMBRI is a deputy governor of the Bank of Canada, where he is responsible for overseeing the bank's analysis of domestic economic developments and their implications for monetary policy.

GEORGE P. SHULTZ is the Thomas W. and Susan B. Ford Distinguished Fellow at the Hoover Institution and has served as US secretary of labor, director of the Office of Management and Budget, secretary of the Treasury, and secretary of state.

About the Hoover Institution's Working Group on Economic Policy

The Working Group on Economic Policy brings together experts on economic and financial policy at the Hoover Institution to study key developments in the US and global economies, examine their interactions, and develop specific policy proposals.

For twenty-five years starting in the early 1980s, the US economy experienced an unprecedented economic boom. Economic expansions were stronger and longer than in the past. Recessions were shorter, shallower, and less frequent. GDP doubled and household net worth increased by 250 percent in real terms. Forty-seven million jobs were created.

This quarter-century boom strengthened as its length increased. Productivity growth surged by one full percentage point per year in the United States, creating an additional $9 trillion of goods and services that would never have existed. And the long boom went global with emerging market countries from Asia to Latin America to Africa experiencing the enormous improvements in both economic growth and economic stability.

Economic policies that place greater reliance on the principles of free markets, price stability, and flexibility have been the key to these successes. Recently, however, several powerful new economic forces have begun to change the economic landscape, and these principles are being challenged with far-reaching implications for US economic policy, both domestic and international. A financial crisis flared up in 2007 and turned into a severe panic in 2008 leading to the Great Recession. How we interpret and react to these forces—and in particular whether proven policy principles prevail going forward—will determine whether strong economic growth and stability returns and again continues to spread and improve more people's lives or whether the economy stalls and stagnates.

Our Working Group organizes seminars and conferences, prepares policy papers and other publications, and serves as a resource for policy makers and interested members of the public.

Working Group on Economic Policy—Associated Publications
Many of the writings associated with this working group will be published by the Hoover Institution Press or other publishers. Materials published to date, or in production, are listed below. Books that are part of the Working Group on Economic Policy's Resolution Project are marked with an asterisk.

The Structural Foundations of Monetary Policy
Edited by Michael D. Bordo, John H. Cochrane, and Amit Seru

Rules for International Monetary Stability: Past, Present, and Future
Edited by Michael D. Bordo and John B. Taylor

Central Bank Governance and Oversight Reform
Edited by John H. Cochrane and John B. Taylor

Inequality and Economic Policy: Essays in Honor of Gary Becker
Edited by Tom Church, Chris Miller, and John B. Taylor

Making Failure Feasible: How Bankruptcy Reform Can End "Too Big to Fail"*
Edited by Kenneth E. Scott, Thomas H. Jackson, and John B. Taylor

Across the Great Divide: New Perspectives on the Financial Crisis
Edited by Martin Neil Baily and John B. Taylor

Bankruptcy Not Bailout: A Special Chapter 14*
Edited by Kenneth E. Scott and John B. Taylor

Government Policies and the Delayed Economic Recovery
Edited by Lee E. Ohanian, John B. Taylor, and Ian J. Wright

Why Capitalism?
Allan H. Meltzer

First Principles: Five Keys to Restoring America's Prosperity
John B. Taylor

Ending Government Bailouts as We Know Them*
Edited by Kenneth E. Scott, George P. Shultz, and John B. Taylor

How Big Banks Fail: And What to Do about It*
Darrell Duffie

The Squam Lake Report: Fixing the Financial System
Darrell Duffie et al.

Getting Off Track: How Government Actions and Interventions Caused, Prolonged, and Worsened the Financial Crisis
John B. Taylor

The Road Ahead for the Fed
Edited by John B. Taylor and John D. Ciorciari

Putting Our House in Order: A Guide to Social Security and Health Care Reform
George P. Shultz and John B. Shoven

Index

Index